WOMEN AND HOMELESSNESS IN EUROPE

Pathways, services and experiences

Edited by Bill Edgar and Joe Doherty

J C S H R

First published in Great Britain in September 2001 by

The Policy Press
University of Bristol
34 Tyndall's Park Road
Bristol BS8 1PY
UK

Tel +44 (0)117 954 6800
Fax +44 (0)117 973 7308
E-mail tpp@bristol.ac.uk
www.policypress.org.uk

ISBN 1 86134 351 5

Bill Edgar and **Joe Doherty** are Directors of the Joint Centre for
Scottish Housing Research at the University of Dundee and the
University of St Andrews.

The research was commissioned by FEANTSA with the financial support
of the Directorate-General for Employment and Social Affairs of the
European Commission. The research was carried out by the 15 national
correspondents of the European Observatory on Homelessness, with the
support of universities and research institutes in the member states of
the European Union.

Cover design by Qube Design Associates, Bristol
Printed in Great Britain by Hobbs the Printers Ltd, Southampton

Contents

SERVICES

EXPERIENCES

List of figures and tables

Figures

Table

Foreword

Somewhere, there is a 37-year-old woman, who, 21 years ago, was my first client when I commenced working in the field of homelessness. As a 16-year-old, Miss X had run away from a violent home, lived some weeks with a relative, and then found herself on the streets. She was, in those days, too young to be considered for a social tenancy and yet too old to be given social services care. Three weeks of continuous and intensive work by a non-governmental organisation (NGO) eventually found the girl a room in a fairly disreputable lodging establishment – but with no support whatsoever – and so she 'disappeared'.

Legislation and practice in European Union countries has progressed since, but what is apparent from the research of European Observatory on Homelessness of FEANTSA correspondents is that the particular position of women who find themselves homeless, has largely been neglected.

Generally speaking around 1 in 5 of homeless persons is a woman. Increasingly these are young women and many of them are hidden from public view because they find their own solutions, temporarily at least, to their homelessness.

As is the norm with European Observatory on Homelessness of FEANTSA research, due to constraints of resources and time, this book uses secondary sources for information, but this in no way devalues its arguments or conclusions. It is also unique in this series in that it contains chapters specifically written by individual correspondents. This has itself made the task of the Joint Centre additionally difficult, but what results is a book uniquely grounded in the context of the 15 individual EU countries. At the same time Bill Edgar and Joe Doherty have drawn out the common threads relating to homelessness and women. In an area of real neglect this book goes at least some way towards redressing the balance. It will, I hope, not only stimulate debate about those factors in homelessness which are unique to women, but also highlight the issues in homelessness which are common to both men and women and this, I believe, is equally important.

There is something here for everyone, researchers, sociologists, academics and practitioners. It is a first step for us all to build on.

Finally, I would like to record thanks to all involved in the production of this research report: the Directorate-General for Employment and Social Affairs of the European Commission, the Joint Centre for Scottish Housing Research, the national correspondents of the European Observatory on Homelessness and their research institutes and the Brussels Secretariat of FEANTSA.

John Evans
President of FEANTSA
May 2001

Acknowledgements

Our primary debt is to the national correspondents of the European Observatory on Homelessness whose national reports provide the basis for this study. We therefore acknowledge our debt to and extend our thanks to the following correspondents and their assistants: Heinz Schoibl and Klaudia Novak (Austria), Pascal De Decker (Belgium); Tobias Børner Stax, Inger Koch-Nielsen, Anders Munk, Mette Raun (Denmark); Sirkka-Liisa Kärkkäinen (Finland); Stéphane Tartinville (France); Volker Busch-Geertsema and Uta Enders-Dragässer (Germany); Aristides Sapounakis and Vasiliki Gamagari (Greece); Antonio Tosi (Italy); Eoin O'Sullivan and Mary Higgins (Ireland); Monique Pels (Luxembourg); Henk de Feijter (Netherlands); Isabel Baptista and Alfredo Bruto da Costa (Portugal); Pedro José Cabrera Cabrera (Spain); Ingrid Sahlin and Catharina Thörn (Sweden); and Robert Aldridge (UK).

We would like to pay special tribute to Amy Mina-Coull for her invaluable contributions during the early stages of the development of the research project on which this book is based. For a variety of work, family and personal reasons Amy had to withdraw from the project prior to its completion. We wish her all success in her new career in Cairo.

We would also like to acknowledge the key roles played by members of the FEANTSA Secretariat in coordinating the project and in organising meetings of the Observatory correspondents in Amsterdam and Lisbon. Finally we would like to express our thanks to Dawn Rushen, Editorial Manager at The Policy Press, for her assistance and forbearance in bringing this book to publication.

FEANTSA and the European Observatory on Homelessness

FEANTSA (the European Federation of National Organisations Working with the Homeless) is a European non-governmental organisation founded in 1989. FEANTSA currently has a total of 74 member organisations in the 15 member states of the European Union and other European countries. FEANTSA is the only major European non-governmental organisation which deals exclusively with homelessness. FEANTSA works to facilitate networking, exchanges of experiences and best practices, research and advocacy in the field of homelessness at European level. FEANTSA maintains regular dialogue with the institutions of the European Union and with national governments in order to promote effective action in the fight against homelessness. FEANTSA receives financial support from the European Commission for carrying out a comprehensive work programme. FEANTSA has very close relations with the institutions of the European Union, in particular the European Commission and the European Parliament, and has consultative status with the Council of Europe and with the Economic and Social Council (ECOSOC) of the United Nations.

The European Observatory on Homelessness was set up by FEANTSA in 1991 to conduct research into homelessness in Europe. It is composed of a network of 15 national correspondents from all member states of the European Union, who are widely recognised as experts in the field of homelessness. Each year the correspondents produce a national report on a specific research theme related to homelessness. The coordinators of the Observatory then analyse those national reports and integrate them into a European research report which focuses on transnational trends.

Contact address: FEANTSA, 1 rue Defacqz, B-1000 Brussels, Belgium; Tel 32 2 538 66 69, Fax 32 2 539 41 74, e-mail office@feantsa.org, website: http://www.feantsa.org

Coordinators and national correspondents of the European Observatory on Homelessness: 1998-1999

Coordinators

Bill Edgar, Co-Director of the Joint Centre for Scottish Housing Research (JCSHR), School of Town and Regional Planning, University of Dundee, Perth Road, Dundee DD1 4HT, UK; Tel (44) (0)1382 345238, Fax (44) (0)1382 204 234, e-mail w.m.edgar@dundee.ac.uk

Joe Doherty, Co-Director of the Joint Centre for Scottish Housing Research (JCHSR), School of Geography and Geosciences, University of St Andrews, St Andrews, Fife KY16 9AL, UK; Tel (44) (0)1334 463911, Fax (44) (0)1334 46 39 49, e-mail jd@st-andrews.ac.uk

National correspondents

Austria: Heinz Schoibl, Helix-Forschung und Beratung, Mirabellplatz 9/3, A-5020 Salzburg; Tel (43) 662 88 66 23 10, Fax (43) 662 88 66 23 9, e-mail helix@salzburg.co.at

Belgium: Pascal De Decker, Sint-Denijslaan, 293, 9000 Gent; Tel (32) 9 220 59 26, e-mail pascal.de.decker@skynet.be

Denmark: Inger Koch-Nielsen, The Danish National Institute of Social Science, Herluf Trollesgade 11, 1052 Copenhagen K; Tel (45) 33 48 08 60, Fax (45) 33 48 08 33, e-mail ikn@sfi.dk

Finland: Sirkka-Liisa Kärkkäinen, STAKES, PB 220, Fl-00531, Helsinki; Tel (358) 9 39 67 20 68, Fax (358) 9 39 67 20 54, e-mail sirkka-liisa.kärkkäinen@.stakes.fi

France: Raphaelle Betton, 38 Chemin de Fonts, 69110 Sainte-Les-Foye, France; e-mail serge.betton@ac-lyon.fr

Germany: Volker Busch-Geertsema, GISS e.v. (Association for Innovative Social Research and Social Planning), Kohlhöstrasse 22,

D-28203 Bremen; Tel (49) 421 339 88 33,
Fax (49) 421 339 88 35, e-mail giss-bremen@t-online.de

Greece: Aristides Sapounakis, Kivotos, Angelou Pyrri Street 9, 115
27 Athens; Tel (30) 1 770 33 57, Fax (30) 1 771 08 16,
e-mail arsapkiv@mail.hol.gr

Ireland: Eoin O'Sullivan, Department of Social Studies, Trinity
College, University of Dublin, Dublin 2; Tel (353) 1 608 2548,
Fax (353) 1 671 2262, e-mail tosullivan@tcd.ie

Italy: Antonio Tosi, Dipartmento di Scienze del Territorio,
Politecnico Milan, Via Bonardi 3, 20133 Milan; Tel (39) 02 239 954
17, Fax (39) 02 239 954 35, e-mail antonio.tosi@polimi.it

Luxembourg: Monique Pels, CEPS/INSTEAD, BP 48 L-4501
Differdange; Tel (352) 58 5855 536, Fax (352) 58 5560,
e-mail moniquep@hermes.CEPS.lu

Netherlands: Henk de Feijter, Planologisch Demografisch Instituut,
University of Amsterdam, Nieuwe Prinsengracht 130, NL-1018 VZ
Amsterdam; Tel (31) 20 525 40 40, Fax (31) 20 525 40 51,
e-mail H.J.Feijter@frw.uva.nl

Portugal: Alfredo Bruto da Costa, Portuguese Catholic University,
rua Eiffel 4, 3 Esq, 1000 Lisbon; Tel (351) 21 796 89 45, Fax (351) 21
795 18 35, e-mail alfredo.bc@mail.telepac.pt

Spain: Pedro José Cabrera Cabrera, Universidad Pontifica Comillas 3,
28049 Madrid; Tel (34) 91 734 39 50, Fax (34) 91 734 45 70;
e-mail pcabrera@tsocial.upco.es

Sweden: Ingrid Sahlin, Department of Sociology, University of
Göteborg, PO Box 720, 40530 Göteborg; Tel (46) 31 773 53 92,
Fax (46) 31 773 47 64, e-mail Ingrid.Sahlin@sociology.gu.se

United Kingdom: Robert Aldridge, Scottish Council for the Single
Homeless, Wellgate House, 200 Cowgate, Edinburgh EH1 1NQ;
Tel (44) 131 2264 382, Fax (44) 131 2254 382, e-mail
robert@scsh.demon. co.uk

Notes on contributors

Robert Aldridge is Director of the Scottish Council for Single Homeless and is a member of the Scottish Executive Homelessness Task Force.

Isabel Baptista is an anthropologist, senior researcher and member of the Board of Directors at CESIS (Centro de Estudos para a Intervenção Social), Lisbon.

Alfredo Bruto da Costa is Assistant Professor in the Department of Social Sciences at the Portuguese Catholic University of Lisbon.

Pedro José Cabrera Cabrera is Director of Research in the School of Social Work at the University of Pontificia, Madrid.

Pascal De Decker is a sociologist and spatial planner working as a researcher at OASeS, a research group on Poverty, Social Exclusion and the City based at Antwerp University.

Uta Enders-Dragässer is a sociologist, educationalist, women's studies researcher, and works as Research Director at Gesellschaft für Sozialwissenschaftliche Frauenforschung e.V., Frankfurt am Main, an independent research association with a special focus on women in difficult life situations and gender studies.

Henk de Feijter is Assistant Professor in Demography in the Department of Physical Planning and Demography at the University of Amsterdam.

Vasiliki Gamagari is a researcher in the Planning Department at the University of Thessaly, Volos, Greece.

Mary Higgins is a researcher and librarian at Trinity College, Dublin.

Sirkka-Liisa Kärkkäinen is a researcher at the STAKES Research Institute in Helsinki.

Inger Koch-Nielsen is head of the research unit of the Danish National Institute of Social Research and is responsible for the research unit engaged in social policy research.

Amy Mina-Coull is an independent research consultant with AMC Research Consultancy.

Anders Munk is a researcher in the Danish National Institute of Social Research.

Klaudia Novak is a social worker in Vienna with long-term practical experience in counselling homeless women and in the prevention of eviction.

Eoin O'Sullivan is a lecturer in Social Policy in the Department of Social Studies, Trinity College, Dublin.

Monique Pels is a researcher at the CEPS/INSTEAD Research Institute in Luxembourg.

Mette Raun is a researcher in the Danish National Institute of Social Research.

Aristides Sapounakis is an architect and town planner and lecturer at the University of Thessaly, Volos, Greece.

Heinz Schoibl is a researcher with the research institute Helix-Forshung und Beratung in Salzburg.

Stéphane Tartinville, during the preparation of this research project, was employed as a researcher by FNARS, Paris.

Catharina Thörn is a doctoral student at the Department of Sociology at Gothenburg University, working on a thesis on homeless women.

Antonio Tosi is Professor of Urban Sociology at the Polytechnic of Milan.

Part One:
The contextual chapters

ONE

Introduction

Bill Edgar and Joe Doherty

Feminist critiques of housing policy and provision have argued that women have been frequently neglected and marginalised in contemporary housing policy and practice. In particular, access to housing, housing design, the meaning attributed to the term 'home' and the interpretations of the concept of 'homelessness' have elicited especial criticism (Watson, 1984; Watson and Austerberry, 1986; Madigan et al, 1990). In seeking to understand the nature of this marginalisation, attention has been directed towards structural disadvantages faced by women, as reflected in their position in the labour market; a position which is seen as particularly important in limiting access to housing. In addition, researchers such as Watson (1999) and Smith (1999), referring to the predominant traditional, male breadwinner family model, argue further that the sexual division of labour within the household has implications for the relationship of different household members to the 'home' and hence to 'homelessness'. A domestic division of labour which places women in a position of economic dependence has implications not only for a woman's place in the 'home', but also for her 'place' in the wider housing market.

This book takes up and develops these themes in the context of Europe as a whole (Part One) and in the context of individual member countries of the European Union (EU) (Part Two). A study of women and homelessness in Europe at this time is particularly apposite for several reasons. First, there is a general concern that the number of homeless women may be increasing in relative and/or absolute terms in most if not all EU countries. Second, it is now widely recognised across the EU that housing and social welfare provision for homeless women is often inadequate (compared to the size of the real problem) and inappropriate (compared to women's felt or expressed needs). Third, although homelessness affects both men and women, there is a growing recognition, on the part of many practitioners and policy makers as well as researchers, that women's experiences of homelessness differ from that of men and that there is an important gender dimension to the problem of homelessness.

Data on homelessness is notoriously difficult to acquire. Homeless people exist outside of the 'normal' structures of society, they comprise a moving target which by its very nature is difficult to access. Subsections of the homeless population are even more difficult to identify and this is perhaps especially the case in relation to women whose homelessness is often 'hidden' among accommodating friends and relatives and whose presence, in consequence, in shelters and on the street (the usual sources of information on homelessness) is unrepresentative of the true dimensions of the problem. However, fragmentary and anecdotal though it may be, available information for EU countries indicates that the relative proportions of homeless women and, in some situations, possibly their absolute numbers are on the increase. While part of this recorded increase is undoubtedly due to a greater willingness on the part of women, particularly younger women, to declare themselves as officially homeless rather than remain invisible in the ranks of the hidden homeless, more fundamental reasons are to be found in European-wide changes in the social and economic circumstances of women, changes which have exposed some to an increased risk of homelessness.

The immediate triggers of homelessness among women – desertion, separation, divorce, domestic violence – associated with the dependent position of women within male-dominated nuclear households, have been compounded in recent years by increases both in the rate of marriage break-up and in the formation of vulnerable single and lone parent, female-headed households. These developments reflect the interaction of a slew of socio-demographic and economic transformations across European society which include the decline in the predominance of the nuclear family, delayed marriage, reduced fertility, increasing longevity especially among women and, importantly, the entry of large numbers of women into the labour market. These developments have, at least in part, been encouraged by feminist inspired attempts on the part of women to break from subordinate and dependent relationships as wives, mothers and carers within male breadwinner households. While many women have benefited from swapping the 'dependency' associated with their position within the traditional nuclear family for the 'freedom' of the market, others have not been so fortunate. An unintended consequence of the drive towards female emancipation – when linked with demographic transformations and social change – has been the increased exposure of some women, particularly those who have joined the lower echelons of the labour force, to an increased risk of homelessness. If there is a single message to be identified in this book it is, we suggest (notwithstanding variations between countries), that increases in the exposure of women to homelessness are at base related to the 'feminisation of poverty'; a condition which erodes the capacity of many female-headed households to establish and maintain independent homes.

While it is important to recognise the similarity in trends and the commonality of experiences among homeless women as they are manifest across Europe, it is also important to acknowledge the heterogeneity of homeless women and not to lose sight of their diversity of situations and individual experiences. This heterogeneity is reflected, for example, in the different pathways that various groups of women (young, old, single, lone parents, immigrant and so on) have in and out of homelessness, the nature of which has important implications for the identification and formulation of policy. It is also reflected in the variable manifestation of the dimensions of homelessness among women from country to country, itself reflecting variability in both the impact of the feminisation of poverty and the effectiveness of equal opportunities and welfare policies. In this respect some researchers have identified a distinction between 'women-friendly' and 'women-hostile' countries. Nordic countries are typically identified as falling within the ranks of the former, southern European countries – which have little or no formal provision for homeless women – within the ranks of the latter.

In Part One of this study the trajectory of demographic and social changes, and their impact on the position of women in European society over the post-war decades is examined. It is argued that the vulnerability of women and their exposure to the risk of homelessness, occasioned by the feminisation of poverty, has been aggravated in recent decades by the failure of the welfare state to offer sufficient social protection (Chapter 2), on the one hand, and, on the other hand, by the changing structures of the housing market which have reduced the availability of affordable and accessible housing (Chapter 3). Chapter 2 also considers recent shifts in the feminist analysis of welfare and homelessness which, while recognising the shared gender experiences of women, has cautioned against 'over-homogenisation' and argued for the recognition of 'difference', particularly in relation to the development of effective policies for resolving and preventing homelessness; a recognition of difference which embraces an understanding of the multifarious origins of homeless women in relation to class, race and generation and a sensitivity to individual life circumstances such as those of lone parents, victims of domestic violence and young single homeless women. An additional objective of Chapter 3 is to draw out the main dimensions of the problem of women's homelessness in EU countries. Drawing on the national reports of the correspondents of the European Observatory on Homelessness, an attempt is made to establish the scale of the problem, whether it is growing, by what amount and what types and groups of women are most affected.

The chapters in Part Two are derived from much larger and comprehensive national reports published in 2000 by the correspondents of the European Observatory on Homelessness. For the purposes of this publication some of the correspondents have produced a summary of their national reports retaining an overall perspective on the issue of women and homelessness in their respective countries, examining causes and dimensions, and the policy attempts to deal with the problem in its various forms. Other correspondents have been more selective, focusing on particular aspects of women and homelessness in each of their countries. Under the section heading 'Pathways' the chapters on Portugal, Spain, Ireland, the United Kingdom, Belgium and Denmark take a broad view. The range of countries considered here has been chosen to represent all the main types of European welfare regimes: Spain and Portugal from southern Europe, Ireland and the UK from the liberal regime type, Belgium from the continental regime type and Denmark from the Nordic grouping. These chapters demonstrate clearly the impact of the issues raised in Part One – feminisation of poverty, deficient social protection policies and changing housing markets – on the dimensions of female homelessness, but they also indicate considerable variation in the individual importance of these issues and the very different ways they combine to produce rather different outcomes in each country.

The chapters gathered under the label 'Services' (Austria, France, Greece, Italy, the Netherlands and Finland) are more selective in their coverage, focusing, often critically, on issues of service provision for homeless women in their respective countries. The first three chapters take a broad view of the nature and limitations of service provision. The Austrian chapter focuses on the fragmentation and lack of coordination in service provision, as well as on its overwhelming male orientation. The French chapter identifies the gaps in service provision for homeless women and examines the difficulties single women and lone parents have in maintaining relationships with partners as well as the problems women as mothers have in accessing services which allow them to maintain the integrity of their families. The chapter on Greece examines the problems of women's access to housing in a country where traditional familial ties are eroding and where social housing provision is limited. The final three chapters in this section focus on service provision for specific groups of women. The chapters on Italy and the Netherlands are concerned particularly with the plight of women members of ethnic and immigrant groups, while the Finnish chapter examines the relationship between substance abuse, homelessness and support provision.

The chapters in the section headed 'Experiences' demonstrate in three very different country contexts how the needs of homeless women are inadequately or inappropriately provided for by extant homeless services. The chapter on Luxembourg reports on the outcomes of face-to-face interviews with a sample of homeless women and service providers. It examines the adequacy of service provision and derives from the interviews a series of explicit recommendations for improvement which range from the better provision of information to suggestions regarding the design of shelters. The German chapter, in the context of a critique of the neglect of the needs of women in welfare and housing policy, considers a variety of issues ranging from coping strategies of homeless women, gender specific requirements for support facilities and rights of women in urgent need of housing. The Swedish chapter, through a series of carefully conducted, in-depth interviews, recounts the personal views of women who have had direct experience of homelessness. These three chapters demonstrate clearly that homeless women are not just hapless victims; they are also capable of active agency both in the way they cope with the problems of homelessness and in the potential they have to contribute to the development of preventive policies.

The concluding chapter, reflecting on the national coverage, attempts an overall assessment of the issue of female homelessness in Europe, particularly with regard to trends and changing composition. This chapter also assesses the overall level of service provision and identifies, with regard to the expressed preferences of women themselves, the types of changes that would contribute to effective resolution and prevention of homelessness among women. It concludes with a brief consideration of future research.

This book draws together, for the first time, research on women and homelessness across the member countries of the EU. It is designed as a contribution to the forwarding of an understanding of the relationship between gender, housing and welfare, and as a contribution to the evaluation of housing policy and practice as it relates to the needs of homeless women. The topicality of these issues has been recently affirmed by the Nice Summit of December 2000 at which the European Heads of State approved a Charter of Fundamental Rights, adopted a new European Social Agenda and a strategy for the development of National Action Plans (NAPs). All of these developments embraced the concept of the need to ensure that citizens of the EU have access to decent housing. The NAPs have explicitly adopted, as one of their objectives, the development and implementation of "policies which aim to provide access for all to decent and sanitary housing as well as the basic services necessary to live normally having regard to local circumstances" (FEANTSA newsletter, 2001, no 9, p 5). Under the umbrella of the right to a decent and affordable home, homelessness is gradually being drawn into the European debate on social and welfare policy. There is still a long way to go, although in the arena of European political debate there is emerging an understanding of homelessness as a multifaceted problem, a manifestation of social exclusion, whose effective solution is linked to issues of poverty and citizenship, and a recognition that homelessness is as much about social relationships and personal welfare as about the material conditions of housing circumstances. As the national chapters in this book demonstrate with reference to homeless women, solutions to the problems of homelessness that provide for successful integration, involve explicit consideration of issues of social participation and of personal security, control and empowerment, as well as of provision of adequate shelter.

TWO

Gendering homelessness

Joe Doherty

Introduction

The causes of women's homelessness are rooted in social and gender specific explanations and any attempt to formulate an understanding of women's encounters with homelessness requires attention to the patriarchal relations which pervade present day European society. Women's experiences of homelessness, while sharing many features with experiences of homeless men, reflect in addition their subordinate and disadvantaged position in society. In seeking an understanding of these issues, we look, first, at the changing position of women within European society during the latter half of the 20th century and the way these changes have impacted on women's exposure to and risk of homelessness. These changes reflect the combined and parallel impact of what has been called by Lesthaeghe (1995) the 'second demographic transition' (changes in the social composition and demography of European households which became apparent in Europe from the 1960s), and the post-war movement for the emancipation of women (which challenged entrenched patriarchal structures and brought about fundamental changes in the attitudes and behaviours of both women and some men)[1]. As behavioural, social and demographic changes pervade European societies, the dependency of women on membership of a male breadwinner household for access to housing – for so long the 'normal' route for women into permanent housing – has, albeit gradually and unevenly, diminished. For an increasing number of women their risk of homelessness is closely related to their capacity to form and maintain independent and autonomous households (Orloff, 1993, p 319); a capacity which crucially depends on access to resources either through the market place in secure and well paid employment or (when rewarding employment is absent) through the social protection policies of the welfare state. The second section of this chapter focuses on the latter of these issues in an examination of the extent to which women's risk of homelessness is recognised and addressed by social and welfare policies, policies which continue to reflect their origins at a time when the male breadwinner household was the dominant social form. The third and final section of the chapter examines the way female homelessness is conceptualised. Here we reflect on the heterogeneity of women as a group, recognising that while they share certain commonalities of experience, for the development of a full and constructive understanding of women's routes into and out of homelessness, the diversity of women's situations and individual experiences has to be acknowledged.

Women and the risk of homelessness

Traditionally, women's 'normal' access to housing has been through the channel of the male breadwinner household in which women played the role of dependent wife, mother and carer (Järvinen, 1993a; Kristensen, 1994; Watson, 1999). While these traditional household structures were indirectly challenged by the first feminist movement of the last century – the struggle for political emancipation in the 1920s and 1930s – it took the second feminist movement of the 1960s and 1970s, with its more explicit focus on social and economic issues, to effectively confront the established structures and the patriarchal ideology of the nuclear household form (de Bruijn et al, 1993; González López and Solsona, 2000). The demands of the women's movement for equality of treatment and opportunity in the home and the workplace were accompanied by the onset of significant demographic changes linked to the so-called 'second demographic transition'. Starting in northern Europe, these demographic changes – increasing longevity, widening sex differences in mortality, ageing and low fertility – in their turn fostered alterations in the social relationships between men and women. From the 1960s, the changing nature of dyadic relationships has been reflected in delayed marriage, increasing cohabiting and 'living-apart-together' as well as rising levels of divorce and separation. With the emergence of the dual-earner household, as more and more women entered the labour force and postponed child bearing or returned to work soon after child birth, the asymmetrical family relationships of the pre-war and early post-war decades have been, in part at least, replaced by more symmetrical relationships with both women's and men's attitudes and behaviour undergoing significant transformations. The changing nature of dyadic relationships has been paralleled by the emergence of non-traditional households – lone parents, single-person households and female-headed households – with non-traditional housing needs and non-traditional residential behaviour. Today, through much of Europe, the two-person, heterosexual family with children is no longer the dominant household form, and a woman's access to a home and position in the household is no longer necessarily determined or characterised by a dependency relationship with a man.

Seeking financial and personal independence women have moved progressively and rapidly into the labour market during the course of the past 30 years. While many have acquired skills and secured well paid jobs with career positions commanding sufficient resources to contribute to a dual-income household or to maintain their own independent households, the dominant characteristics of women's employment patterns across Europe are high levels of gender occupational segregation, low pay and high levels of unemployment (Cousins, 1999)[2]. Female labour market participation is typically in the service sector and is predominantly part time, temporary and low paid. The transition from the 'safe haven' of the nuclear family to the 'freedom' of the market place has been closely linked with the 'feminisation of poverty'; poverty which has exposed many women to an increased risk of homelessness (Millar and Glendinning, 1989; Agee and Walker 1990). There are several contributory explanations for the feminisation of poverty, for women's concentration in low paid employment – lack of skills, interrupted careers, need for (re)training and persistent workplace discrimination which continues to deny women equal pay for equal responsibility. Additionally, however, the feminisation of poverty is also explained by the coincidence of increased female labour force participation with the erosion of the standard employment contract and its replacement by the concept of flexible labour. The full-time, life-long and permanent job, which underpinned social policies in earlier decades, has been undermined in the new labour market by temporary, short-term employment contracts, many of which are part time and often low paid. It is the disproportional concentration of women in these occupations which leads to their marginalisation and to their poverty (Schmid et al, 1996).

Experiencing conditions of relative poverty, access to affordable housing has become problematic for many female householders as deregulation (escalating rents in a declining or static social housing sector) and privatisation (the drive to owner occupation) increasingly govern the development of European housing markets. Despite recent improvements, housing markets in Europe still respond predominantly to stereotyped gender roles and relations and their operation remains geared to the presumed prevalence of the traditional nuclear family. Low income, relatively poor women, denied access to mortgage finance, depend disproportionately on social housing for affordable accommodation, but even here women's housing needs, particularly when they are triggered by sudden life events such as pregnancy, relationship breakdown, sexual or physical violence, are not properly addressed or even necessarily recognised. Many social housing agencies, for example, require legal proof of separation from former partners before granting a tenancy; many show a lack of sensitivity in offering tenancies in locations near to former violent partners and continue to contribute to the destabilising of parent–child relations in providing only temporary and often inadequate accommodation for lone women with children.

In such circumstances women, threatened with homelessness, fall back on coping strategies which call on supportive social networks; networks of "kinship groups or simply of ... friends and neighbours within the community" which provide "interdependency and reciprocity" between women members (Ackers, 1998, p 38). Reliance on such 'resource frameworks' to provide shelter effectively removes many poor and destitute women from the ranks of the visibly homeless and hence from official statistics. In conditions of inadequate provision of affordable housing, hidden homelessness has become a significant dimension of homelessness among women across Europe.

The gender revolution of the second half of the 20th century has been accompanied by a retreat from the nuclear family as the dominant household form. Women's access to housing now depends less on the 'protection' offered by a male breadwinner and more on their capacity to independently access resources to form and maintain independent households. For those women, ghettoed in poorly paid and insecure employment, access to such resources is increasingly problematic, especially in conditions of changing housing markets which do not explicitly address their needs. In such circumstances, if women are to avoid the risk of homelessness, the capacity of the welfare state in providing social protection becomes critical.

Feminist critiques of the welfare state centre on the gendered nature of social policy formulation which continues to be prescribed on the basis of the male-based, standard employment contract with woman viewed as homebound wives, mothers and carers. Notwithstanding attempts to break through the stereotypes, the nuclear family remains the assumed norm and the needs and requirements of women as low paid employees in an increasingly flexible and unstable labour market, often with parental caring responsibilities, remain relatively neglected. In the next section we examine these issues through a consideration and critique of Esping-Andersen's influential first study (1990) of European welfare states, in which the degree of 'decommodification' (the extent to which risk is taken out of the market and absorbed by the state) was considered paramount and the process of 'defamilialisation'[3] (the extent to which risk is taken out of the family and absorbed by the state) was rendered inconsequential. The argument here is that the degree to which social policies address the resource needs of women can, to some extent, be measured by the degree of defamilialisation. The more that defamilialisation is an established characteristic of welfare states, the more likely it is that social policies at least begin to address the needs of women and offer them appropriate and sufficient social protection in relation to access to housing.

Welfare state: decommodification and defamilialisation

The importance of Esping-Andersen's (1990) welfare state regime typology in contributing to the debate on social welfare and social policy development in Europe is widely acclaimed. For the first time a set of criteria was identified which permitted welfare comparison across countries on the basis of multidimensional rather than one dimensional measures. In deploying and concretising the concept of 'decommodification', Esping-Andersen also presented a measure of the emancipatory potential of welfare states in terms of the ability of the commodified labour force to maintain a livelihood independent of the market. Seminal though this work has proved to be, it has nevertheless been subjected to considerable criticism and arguably, in many respects, it has been as influential in its lacunae as in its insights.

In the context of this book, two criticisms are of particular relevance. First, the inadequacy of the threefold typology and the need for a fourth regime type to mark out the distinctiveness of the southern countries from Continental, Nordic and Liberal regimes and second, an inattention to issues of gender. These criticisms are related in that the identified need for a fourth category is, in part, based on the claimed distinctiveness of the southern European countries (Portugal, Spain, Italy and Greece) in terms of their weak development of state provision of social protection and the concomitant central role of the family in the delivery of welfare (Orloff, 1993; Kilkey and Bradshaw, 1999).

Esping-Andersen, in a recent reappraisal of his 1990 typology, accepts much of these criticisms, belatedly recognising that the family,

> ... cannot be dismissed as a haven of intimacy and consumption. It is an all-important actor whose decisions and behaviours directly influence, and are directly influenced by, the welfare state and the labour market. Welfare regimes must be identified much more systematically in terms of the inter-causal triad of state, market and family. (Esping-Andersen, 1999, p 35)

Esping-Andersen accepts that the notion of decommodification assumes that individuals are already commodified and that his original conception of welfare was too tightly drawn "through the lens of the standard male production worker" and in terms of an "emphasis on income maintenance programmes and state–market duality" (1999, p 44). He further concedes that decommodification is not easily applicable to women, in that welfare states, unless they help women to become commodified first, merely cement women's pre-commodified status, doing little to alleviate the dual burden of employment and family responsibilities. Nearly 10 years after his original formulation, Esping-Andersen recognises that the "functional equivalent of market dependency for many women is family dependency", in other words, "female independence necessitates 'defamilialising' welfare obligations" (1999, p 45).

Yet, while accepting the overall gender critique of his regime analysis, Esping-Andersen is resistant to any adjustment to his simple trichotomy. By means of an examination of a variety of defamilialisation measures across European countries (1999, pp 61-2)[4] he provides a dogged defence of his original typology and argues strongly for the retention of decommodification as the central analytical concept. In the conclusion to his empirical analysis, Esping-Andersen argues that while southern countries emerge much lower on some counts, on other dimensions "other Continental regimes (like Belgium, Germany or the Netherlands) appear more familialistic" (1999, p 66). This, he suggests, "confirms more than disconfirms" (1999, p 46) the validity of the original schema. Esping-Andersen absorbs defamilialisation within the decommodified regime typology arguing that "active defamilialisation of welfare burdens" is closely associated with the social democratic regime, while an "essentially passive or at most targeted assistance approach" characterises the liberal regime, and a policy of "sustained familialism" marks out the Continental European regime (1999, p 161).

Other analyses of the gender dimensions of welfare, as Sainsbury (1999) has recently observed, take a rather more radical and critical view, not only pointing out the gaps in mainstream approaches but also proposing alternative and rival schema which cut across that of Esping-Andersen. Lewis (1992), for example, has proposed a typology based on a juxtaposition of 'male breadwinner societies' (differentiated in terms of strong, moderate and weak and dual breadwinner versions) with 'female homemaking/caring societies'. Sainsbury (1996) herself has identified a putative typology based on 'male breadwinner' and 'individual' models, differentiated on the basis of whether social rights are 'familialised' or 'individualised'. In a more recent analysis Sainsbury, admittedly with a smaller range of data, has presented empirical evidence, in direct contradiction of Esping-Andersen's conclusions, which suggests that "... in the area of care [for older people] and the provision of childcare services ... countries do not cluster into distinct groups corresponding to welfare state regimes" (1999, p 246).

The disjuncture between some feminist interpretations and those of the mainstream as represented by Esping-Andersen, is not, however, simply a question of empirical interpretation; rather it reflects a more fundamental issue of how gender is conceptualised. In attempting to come to terms with the gendered nature of welfare state regimes, Esping-Andersen effectively evades the nub of feminist criticism by moving away from a focus on 'women as individuals' to a focus on 'women in the family'. Feminists cogently argue that viewing 'women as individuals' focuses on issues of personal autonomy and provides a more effective means of assessing the impact of welfare systems on a variety of interrelated aspects of dependency – on male breadwinners, the labour market, and on the state – and in practice provides us with a clearer assessment of women's ability to exercise choice and independence (Ackers, 1998, p 37). The personal autonomy of women and their ability to exercise choice and independence is enhanced under different welfare regimes by the degree to which social policy is characterised by defamilialisation, taking on responsibility for child care, care of older people and disabled people; the level of personal autonomy that can be exercised determines, among other things, the capacity of women to form and maintain an independent household (Orloff, 1993)[5].

The 'principle of individual provision' of social welfare has been used to differentiate countries along a continuum from 'women-friendly' to 'women-hostile'; the former are likely to offer a high degree of protection for women against the risk of homelessness, the latter a low degree of protection. Early attempts to place groups of countries on this continuum identified Scandinavian countries such as Sweden and Denmark as 'women-friendly' and southern countries such as Greece as 'women-hostile', with the UK and Ireland occupying intermediary positions (see Ackers, 1998, p 224). Such categorisations, however, as well as echoing aspects of Esping-Andersen's analysis in that they leave his trichotomy virtually unchanged, have been criticised for conflating theory with practice, of confusing nominal provision with actual provision, and for a universalising tendency which does not take into account the heterogeneity of women in relation to their varying requirements for social protection.

More recent analysis (Pfau–Effinger, 1998; Bang et al, 2000; Duncan, 2000) has suggested that the problem with many gendered models of European welfare states, and the reason why they tend to reproduce Esping-Andersen's typology, is that they are too concerned with the economic, labour market dimensions of gender relations; dimensions which are treated as "an empirical, almost optional, add–on" to analysis based on 'conventional' decommodification (Duncan, 2000, p 10). In Duncan's view, in any consideration of the gendered nature of welfare states, gender relations need to be embraced as "the central causal dynamic" (2000, p 15) by taking explicit account of the dominant social norms and values within the home (the 'gender contract') as well as gender relations in the labour market (the 'capital-labour contract'); gendered models of the welfare state need to reflect decommodification and defamilialisation simultaneously. Pfau-Effinger's (1998) six–part typology (family/economic; male breadwinner/female home carer; male breadwinner/female part-time carer; dual breadwinner/state carer; dual breadwinner/dual carer; dual earner/marketised female carer) comes close to embracing these criteria in explicitly juxtaposing the gender relations of the labour market with those of the family/household.

Pfau-Effinger's typology – to the extent that it captures the fundamentals of presently existing gendered welfare states across the EU – exposes the manner in which the social policies of all European welfare states are still wedded to a greater or lesser degree to the concept of traditional dyadic relationships as the household norm. The 'misfits' of society, that is, those households which do not fit the dyadic model (see Bang et al, 2000, p 121), do not figure explicitly in these classifications, indicating their relative neglect by social protection policy. Yet it is precisely among the 'misfit' households, which include poor, lone female households, lone parents, divorcees, and women fleeing from domestic violence, that the risk of homelessness is at its most acute and the requirement for social protection highest. In determining the extent to which welfare states serve to protect and reinforce the capacity of women to form and maintain autonomous households, this neglect of alternative, non-dyadic household structures is critical in contributing to increases in the level of homelessness and the risk of homelessness among women. As the 1999 national reports of the correspondents of the European Observatory on Homelessness indicate (see Chapters 4 to 18), the provision of social protection for women exposed to the risk of homelessness, even in those countries with well established welfare states, is at best patchy, providing reasonably well for some categories of women, but rather poorly for others. Most countries, for example, reflecting the attachment to family values and a recognition of childhood vulnerability – values captured and emphasised in Pfau-Effinger's typology – can claim provision for lone parents; most, however, are neglectful of older women and few can claim adequate provision for young, single women or for victims of domestic violence. All fail to adequately to address the plight of immigrant women or asylum-seekers. The effectiveness of social and welfare policies in supporting women's personal autonomy and independence – and hence their capacity to maintain an autonomous household – requires not only that they address the economic circumstances (feminisation of poverty) of women within the dual household, but that they are also sensitive to the heterogeneous composition of female households and are attuned to the specifics of individual social (and political) circumstances.

Conceptualising homelessness among women

Feminist analysis of welfare issues has undergone several shifts of focus in recent years and these have had an impact on the study of female homelessness. As Bang and his colleagues suggest, in relation to research on the way in which the welfare state affects the position of women, two opposing theoretical viewpoints have tended to predominate: a radical 'patriarchal' perspective which characterised the welfare state as "an instrument used by men for the oppression of women", and an 'empowerment' perspective which viewed the welfare state as offering the potential for the improvement of "women's lot as workers, mothers and citizens" (Bang et al, 2000, p 115). Current disputes, however, while reflecting some of the earlier debates, tend to focus more on the opposition between 'essentialist' and 'anti-essentialist' perspectives. The former start with the concept of 'a unified gender identity' and argue that the modern welfare state ought to be constructed to meet the common needs and aspirations of women. Anti-essentialist perspectives, in contrast, argue that such normative thinking is inappropriate and that "institutions and individuals cannot be analysed independently of the historical and social conditions that constitute them" (Bang et al, 2000, p 115). Such social and historical contextualisation is to be welcomed in that, in encouraging disaggregation, deconstruction and recognition of difference, it counters the homogenising effects apparent in many taxonomic schema and permits the development of a more sensitised and nuanced understanding of the female predicament. However, to then argue, as some anti-essentialists do, that the dimensions of women's equality should be determined by those same historical and social conditions and not be addressed in broader, more universalistic terms, would seem unnecessarily limiting. While it is important that we are sensitive to context and recognise heterogeneity among women, it is also important, as Neale (1997) reminds us, that we do not lose sight of women's "shared gender experiences". An anti-essentialist viewpoint in neglecting the commonality of women's position and experiences in male-dominated societies, is in danger of descending into a 'formless relativism' where research becomes immersed in specifics, producing empathetic accounts, but losing sight of the wider agenda and, indeed, of dispensing entirely with the idea of improvement and progress in the condition of women.

As the national reports in Part Two of this book demonstrate, effective social policies for preventing and resolving homelessness among women should recognise and address the heterogeneity of women's needs. This involves not only a recognition of difference based on class, race, generation, family status, citizenship, disability and sexual orientation, but also of the individual support needs of, for example, women caught up in the so-called ADM (alcohol, drugs and mental illness) syndrome (see Fischer and Breakey, 1991; Blasi, 1990). Further, reflecting the complexity and multidimensionality of homelessness and of women's homelessness in particular, effective social policy requires sensitivity to women's individual life circumstances – young women deserting or being evicted from the parental home, women suffering from domestic abuse, lone parents, divorcees, older women and widows – circumstances which, in part at least, reflect structural and behavioural changes associated with the 'second demographic transition'.

The national reports also indicate that effective prevention and resolution of homelessness among women requires a detailed understanding of women's coping mechanisms when faced with actual homelessness or the threat of homelessness. The stigma associated with homelessness for women in their pejorative labelling as 'victims' or as 'fallen women' (prostitutes), the potential threat of the violence of the streets and the iatrogenic maleness of homeless shelters, all operate as deterrents to women owning up to homelessness. The ability of women to hide their homelessness within the supportive confines of their social networks not only demonstrates an effective coping strategy, but, importantly, also has the potential of disguising the full extent of the problem from public gaze and hence as a welfare issue.

The necessity of a contextualised analysis is further demonstrated in the evaluation of the contribution of specific welfare provisions in facilitating the ability of women to form and maintain their own home and hence to obviate the risk and threat of homelessness. In relation to the provision of day care facilities for children, Bang and his colleagues, for instance, indicate that their impact may vary between different social contexts:

> First, day care may be constructed in order to improve socialisation, life quality and welfare of children vulnerable to neglect or abuse. Second, day care may be constructed to bridge the needs of mothers in combining childrearing with paid employment. Third, day care may be considered as an institution of relief in order to improve the welfare and functioning of the family. (Bang et al, 2000, p 121)

Thus, as Bang observes, while in Britain public day care (until recently) focused predominantly on problem children, in Nordic countries it is designed to enable women to combine motherhood with participation in paid employment, and in Italy and Germany educational motives predominate.

Contextualisation, however, has another dimension beyond the social and historical identified by anti-essentialists. That is the context of the shared experience, the commonalities that all women share in their experience of patriarchy and the commonalities that homeless women share in their experience of homelessness or the threat of homelessness. The key issues here, for women at risk of homelessness, are those identified in the preceding sections of this chapter: the experience of (relative) poverty (a consequence of the disadvantages of being a woman in a discriminating and flexible labour market) and the problems of accessing decent and affordable housing and appropriate and sufficient social protection in the context of welfare states which remain largely in thrall to traditional notions of household formation. These contextual commonalities as well as the social and historical context identified and emphasised by anti-essentialists are addressed in the following national chapters.

Notes

[1] The question of whether the position of women is primarily the determinant of demographic change or its outcome is set aside here in favour of a view which sees them as mutually interacting (see Frederici et al, 1993).

[2] Even in Scandinavian countries where the labour market position of women is perhaps most secure, women's wages are on average only 80% of those of men employed in equivalent occupations.

[3] See Lister (1994) for an early use of this term.

[4] Esping-Andersen's empirical tests involve an examination of the percentage of GDP public spending on family services, the provision of public day care services for under three-years-olds and home-help provision for older people. He also looks at the percentage of older people living with their children, the proportion of unemployed youth living at home and weekly unpaid hours of women in the home and at the way benefits and taxes contribute to defamilialisation.

[5] The evaluation of welfare states in terms of their contribution to the development of personal autonomy and individual entitlements can be identified in the wider literature on the retrenchment of the welfare state. Claude Offe, for example, has recently argued for the decoupling of individual income entitlement from income-earning capacity. For Offe, decoupling can be given concrete form by "doing away with means-testing and assessment of willingness to work, by the gradual replacement of the principle of equivalence by that need" and by introducing "the principle of the individual as the basis for entitlement" (Offe, 1996, p 210, quoted in Bauman, 1998, p 95). Zigmunt Bauman – in a direct link with feminist critiques of Esping-Andersen – observes that Offe's postulate needs to be supplemented by another, that of decoupling of work from the labour market, from that historically derived definition which "demarcated work as part of a man's world, leaving outside virtually everything which was cast as the exclusive domain of women" (Bauman, 1998, p 97).

THREE

Women, the housing market and homelessness

Bill Edgar

Introduction

The national reports of the research correspondents of the European Observatory on Homelessness suggest that there is little official recognition that homelessness among women is a particular problem, or that the nature of the problem merits closer policy scrutiny. Several factors may account for this situation. Since homelessness has traditionally been perceived as a male experience, gender does not enter the "analytic or explanatory account" (Novac et al, 1996, p 1) beyond the inclusion of women in the basic demographic profile of homeless people. Where homelessness is perceived in the more narrow conception of 'sleeping rough' then the visibility of homelessness as a women's issue is less evident (Baptista and Bruto da Costa, 2000). Furthermore, since women often avoid homelessness services which leave them feeling vulnerable or unsafe, the extent of women's homelessness is often "underestimated in official figures and statistics from hostels and night shelters" (Jones, 1999, p 12). Contributing to this lack of official awareness of the vulnerability of women to homelessness, despite the recent emergence of a literature on gender and housing (Enders-Dragässer, 2000), is the absence of sustained gender specific research on the subject of homelessness.

This chapter provides a context for discussion of the nature of homelessness among women in Europe. The context is established in two main ways. First, the chapter considers the housing market constraints facing women, and how these vary between countries. This discussion suggests that changes in housing markets across Europe may make female-headed households more vulnerable and thus increase their risk of living in poorer quality or insecure housing as well as increasing their risk of homelessness.

Second, the final section of the chapter describes the pattern of homelessness among women in Europe. The aim of this description is to determine the scale of the problem, whether it is growing, what types/groups of women are most affected, what factors may be most important and whether there are differences in these dimensions between the countries of the European Union (EU). This provides the background for a discussion of the national situation of homelessness among women in each member state of the EU.

The changing housing market in Europe

The changes in the housing market which have been evident across Europe, during the last 20 years, are well documented in the literature (McCrone and Stephens, 1996; Kleinman et al, 1998; Balchin, 1996; van der Heijden and Haffner, 2000). These reviews demonstrate that, overall, there has been a retrenchment in state involvement in housing in most European countries. Government preference in most countries, since the mid-1990s, has been for a "weakly regulated market framework" (Ball and Wood, 1999, p 191). The way these twin themes, of a less prominent regulatory and subsidy role of the state and a more prominent role of the market, are elaborated varies between countries (van der Heijden and Haffner, 2000). This variation reflects the level of interaction between housing policy and housing market developments in the context of exogenous factors related to economic and demographic changes (van der Heijden and Haffner, 2000).

Ball and Wood (1998) demonstrate convincingly how the impact of financial deregulation has made housing provision more dependent on general macro-economic performance and on the policies and structures of key financial institutions rather than government policy. This shift towards more market-oriented mechanisms has led to a greater volatility and uncertainty as housing markets follow general economic cycles (Kleinman, 1998; Ball and Wood, 1999). A key outcome of this has been a closer link between a household's economic circumstances and its housing circumstances.

Some of the key effects of the desire of governments to disengage from housing provision (and housing subsidy) include rising housing costs, an increasing difficulty of access to housing resulting from tenure change combined with high rates of household formation, and a decline in social housing production. Housing consumption patterns are now more determined by people's position in the labour market relative to the wider economy. The link between poverty and poor housing is re-emerging, levels of homelessness rising and mortgage repossessions and evictions for rent arrears becoming a permanent feature in most countries. The problem of accessible and affordable housing, and the link between a household's economic circumstances and housing quality, must be central concerns if the European policies of social inclusion are to be realised (McCrone and Stephens, 1996; Balchin, 1996; MacLennan et al, 1996).

Demographic changes, in an era of high household formation rates, together with economic factors, combine to ensure that "tenure is a major contour of social exclusion" (Maclennan et al, 1996, p 3). Housing policies across Europe, with the possible exception of Sweden which pursues a tenure-neutral policy, have aimed at promoting home ownership. Such policies have co-existed with a stagnation or decline in social rental sectors resulting both from a decline in production (in most countries) and from the transfer to owner-occupation (in some countries). From a peak in the late 1960s/1970s housing supply has declined in most states. During the 1990s housing production has continued to show an absolute decline with the exception of Portugal and Spain and, more recently, Ireland (see Figure 3.1).

Hence there is an absolute shortage of affordable rented housing in most EU countries. One effect of this is that the larger social rental

Figure 3.1: Percentage change in annual dwelling completions (1980 and 1999)

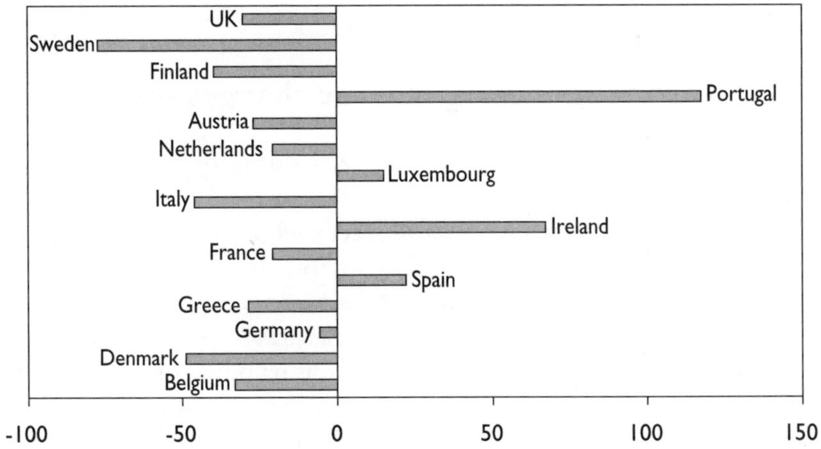

Source: Haffner and Dol (2000)

23

sectors in Europe have, over the last 20 years, come to house a larger proportion of the poor, including older people, unemployed and single-parent families as well as people from ethnic minorities and migrants.

Ball and Wood (1999) argue that "housing is becoming more expensive relative to incomes over the medium term, even when cyclical effects are discounted" (p 63). The worst phase of house price increases occurred in many European countries between 1975 and 1990 (Boelhouwer and van der Heijden, 1992; Myers et al, 1992; Bramley, 1994; Ball and Wood, 1999). Housing costs have continued to increase during the 1990s in many countries. While house prices for owner-occupation have shown considerable volatility, there is evidence that rents have continued to increase (Haffner and Dol, 2000). In countries with housing allowance systems rents rose ahead of inflation throughout the 1980s and this pattern has continued into the 1990s, while the Mediterranean countries (with no housing allowance systems) had rent increases below inflation rates (MacLennan et al, 1996). Van der Heijden and Haffner (2000, p 75) show that on average "rents have risen more steeply than incomes, whereby the proportion of household income spent" on (net) rent has risen, with the exception of the Netherlands and France where housing allowances have mediated net increases. The effectiveness of housing allowances, and of increased targeting of subsidies, in combating renter poverty is a complex issue but it is probable that such protection measures create poverty traps especially for households whose labour market position is marginal. In all six countries studied, van der Heijden and Haffner (2000) describe an increase in the concentration of low-income groups in the social rented sector, where their presence was already strong.

The impact of housing market changes on women

While it has been possible to review the nature of housing market changes, using a wide range of available research and literature, it is more difficult to determine what impact such changes may have had for women, or rather for female-headed households. It is argued that "market-dominated housing policies disadvantage women, particularly female-led households" (Novac et al 1996, p 1). To the extent that this is true, then the retreat of the state from housing provision and the shift of policies towards a weakly regulated market framework may have increased the vulnerability of women to homelessness or increased the precariousness of their housing circumstances. This section, using the framework presented in Chapter 2 and the evidence in the national reports of the European Observatory on Homelessness, examines three main factors: the economic status of women, their family status and the extent to which housing and social protection policies mediate their vulnerability in the housing market.

The first issue to consider is the extent to which the economic status of female-headed households exposes them to vulnerability in the context of weakly regulated housing markets. Stable, secure and well-paid employment ensures success in the housing market, while low-wage employment and unemployment leads to the risk of housing exclusion. This risk will be moderated by the nature of social security and by the strength of family protection.

Since 1994, women have accounted for most of the growth in the EU labour force (approximately 85%). While this increase was widespread across the EU, it was especially marked in those countries with the lowest levels of participation. However, much of this growth was accounted for by part-time employment. As a result, in 1999 a third of all women in employment worked part time compared to 28% in 1994 (see Figure 3.2). Part-time employment is highest in the Netherlands (almost 70%) and the UK (45%) and lowest in the Nordic countries and in the southern European countries. Despite this improvement in

Figure 3.2: Women's employment rates and women's part-time rates (1998)

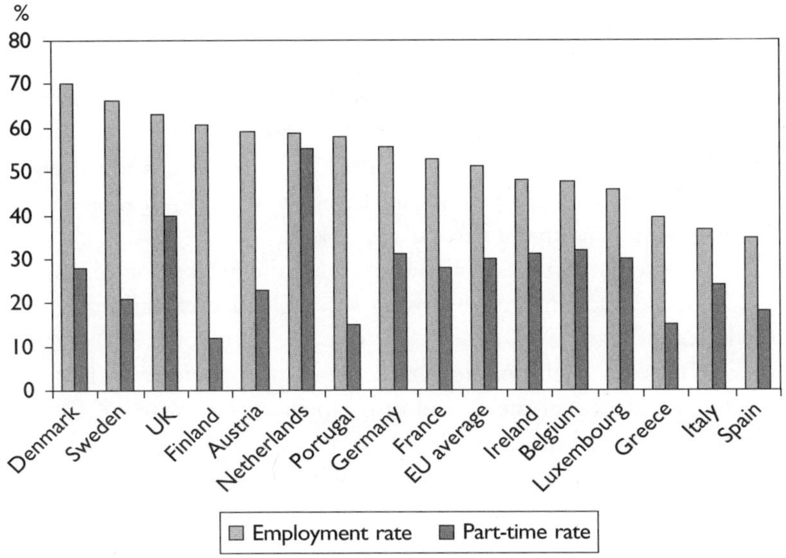

Source: OECD (2000)

participation rates, unemployment rates remain higher for women than for men. In Belgium, Denmark, Spain, Italy, the Netherlands and Portugal the female rate is between 55 and 92% higher, while active women in Luxembourg and Greece are twice as likely to be unemployed (European Commission, 2001). Only in Ireland, Sweden and the UK is the situation more favourable for women.

Muehlberger (2000) argues that both partnership and care responsibilities have a strong negative impact on women's labour market participation, while care responsibilities have a positive impact on part-time employment. While these effects are particularly strong in Germany and the UK, they are weaker in Denmark, Italy and Greece. The explanation can be found in the strength of family ties in child care provision in Italy and Greece and the strong public provision of facilities in Denmark (see also Sainsbury, 1999). In Germany, the lack of public caring infrastructure reduces women's chances of integrating in the labour market.

Although their employment prospects may have been improving, the susceptibility of women to poverty is only partially mediated by their improved employment situation. Muehlberger (2000) cites recent economic research on the gender wage gap to demonstrate that gender and family status (notably motherhood) result in a substantial negative impact on women's wages (Waldfogel, 1998; Gupta and Rothstein, 2000; Lissenburgh, 2000; Meurs and Ponthieux, 2000). In the Nordic countries, Belgium, Luxembourg, France and Germany women's average wages are between 80-84% of men's, while in the remaining countries they are around 70%. However, it is significant that female-headed households stand out as having higher than average levels of poverty according to the EU definition of poverty (European Commission, 2001), including lone parents (36%) and single women (26%). In the UK and Ireland more than half of single parents are in poverty, while in Greece and Portugal older women are particularly at risk.

It is reported in a number of countries that the proportion of female-headed households in poverty (using the EU poverty definition) has risen in recent years. De Decker (2000; quoting Cantillon, 1999) suggests that, in Belgium, "within the active population there is a clear and structural tendency in the direction of an increasing share of females who head a household in poverty" (p 11). Similar situations are in evidence, for example, in Ireland (O'Sullivan, 2000), the Netherlands (de Feijter, 2000), Spain (Cabrera, 2000) and Portugal (Baptista and Bruto da Costa, 2000) where lone parents and single retired women are reported as the main risk groups. However, in Finland, Denmark, Sweden and

France income transfers are effective in protecting some groups from poverty (Ritokallio, 2000). In the Nordic countries especially the poverty risk of lone parents is not much higher than for the population generally (Ritokallio, 2000, pp 34-35). On the other hand, Kärkkäinen (2000, p 21) suggests that, in Finland, "the proportion of young single women in the lowest income fifth rose from 26 to 38 per cent in the 1990s".

An understanding of the effects of economic status on the housing situation of women requires consideration of their family status. Overall, more than a quarter of households in Europe are headed by a woman. It has been argued that women's housing prospects are tied closely to their family status (Pascall, 1997). This arises for different reasons. First, a woman's marital and parental status affect her labour force participation which in turn affects her level of autonomy and independence within and outside of marriage (Watson and Austerberry, 1986, p 148). Second, a woman's security of housing tenure and property rights may be affected by her relationship or family status – whether she is single, cohabiting or married. Third, relationship breakdown changes a woman's housing circumstances (often for the worse).

The demographic changes occurring across Europe are well documented and have been discussed in Chapter 2. The relative stability of the birth rate since the mid-1970s in northern Europe and the steep falls in southern Europe were accompanied by trends towards later marriage, a growth in single-person households and in cohabiting among young people, and more divorce (Ermisch, 1996). In addition, the ageing of Europe's population and the social and economic impacts, although they vary considerably between different European countries, are much debated. The relative importance of women in the older population is a further factor in the increase in female-headed households. We can identify three main types of female-headed households: single adults of working age living alone, single older women and lone parents. The proportion and mix of these household types varies between countries. Equally the vulnerability of these different female households will vary and will tend to be influenced respectively by labour market differentials in income, by gender power relationships following divorce, and by the differential effects of social protection systems.

A quarter of all households in Europe are composed of a single person. While population ageing plays a role in this increase the pattern across Europe shown in Figure 3.3 illustrates that, at least in northern Europe, there is an increasing tendency for people below retirement age to live alone. People reliant on a single income are least able to cope with the financial burden of housing costs (Sandeman et al, 2000), particularly

Figure 3.3: Single-person households as a percentage of all households (1999)

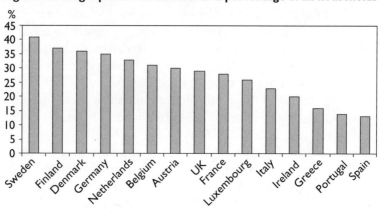

Source: Haffner and Dol (2000)

among those in rented accommodation (Siikanen et al, 1999). More than a quarter of single women are in poverty according to the EU definition.

As a result of high and increasing divorce rates and births outside marriage, single-parent families now account for between 5% and 17% of all families in different countries. The lowest levels of lone parenthood are found in Sweden, Denmark, the Netherlands, Germany and Greece, while the highest occur in the UK, Finland and Ireland. In the UK one fifth of families with dependent children are lone-parent households. The English Housing Survey found that one third of lone-parent (mainly women) households had experienced homelessness within the previous 10 years compared to 6% of all households (Webster, 2000) and three quarters relied on local authority rented housing to escape their homeless situation. In a 1999 assessment of homelessness in Ireland over a quarter of households were single parents; the assessment of housing need showed that 37% were unable to afford their existing accommodation. However, in Finland low-income single parents have priority for social housing and hence their circumstances are probably better than other groups, such as young single women without children (Kärkkäinen, 2000).

The third set of factors which may influence the ability of women to maintain an independent autonomous household relate to the extent to which housing and social policies enable them to realise housing opportunities in the local housing market. Although gender-based national housing statistics are rare in Europe, it is claimed (Gilroy and Woods, 1994; Pascall, 1997) that women-led households are predominantly renters. To the extent that this is true, it is then argued that "their severe affordability problems in the private rental sector, and the lack of sufficient subsidised housing, are obvious factors in their vulnerability to homelessness" (Novac et al, 1996, p 1).

Because of the paucity of gendered housing statistics, there is very little available data on the tenure distribution of households headed by women. Balchin (1996) describes three categories of countries based on tenure distribution. In countries with a high level of owner-occupation the housing status of female-headed households will be more dependent on access to mortgage finance or the availability of family and personal finance and support. Sapounakis (2000) highlights the importance of the tradition of the dowry system in Greece by which the bride's family provides accommodation where possible and over which the woman retains full rights. In countries with a high level of private rented accommodation, the position of women will reflect the prevailing systems of allocation and of housing allowances and will be more precarious in countries with high rent levels and weakly developed systems of housing allowances or of allowances which discriminate against female households. Private renting is higher than the European average in Germany, Belgium and Luxembourg. However, it represents over 80% of all rental accommodation in five countries – Greece, Luxembourg, Spain, Portugal and Belgium – and 50% or over in Germany, Denmark, Italy, France and Austria (see Figure 3.4).

Elsewhere social rented housing is a more significant contributor of rental housing. It is well documented that female-headed households

Figure 3.4: Private rental housing and total rental stock (1999)

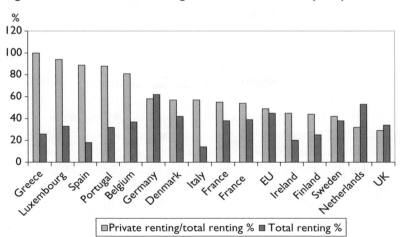

Source: European Commission (2001)

(that is, single parents and older people) are overrepresented in, and hence more reliant on, the social rented housing stock. In countries with relatively high levels of social rented accommodation, then, women tend to benefit if they have dependent children but otherwise face the same discrimination as single men (Aldridge, 2000; Kärkkäinen, 2000; O'Sullivan, 2000). Decline in the provision of social housing in most countries in Europe since the mid-1980s (Haffner and Dol, 2000) is likely to have exacerbated the precarious situation of female-headed households and, particularly, of single women under retirement age.

In the context of the rapid increase in housing costs and rents described above, the vulnerability of women in the housing market is exacerbated by their relative poverty and reliance on part-time employment. Increased incidence of renter poverty and rising rents, at least in northern Europe, in all rental tenures are increasingly being met by housing allowances and other income-related rent measures (MacLennan et al, 1996). Studies of housing affordability in the rented sectors, where these exist, show that it is single adult households (of either gender) and female-headed households who pay a larger proportion of their household expenditure on direct housing costs (Pleace et al, 1999). De Decker (2000) suggests that, in Belgium, single women under retirement age pay more than average for housing while lone parents pay less than the affordability threshold of 20% of income (p 28). A similar picture is apparent in the Nordic countries. O'Sullivan (2000), on the other hand, quotes national housing data to demonstrate that single parents face the greatest difficulties in housing affordability. The housing poverty of female-headed households is mediated only by their increased dependency on housing benefits. However, housing allowances may create poverty traps, especially for people in part-time employment.

The pattern of homelessness for women

This section reviews the evidence presented by the researchers of the European Observatory on Homelessness on the nature of homelessness among women in Europe in the national reports. This provides an overview of the situation across Europe to set the context for the more detailed discussion of specific issues arising in each of the member states. The available evidence is reviewed with the aim of addressing three main questions:

- What is the scale of homelessness among women, and is the problem growing?
- Which women are most affected by homelessness?
- What factors lead to homelessness?

In addressing these questions the diversity and commonality of experience across Europe is considered. However, the findings presented here must be interpreted with caution due to the well-known problems, especially in the field of homelessness research, of a lack of consistent quantitative data across Europe. These difficulties arise from several factors which pertain in all comparative homelessness research: the lack of official statistics, the consequent reliance on service user statistics, the measurement problems which pertain to homelessness research and different operational definitions between areas and between time periods. In the current context they also arise because of the lack of gendered statistics in many countries or of historic gendered data. Importantly, however, analysis of homelessness among women is compounded by the conceptual problems discussed in Chapter 2 and reflected, in particular, in the extent of hidden homelessness among women and in the extent to which, for example, women fleeing domestic violence are classed as being homeless. Equally, women in institutional care are omitted from national analysis even though, according to the FEANTSA definition, they should be regarded as 'houseless'. We may also assume that measurement of homelessness among immigrant women may be difficult if the legality of their status is in doubt. Finally, our analysis of the nature and scale of homelessness for women cannot escape the 'service-statistics' paradox. That is to say, that measurement, especially using official statistics, will often be a reflection of current service provision rather than actual needs.

What is the scale of homelessness among women and is the problem growing?

Given the difficulties described above, any estimate of the scale of female homelessness across the European member states is likely to be an underestimate of the true extent of homelessness among women. The estimates provided here may, nevertheless, be helpful in providing, for the first time, a benchmark against which the nature and trends of homelessness can be assessed. It allows some comparative analysis to be undertaken and will, hopefully, raise awareness of the scale and nature of the problem and provide a basis for further debate.

The evidence suggests that a common pattern across Europe appears to be that women represent approximately 11-17% of the street homeless population and between 25% and 30% of all homeless people. While males remain overrepresented in counts of homelessness, the number of females appears to be increasing in some countries (although not everywhere). In view of the difficulty of obtaining figures from official sources or service providers on a consistent basis, we will consider the issue in relation to the three broad groupings of countries described by Harvey (1993).

First, there are the larger nations where the level of homelessness is relatively high (between five and 10 persons per thousand of the population): Germany, France and the UK. In Germany, it has recently been estimated that there are about 530,000 homeless people, of whom 26,000 are street homeless (Specht-Kittler, 1999). Steinert (1991) estimated that 15% of the homeless ('persons without fixed abode' – *nichtsesshaft*) were single women. More recently, the National Campaign for the Homeless estimates that 11% of the street homeless (about 3,000), 21% of all homeless single-person households (about 38,000) and 30% of all homeless persons (about 160,000) are women (BAG Wohnungslosenhilfe, 1999). It is uncertain whether this apparent increase from the early to the late 1990s indicates a real increase or greater visibility of homeless women. These figures do not include women fleeing domestic violence who find protection and support in shelters for battered women (*Frauenhäuser*). There are about 390 shelters in Germany which operate under the political responsibility of the municipalities and belong to an independent support system separate from the support system for homeless people.

In the UK, it is difficult to obtain gendered statistics on homelessness. Evidence, therefore, has to be derived from service user statistics. In 1999, local authorities accepted responsibility for housing 104,770 homeless households (statutorily defined as in priority need of housing), a quarter of whom lost their last home as a result of relationship breakdown (DETR, 2000). Shelter has reported that in 1996/97 more than 36,000 women approached its network of advice centres in England and that, of that number, 21,000 were homeless, either living rough or in temporary accommodation. In 1995 20,000 women lost their home because of domestic violence. Women's Aid, which operates refuges for women who have experienced domestic violence, reports growing numbers of women approaching them for assistance. Studies in England

(Anderson et al, 1993) found that 15% of rough sleepers were women, while studies in Scotland (Shaw et al, 1996) showed a similar figure. Recent surveys indicate that a quarter of homeless young people arriving in London are women. Comparing surveys of homeless women in hostels between 1972 and 1991, the clear trend is that there is an increase in younger homeless women using services. Centrepoint, offering emergency accommodation to young people, shows the proportion of young women admitted to projects rose from 25% in 1987 to 44% in 1997.

Data on women's homelessness in France largely reflects the situation in Paris and its environs with few statistics for the rest of the country. In common with all other countries, most data on homelessness is gathered from service providers thus reflecting more accurately the extent of service use rather than actual need. A survey undertaken on one night in Paris found that women made up 23% of service users in emergency shelters in Paris increasing from 21% in the previous year (Tartinville, 2000). Women accounted for 15% of callers on the homelessness helpline (115) in Paris (1998) and 20% of callers in provincial regions (1999). In longer-term provision with support (CHRS: Centre d'Hebergement et de Readaptation Sociale), women make up between 34% and 40% of service users, reflecting, perhaps, their preference for this type of self-contained supported housing on the one hand, and the recognition of their needs by these types of service providers on the other.

In the second group of countries, it is estimated that about two people in every 1,000 are homeless in countries including Italy, Belgium, the Netherlands and Luxembourg.

In Italy, according to 1999 estimates, women account for between 13% and 16% of the 'no abode' homeless population, a percentage which corresponds to local survey evidence and which would indicate a figure of 9,000-10,000 'no abode' women in Italy. If account is taken of "the latency of homelessness among women and the high percentage of implicit homelessness, the number of women that can be considered homeless must certainly be higher" (Tosi, 2000a, p 9). Evidence indicates that much higher percentages of women are found among the users of social services for persons 'in difficulty' (the UAD – municipal offices for adults in difficulty). Thus, while it is difficult to garner evidence that explicit homelessness is increasing, it is probable that there is an increase in the vulnerability and risk of homelessness among women.

In Belgium, figures are available in relation to the users of reception houses in the Flemish region which indicate that 17% of the homeless are women. Trends indicate that, despite a rising capacity in service provision, the numbers of women using these services has probably declined slightly since the early 1990s. This cannot, however, be taken to indicate that homelessness among women has been declining per se. Rather it indicates a shift in the role of such centres where the average duration of stay has been increasing, reflecting a recognition of the support needs of women as well as the difficulty of accessing permanent move-on accommodation.

The number of homeless people in the Netherlands has remained fairly constant in recent years. Despite projections that the number of homeless people would increase to 53,000 by the end of the 1990s (Heydendael et al, 1990; Avramov, 1995), it is estimated that there are approximately 25,000 to 30,000 homeless people in the Netherlands at this time (Wolf et al, 2000). Social shelters in the Netherlands are a relatively small and recent sector comprising some 100 organisations running about 300 (mainly) small-scale facilities with a placement capacity of around 10,000 (3,000 in women's shelters and 7,000 in other shelters). Homeless women are mainly provided for in special shelters for women (90%). In 1999 there were 10,367 admissions (from 32,581 applications) to women's shelters (including women's refuges, shelters for single mothers and women's shelters). A total of 1,600 women asylum-seekers stayed in women's shelters in 1999. A small number of special shelter facilities have recently been established by youth care organisations to provide accommodation for young prostitutes (up to 21 years of age); it has been estimated by Childcare Worldwide that there are over 1,000 prostitutes (mainly girls) aged between 12 and 18 in the Netherlands.

All currently available data on the homeless population in Luxembourg shows that, over the past five years, the number of women using reception centres and foyers has increased considerably. A survey of reception services conducted annually since 1995 shows that the number of women entering services has doubled, with women currently accounting for 46% of service users. Even this figure is likely to be an underestimate of the true extent of the problem, since it only includes women who have approached services. Data on number of applicants as compared with number of women entering services may be indicative of the greater level of unmet need. Figures from 1995 and 1998 show that more women were unable to access services than were actually admitted despite an increase in the supply of women-specific provision.

The third group of countries, where homelessness is defined as being low as a proportion of the population, can possibly be subdivided into two main categories. First, there are countries where the level of homelessness is low as measured by rooflessness and houselessness, and where insecure and inadequate accommodation is also low; this includes Austria, Denmark, Finland and Sweden. Second, there are countries where rooflessness is apparently low, but where there are high numbers of people living in insecure or inadequate accommodation, including Greece, Ireland, Portugal and Spain.

The Austrian federation of service providers for the homeless (BAWO) has recently implemented a national project to register all services which are concerned with issues of poverty and homelessness (Eitel and Schoibl, 1999). On the basis of this secondary data, Schoibl and Novak (2000) estimates that, in towns of more than 10,000 people, in the course of a year about 70,000 are threatened with eviction and are thus potentially homeless. More than half of these are women (FAWOS, 1996). About 12,500 are manifest homeless living either in supported accommodation, in emergency shelters or sleeping rough; Schoibl estimates about 17%, or 2,125, are women.

According to the latest Housing Market Survey of the National Housing Fund, municipal authorities in Finland estimated that there was a total of 10,000 homeless single people in November 1999. This figure excludes groups such as people receiving treatment for substance abuse, people receiving treatment in institutions, and people in transitional supported accommodation, all of whom would require permanent housing following their treatment. According to the Housing Market Survey, approximately a fifth of homeless people are women (1,800), of whom nearly 1,200 live in the Helsinki region (Tiitinen, 2000). There is no clear evidence to suggest that the number of homeless women is increasing. This is in a context where the extent of homelessness in Finland as a whole has remained static, while there has been a growth in Helsinki and other major cities. This trend appears to be indicative of the extent to which housing market imperfections have impacted on homelessness for women. The housing market has over-heated in the Helsinki region and other major cities in recent years resulting in rapidly increasing housing costs, increasing evictions and a lack of social housing. Altogether 76,000 households are on the waiting list for social housing in the major metropolitan areas. Women fleeing domestic violence, therefore, have to resort to living with family or friends as a result of a lack of shelters and of alternative accommodation. Relationship breakdown is thus more likely to lead to homelessness for one or both partners. Evictions resulting from rent arrears is increasing and may affect female-headed households disproportionately.

According to the most recent national survey carried out in Sweden,

8,440 individuals were homeless in the specific census week in April 1999. Among these, 1,772 individuals (21%) were women (NBHW, 2000, pp 26, 31). The proportion was slightly higher in Stockholm (23%) and in Malmö (22%). In a separate study, it was estimated that the proportion of women among the homeless in Stockholm city had increased from 17% in 1993 to 23% in 1997 (Finne, 1999, p 8). Although half of all women counted in the national survey had the formal custody of children (younger than 18), only 36 children were reported as homeless, which was taken to mean that most of their children were either living with their fathers or in foster care (Finne, 1999, pp 7, 37). Municipal surveys, using a wider definition than the national survey, would indicate almost a doubling of this estimate (Sahlin and Thörn, 2000). This survey included people who were in touch with authorities and voluntary organisations in one specific week, and who were staying in shelters, sleeping rough or in very temporary accommodation with friends. Among the 1,182 individuals who were sleeping rough or in temporary shelters, 200 of these (17%) were women (Sahlin and Thörn, 2000, pp 53 f). This share is double the 1993 census, but the figure might very well reflect the increase of services and shelters targeting homeless women.

It is estimated that, over the variety of categories, there are about 10,000 homeless people in Greece. The number of women in these groups is estimated to be 4,000. These figures do not include people with marginal accommodation, people living in substandard housing and those who are forced to cohabit or share accommodation. Neither does it include immigrants of non–Greek origin who have not managed to integrate into proper housing (a conservative estimate may be 50,000 people), nor the 50,000 gypsies and nearly 10,000 earthquake victims in the greater Athens area who still wait to be rehoused by the state. Of the estimated 4,000 women experiencing homelessness, it is estimated that half are in the Athens region, of whom less than 100 women are sleeping rough.

In Ireland, the 1999 Assessment of Housing Need carried out by the local authorities on behalf of the Department of Environment and local government showed a considerable increase in housing need since the previous assessment conducted in 1996. In addition, a separate assessment of homelessness was carried out by local authorities. This also showed a dramatic increase in assessed rates of homelessness between 1996 and 1999, during which period the number more than doubled to 5,234, of whom 2,947 were single-person households. The 1999 assessment of homelessness provided for the first time a breakdown by gender of homeless adults. Of the 5,234 people assessed as homeless, 26.7% were female adults, almost half were males and the remaining 27% were children.

A survey conducted in 1999 by the Economic and Social Research Institute and the Homeless Initiative in the Dublin Region identified a total of 2,900 homeless people, of whom 1,050 were females. Two categories of homeless were defined: those on local authority lists (710 females, mainly families or single parents) and those using homeless services (340 females). Of those on local authority lists, nearly 65% of women had child dependents (compared to 14% of males). Of those using homelessness services, 68% of women were single (compared to 94% of men). Women, whether using homelessness services or on local authority lists, were significantly younger than men: 44% were aged under 25 compared to only 20% of men. Men experienced a greater duration of homelessness across all age cohorts, except for those aged under 20 and those aged over 65.

Examination of existing research in Portugal (Bento et al, 1996; Figueira et al, 1995; Pereira and Silva, 1999) suggests that up to 17% of the homeless population are women (at least in the major cities where homelessness is concentrated). Analysis of the marital status of homeless women in Lisbon indicates that 43% are single, 7% divorced and 20% widowed, while the remaining 30% are either married (13%) or in partnerships (17%). This suggests that marital conflict and domestic violence is not a major cause of women's homelessness. On the other hand a high proportion of women present psychiatric illness or addiction problems.

There are no recent studies which cover all of the autonomous regions of Spain which would allow us to establish the number and the profile of the homeless. For this reason it is difficult to know the exact proportion that women represent within the totality of the homeless. In those few national studies which are available, the Caritas study (in 1985) estimated the percentage of women at 15.6%, while the IOPE-ETMAR study for the Ministry of Social Affairs (in 1991) found 10.6% of the homeless were women (Cabrera, 2000). In a 1996 survey of the homeless population in Madrid, Cabrera (1998) used the figure of 13% for women, obtained from sample data and provided by the files of the services for the homeless in Madrid (with Spanish nationality) cared for during 1995. Other studies obtained similar proportions in Gijon (Vega González, 1996), in Barcelona (Lucas et al, 1995), and in Extremadura (Barroso and Martín Símón, 1994). If we accept the figure of 8,500 homeless on average cared for daily, then the number of homeless women on any day would be around 1,300. However, these figures were taken exclusively from the users of transient shelters and did not include other services and hence tend simply to reflect the number of places in the existing shelters for each sex. To this number should be added the women who are not cared for by homelessness services, so that it would not be an exaggeration to speak of 2,000 or 2,500 homeless women in Spain on an average day.

Which women are most affected by homelessness?

It is apparent in all countries that there is not a single female homeless population. The common description is of different groups of women (often) in different service areas. Women in urgent need and using emergency services are typically younger, women with children are more likely to be provided for in temporary accommodation, women with particular needs are provided for in supported housing and in longer-term provision. A study of homelessness in Paris, for example, emphasises that there is not a single female homeless population with a clear continuity and trajectory from one state to another but rather there "are distinct groups of homeless women with different trajectories, different origins, of different generations and finally, in different situations at the heart of services at any given moment" (Tartinville, 2000, p 8).

Although there is some diversity across the member states in the characteristics of homeless women, the trends suggest an intriguing degree of commonality. The evidence that there is a clear change in the composition and in the profile of homeless women is repeated across most countries. Almost without exception, data on service use indicates that, among women service users, a higher percentage are in the younger age groups compared to men. Typically, the average age of homeless women using services is under the age of 25, leading De Decker (2000a), for example, to conclude that "homeless women in Belgium are young and they tend to be younger than homeless men" (p 32). The data also suggests strongly that this is a growing trend (see, for example, the evidence quoted above for Centrepoint in the UK). Equally, while the majority of the homeless in Spain are still men, it seems clear, according to Sánchez Morales (1999, p 57), that a new type of homeless person is emerging in which it is easy to detect a greater number of women and of young women in particular (see Figure 3.5).

This change, characterised by the appearance of increased numbers of young women, is frequently associated with drug addiction and/or

Figure 3.5: Taxonomy of the homeless in Spain

Traditional 'homeless'	New types of 'homeless'
– Middle-aged or elderly men	– Middle-aged men – separated or divorced
– Single	– Young men with employment problems
– Alcoholism	– Young and middle-aged men – drug addicts or ex-drug addicts
– Unfavourable social roots	
– Low training level	– Young and middle-aged women – mistreated, separated or divorced
– Low educational level	
	– Young and middle-aged women – drug addicts or ex-drug addicts
	– Higher cultural and educational level
	– Those with mental health problems
	– Immigrants

Principal tendencies detected in the homeless in Spain
- More young people
- More women
- Legal solitude (separated or divorced)
- Drug addictions
- Higher educational level
- Higher training level
- Internationalisation

Source: Sánchez Morales (1999, p 58)

psychiatric problems. The evidence from Finland is typical: "Homeless women are now younger; nearly half the clients of the Special Social Welfare Office (responsible for services for homeless people) are young women mainly with drug addiction or drug related problems" (Kärkkäinen, 2000, p 29). However, studies in Spain (Sánchez Morales, 1999), Italy (SAM, 1999), Ireland (O'Sullivan and Higgins, 2000), Greece (Sapounakis, 2000) and the UK (Crane, 1997) also describe distinct clusters of older women among service users, as well as reporting the growth of young women using emergency homeless services.

An important response of women to an unsatisfactory labour market situation, family situation or poverty – and one which has been neglected in the housing literature – is that of migration (Ackers, 1998). In some countries, an increase in the number of foreign immigrants among the female homeless is reported as a significant and recent trend, changing the composition of the female homeless population. This occurs even though the true scale of the problem cannot be assessed because of the precarious position of illegal immigrants who are unable to access certain types of service provision. This trend is in evidence in many countries.

In Finland, municipal authorities record large numbers of single immigrant persons and immigrant families in the major cities. In Sweden, a quarter of all the homeless were born abroad while two thirds of the women reported from women's emergency centres were born abroad or had a parent born abroad (NBHW, 2000, p 34). In the Netherlands, women from ethnic minority groups represent well over half the population of women's refuges, a proportion which is steadily growing despite the 1998 Koppelingswet law, which explicitly denies social benefits and healthcare to 'illegal aliens'. Since 1998 some 1,200 female asylum-seekers, who would otherwise seek asylum in another EU country, have turned to shelters for the homeless (de Feijter, 2000). However, it is not only among illegal immigrants that the risk of homelessness is severe. In the urban areas of Italy, women immigrants constitute a growing component of female homelessness (Tosi, 2000a). In Greece, Sapounakis (2000) suggests that 1,000 women experience temporary or transitional accommodation including women staying in the refugee centre in Lavrion and those enjoying the benefits of the EIYAPOE programme for people of Greek origin repatriated from former communist countries.

What factors lead to homelessness?

The factors causing homelessness among women in Europe are diverse (and multi-dimensional), reflecting the heterogeneity of women as much as the divergence between countries. It is also likely to be the case that, given the changing composition of the population of homeless women described above, the causes of homelessness have been changing over time. As Tosi (2000a, p 33) suggests, "the heterogeneity of the phenomenon and its evolution emerge quite clearly from an analysis of its stratification over time".

A key feature to emerge from our overview is not so much the growth in homelessness among women, although this appears to have occurred in many countries, but rather the changing composition reflected in the increase in homelessness among younger women. Accounting for this change on the basis of available research remains difficult. An element may indeed reflect an actual increase in youth homelessness reflecting more strongly among women than men. Equally, it may indicate a greater willingness on the part of younger women to use services for visibly homeless people (or an improved responsiveness of such services to their needs). However, this in itself may also reflect a narrowing of housing options for young women who are then forced to use hostels. In the latter case we would also expect to detect signs of an increase in hidden homelessness among younger women and this does appear to be supported by the evidence. On the other hand, De Decker (2000, p 40) speculates whether the fact that in Belgium a fifth of women enter homeless services from the parental home is a reflection of the blurring of welfare responsibilities which result in younger women being accepted into such services rather than youth care services. In the context of the UK, Aldridge (2000, p 11) also discusses this policy blurring, and points to the research evidence that a high proportion of young homeless women using hostels had formerly been in child care or foster care (Anderson et al, 1993).

Existing literature tends to describe the pattern of female homelessness as a one-off or infrequent experience often associated with a relationship breakdown, where periods of homelessness are of shorter duration and are less likely to be repeated than is the case for men (Kennedy, 1985; Watson and Austerberry, 1986; Novac et al, 1996). The trends reported here question this analysis and raise the issue of whether the nature and causes of homelessness among women are changing. If social exclusion is occurring at a younger age than previously then perhaps the pattern of more frequent episodes of homelessness, which may be of longer duration, may come to characterise the experience of these homeless young women in a manner which contrasts strikingly with the experience of previous generations of women. In this context, perhaps the role of the family and of the changing family status of women (the growth of cohabitation and of single female-headed households) are important variables, both at a structural and a personal level, to explain the rise in younger female homelessness.

The literature also stresses the importance of relationship breakdown as a trigger in female homelessness. It is typically reported that four fifths of women reported relationship problems as a cause of their homelessness (Enders-Dragässer, 2000). Relationship breakdown can include leaving the parental home, fleeing from domestic violence, non-violent separation and widowhood. We may expect that the nature of these relationship problems will differ between youth pathways into homelessness and adult and later-life pathways (see Anderson and Tulloch, 2000). However, the dominant impression from the literature on women's homelessness is of the importance of domestic violence as a cause. The significance of this factor is in evidence across Europe and is well documented elsewhere.

However, there is less discussion in the existing literature on the role of the family in mediating the effects of visible homelessness among women. In this context, the changing, weakening role of the family, especially in southern European countries, is highlighted by the national reports of the European Observatory on Homelessness. It is suggested that the family has an important role to play in preventing the exclusion of women from the housing market which, by delaying the onset of homelessness, also helps to account for the existence of older women in the homeless population (Tosi, 2000a). This is particularly the case in Spain, Ireland and Italy, where data on services also confirms a considerable cluster of elderly women among service users (Kennedy, 1985; Sánchez Morales, 1999; SAM, 1999). Cabrera (2000) argues that, in Spain, there is currently a larger number of women who could move beyond "the limits of precarious living situation" (p 36) and into homelessnes. He suggests that the family is usually more active and intervenes more frequently in the cases of women than in the cases of men, in an attempt to make women who are homeless or are under threat of homelessness return to "a normal life".

In Italy, data on service use as well as analyses of case histories also suggest that the relationship with the family and family networks is a critical factor in the path towards female exclusion. While the importance of this type of factor is not unique to Italy, Tosi (2000a, pp 29-30) suggests that, to understand what is typical of Italy, account must be taken of the particular importance of family networks, the protection by the family that women in Italy enjoy, and the characteristics of the welfare system. It is also argued that the longer latency of female homelessness makes it more difficult to reverse the outcomes of marginalisation: "... women try in every way to save family relationships, to maintain some tie, so they delay leaving the home: but when the ties are broken it is final, with no return" (Gazzola, 1997, p 13). The negative effects of family protection are also indicated in relation both to young women:

> ... if a family is willing to welcome back a son with the justification that it was external factors that 'ruined' him, there is much less likelihood of them welcoming back a daughter, especially if she is addicted to drugs or been in prison. (Ianello, 1997, p 13)

and older women:

> At times women just put off the event and end up with no home and no resources at the age of 50. When low threshold services

arrive they have spent all their resources ... it is difficult to make a plan with them. (Tagliaferri, 1999, p 10)

The importance of the role of the family also needs to be understood in the context of the growth of homelessness among young women. The age at which young adults leave the parental home and the reasons for doing so vary across countries, regionally and by social class. In the Nordic and central European states most women will leave the parental home relatively early. In the UK, for example, it is clear that young women aged under 25 move into lone adulthood (single-person households) earlier than their male counterparts and a higher percentage move into partnerships (Coles et al, 1999). However, in southern Europe most young adults leave the parental home very late (Health and Miret, 1996). It is suggested that this Mediterranean path to adulthood is particularly important from the gender perspective because women, generally more disadvantaged in the labour market than men, can afford to acquire sufficient resources to form an independent autonomous household because of their long stay in the parental home (González López and Pairó, 1998).

Conclusions

The capacity of women to form and maintain an autonomous household has been shown to be dependent on their economic status, their family status and also on the extent to which social protection systems support their housing needs. Within the context where housing market changes are re-establishing a closer link between a household's economic circumstances and their housing situation, the economic status of female-headed households has become a critical factor in their vulnerability to homelessness. Despite the increase in female labour market participation in recent years, their reliance on part-time jobs and relatively lower wage levels leave women vulnerable if they do not have a secure tie to a male income earner. Esping-Andersen's welfare regime types (1990) do not fully predict women's employment patterns. Thus, for example, limited child care service provision in the Netherlands and Germany constrains the growth of female employment in those countries. Responsibility for dependent children is a key factor in the exclusion of women from the labour market both for women in relationships (see Belgium, the Netherlands, Luxembourg and France) as well as for single parents (see Ireland and the UK). An important aspect of social protection systems is the extent to which they individualise or familialise recipients (Orloff, 1993). The extent to which single women with dependent children gain priority access to housing distinguishes these countries (for example, Finland, Denmark and Sweden) as women-friendly.

While homelessness, in the form of rooflessness, is still predominantly a male problem, the overview presented here demonstrates that the nature and causes of homelessness among women exhibits a number of gender specific aspects. In particular the typical manifestation of homelessness for women is the hidden forms of, for example, houselessness, insecure housing and institutional living. However, there is evidence that the level of female visible homelessness is increasing in some countries. This increase, as measured in terms of service use, is mainly evident among particular categories of women – the young (under the age of 24), immigrant women and women from ethnic minority groups, and women who have low educational attainment and limited employment experience. Even where there is limited evidence of an actual increase or high level of increase in visible homelessness or in service use among women, we cannot conclude that there is no problem of homelessness or vulnerability to homelessness among women. For example, there is evidence that women are avoiding homeless accommodation and services which are male-run or male-dominated out of fear of harassment and abuse (in Germany, for example). The static level of service use may simply reflect the static level of provision and be indicative of an under-capacity (for example, in the Netherlands). Additionally, the numbers catered for by services may reflect changes in the form of service provision where support is provided for a more realistic period, hence leading to 'service blocking' and access difficulties for women at risk of homelessness (for example, in Belgium). This last issue may point to the need for a wider range of service provision for women including more low threshold services and an increase in the level of supported accommodation.

Our evaluation of both the changing composition of the homeless population and the scale and trends in homelessness each have implications for the nature and delivery of services to women. The hidden nature of homelessness and the avoidance of existing services by some groups of women is, we would suggest, indicative of the need for more targeted prevention strategies and for more appropriate gender specific services. Similarly, the changing composition of service users is indicative of the need for more diverse service provision and for new approaches to service delivery to respond to the changing needs of these new client groups.

An overview of the existing literature suggests a particular scenario of homelessness among women where the immediate cause is typically related to a crisis situation, typically linked to a relationship breakdown or violence, and where the experience of homelessness is of a single and short-term episode. On the other hand, the popular perception of the visible homeless woman is of the 'bag-lady' whose homelessness is related to her mental health. However, recognising the heterogeneity of women and the increasing significance of young women and immigrant women among the homeless population leads to a different perspective or interpretation. It may point to the need for greater awareness of the impact of structural changes on women – for example, the increase in single-person households and the changing role or capacity of the family resulting in changing living circumstances. Equally, the effects of economic restructuring and of increased labour market participation may be impacting both on the economic independence and on the housing market vulnerability of women. As well as emphasising the need to reflect on the structural causes of homelessness for women, these trends also demonstrate the need to recognise the diversity of process leading to homelessness. A more detailed understanding of the youth pathways, adult pathways and old age pathways to homelessness requires further research. Equally, understanding the nature of homelessness among immigrant women demands an understanding of the process rather than simply viewing this as a specific category of the homeless problem. Migration, for some women, is itself a strategy to deal with labour market or housing market exclusion, family breakdown or relationship abuse. The reasons why homelessness is the end product of that strategy for some women requires further research.

Part Two:
Homelessness trends and services in Europe

Introduction

The chapters in Part Two are derived from much larger and comprehensive national reports produced in 2000 by the correspondents of the European Observatory on Homelessness as part of FEANTSA's annual research programme[1]. In these reports the correspondents, within the limitations of information available within each country, addressed three broad topics. First, *awareness* about the scale and composition of homelessness among women which includes a consideration of prevailing attitudes on the part of government authorities to the problem of female homeless and the identification of gaps in social protection and the problems of women's access to affordable housing. Second, a consideration of the level and appropriateness of service *provision* for homeless women and third, women's *experiences* of homelessness and of homeless services. It is around these three themes that the chapters in Part Two have been organised.

The countries represented under the section heading 'Pathways' represent all the main types of European welfare regimes: Spain and Portugal from southern Europe, Ireland and the UK from the Liberal, Belgium from the Continental regime type and Denmark from the Scandinavian grouping. These chapters take a broad view of the issue of female homelessness, examining, where data are available, both the scale of homelessness among women and the type of female households that make up this group. They also examine the extent to which the issues raised in Part One – feminisation of poverty, deficient social protection policies and changing housing markets – impact on the dimensions of female homelessness in their respective countries. While many similarities emerge, for example all countries indicate a growth in homelessness among younger women (especially single women and lone parents), there is also evidence of considerable variation in the importance of issues such as poverty and welfare policies in contributing to female homelessness. The situation in 'woman-friendly' Denmark, for example, where the incidence of poverty among females is apparently much lower than elsewhere and where social policy, in terms of offering protection to marginalised groups, is relatively effective, is very different from that which prevails in, for example, 'woman-hostile' Spain. In the latter, social protection for homeless women is not well developed, yet women's homelessness – which has grown steadily over recent years – is effectively 'hidden' by the prevalence of informal, family care and assistance.

The chapters on Austria, France, Greece, Italy, the Netherlands and Finland, gathered under 'Services', are more selective in their coverage. The first three chapters examine, often critically, the overall nature and limitations of service provision for homeless women in their respective countries. The Austrian chapter focuses on the fragmentation and lack of coordination in service provision and identifies its limitations for women's needs in demonstrating its overwhelming male orientation. The French chapter starts by identifying the gaps in service provision for homeless women and then moves on to examine in more detail, given these deficiencies, the difficulties faced by homeless single women and lone parents in maintaining relationships with partners as well as the problems women as mothers have in accessing services which allow them to maintain the integrity of their families. The chapter on Greece examines the problems of women's access to housing in a country where traditional familialistic ties are eroding and where social housing provision is limited. The final three chapters in this section focus on the provision of services for specific groups of women. Italy and the Netherlands examine the plight of women members of ethnic and immigrant groups, while the focus in the Finnish chapter is on the relationship between substance abuse, homelessness and support provision.

The chapters in the section headed 'Experiences' demonstrate in three very different country contexts how the needs of homeless women are inadequately or inappropriately provided for by the present level of homeless services. The chapter on Luxembourg first identifies the broad parameters of the position of women within Luxembourg, demonstrating that in contrast to other countries of northern Europe, there is a relative under-representation of women in the labour force. This is followed by an examination of the adequacy and appropriateness of service provision for homeless women, an examination which is supported by evidence derived from face-to-face interviews with a small sample of women. These same interviews also provide the source for a series of suggestions on how service provision for homeless women and women at risk of homelessness in Luxembourg could be improved. These suggestions range from better information about service provision to the need for assistance with rental payments. The German chapter identifies the neglect of the needs of women in welfare and housing policy, and, in this context, examines the coping strategies of homeless women. The chapter finishes with a discussion of gender-specific requirements for support facilities and rights of women in urgent need of housing. Through a series of carefully conducted, in-depth interviews, the chapter on Sweden recounts the views of women who have had personal experience of homelessness. In opposition to the notion that women conceal their homelessness out of shame of their behaviour, this chapter demonstrates that concealment should be seen more as a deliberate strategy on the part of women designed to avoid the stigma of homelessness. These three chapters demonstrate clearly that homeless women are not just hapless victims; they are also capable of active agency both in the way they cope with the problems of homelessness and in the potential they have to contribute to the development of preventive policies.

Note

[1] Each year the European Observatory on Homelessness, the research arm of FEANTSA, supported by the Directorate-General for Employment and Social Affairs, produces a series of 15 country specific reports on aspects of homelessness in Europe. From these a transitional report is published by the convenors of the Observatory; see Edgar et al, 1999 and 2000 for recent productions. Details of the national reports are given in a footnote to each of the following chapters and copies are available from FEANTSA.

PATHWAYS

FOUR

Women and homelessness in Portugal

Alfredo Bruto da Costa and Isabel Baptista

Introduction

The problem of women's homelessness has been a neglected area of research in Portugal. The reasons for this gap are partly related to the fact that homelessness is widely understood in Portugal essentially in its extreme form of 'sleeping rough'. In this sense, the homeless are mainly men and, hence, homelessness is perceived as a male phenomenon. It is also partly related to the disparate nature of studies on women produced by various public and private organisations. Although no institution has emerged to collect the existing piecemeal studies and integrate them into a coherent framework, it has nevertheless been possible to identify some major characteristics of homeless women: they represent between 10% and 17%[1] of the homeless population in the city of Lisbon; more than 40% are single; and, although the number of younger homeless people has been growing[2], older homeless women have been reported by the existing studies as one of the most vulnerable groups (Figueira et al, 1995; Borges, 1995), among whom there is a high incidence of psychiatric problems.

In this chapter we examine the origins and objectives of service provision and relate this to be perceived expressed needs of homeless women.

Origins and objectives of service provision

Various private organisations and public agencies deal with different aspects of the vulnerabilities that affect women. Agencies tend to focus on, and specialise in, one particular aspect of the problem (for example, lack of shelter, prostitution, domestic violence). The general situation with regard to services seems to point to the existence of different kinds of services for homeless (or virtual homeless) women: *general services for homeless people* and *specialised services for women* (see Figure 4.1).

The lack of services and their suitability can be identified as two of the major bottlenecks in the provision of services, both in the generalist services for homeless people and in the specialist services for women. However, the very nature of the services, their origin and their recent evolution, provide an interesting insight for a better understanding of both these problems.

One characteristic concerns the dual nature of the specialised services for women: those emerging from religious concerns about women's vulnerable situations (usually with children) and those that developed from feminist concerns (feminist-oriented services). These different origins are closely related not only to the kind of action developed within the services, but also to the priorities attached by the different service providers to the specific problems identified and addressed by them. Equally, there is a clear time lag between both types of service: most of the services that have a religious background have a much

Figure 4.1: Nature of service provision

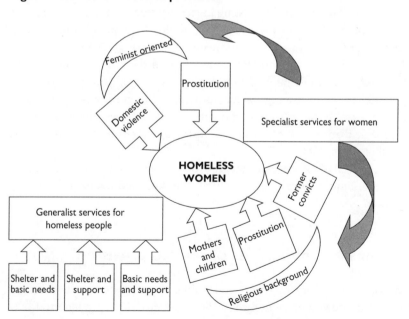

earlier origin than those that emerged from feminist concerns. The latter, though more recent, have been growing rapidly.

Specialist services for women have given priority mainly to issues such as domestic violence, prostitution, the situation of young mothers with children and former female ex-prisoners. The services with religious origins have concentrated mainly on young single mothers and ex-prisoners. Prostitution and, particularly, domestic violence, are the two major issues addressed by feminist initiatives and services. The religious institutions have also supported abandoned women, and also battered wives, but their focus has not overtly related to these situations.

The types of provision made available also seem to reflect different concerns and underlying philosophies. In the case of religious institutions, priority has been given to the provision of temporary shelter for women and their children, and to the promotion of their participation in activities (such as cooking and laundry) which are typically described in service objectives as "aiming at the global development of the woman and her child" and at the "awakening of latent values". These services – small units for 10 to 20 women – also provide child care facilities and, in one case, guidance for occupational training and education. Feminist-oriented services, on the other hand, have different priorities and strategies. They specialise in dealing with situations of domestic violence and prostitution and the services available very rarely include the direct provision of temporary shelter. Information services, medical, juridical, psychological and emotional support are some of the areas which can be found in feminist-oriented services. Their location in areas where some of these problems have long been identified – particularly with regard to prostitution – or the utilisation of mobile units, has recently been one of their strategies for reaching their potential users. These are basically non-shelter services that rely on networking with other institutions in order to provide shelter and other basic needs.

Generalist services for the homeless can be roughly divided into three categories, according to the kind of services provided: (a) temporary shelters (traditional hostels); (b) accommodation with support (transitional accommodation); and (c) day centres providing basic needs and other support. In all of these services homeless women represent a minority among the users, although in some of them their percentage reaches as much as 30% of the total.

Most of the services providing temporary shelter and the satisfaction of other basic needs (for example, meals, showers, clothes) have been long established. However, some more traditional services have recently undergone major changes in order to be able to offer a more comprehensive and integrated response to the needs of the users.

General services providing accommodation and support are either some of the most recent structures available, in major urban centres such as Lisbon and Porto, or are older services which have been recently restructured. Apart from providing for the basic needs of homeless people (for example, accommodation, food, clothes, personal hygiene), they also provide, inter alia, medical support, counselling (social and legal) and information services, occupational training and job orientation. It is particularly striking that while occupational training, job orientation and labour market insertion can be easily identified in most of these general shelter and support services, as well as in specialised services for homeless men, the labour component was practically absent in specialist services for women.

Finally it is also possible to identify day centre services – most of them local initiatives specifically addressing problems of the homeless population – which provide for many of the same basic needs (such as food and clothing) and even, in some cases, counselling and guidance in areas such as emotional and legal support and job and training orientation. These services are usually either linked to religious institutions or have emerged through specific national or EU programmes to combat poverty and social exclusion.

The different types of support available for homeless women – either general or women-specific – the kind of services they provide, and the underlying philosophies, seem to be influenced by what one might call an image of women as victimised and fragile. Hence the emphasis given by the specialised services to psycho-social and emotional support, solutions of 'temporary' shelter in highly protected environments often creating other types of dependency and the relative absence (or inadequacy) of labour market integration or occupational training initiatives. Homeless women – actual or potential – seem to be looked on as either extremely vulnerable, disorganised and psychologically fragile (often suffering from mental illness), or at risk of entering into the process of marginalisation, unless they are protected and looked after. They seem unable to step out of the vicious circle of dependency in which they have lived: dependency on their husband/partner/child and, in the absence of this support, dependency on social services.

In the case of women who sleep rough, even the staff working with them mention that, compared to men, women present more psychiatric or psychological problems. In interviews they frequently commented that "women are more disorganised, they have more frailties than men;

the solutions are much more difficult". These women – usually older women – have often already used all the resources available in order to avoid falling into the most extreme situation of sleeping rough. However, in some cases they have not succeeded, and they arrive at this homelessness situation after having endured severe hardships. At this stage their need for psychological support appears to be unavoidable. This does not mean that the focus of the support given to homeless women should always be in the psychological domain. Younger homeless women's expressed needs concerning support in areas such as training and labour market insertion (referred to below) will show how important it is to consider homelessness in its various forms. In this context an effort should be made to assess – as far as possible – the relationship between perceptions and reality.

Expressed and perceived needs and the evaluation of services

It is extremely difficult to compare the socially constructed images of homeless women's problems and needs with reality. In fact, there is an overall lack of evaluation of the provision of services aimed at meeting the expressed needs of women.

In the following section, an analysis based on data collected by Santa Casa da Misericórdia de Lisboa (the social welfare institute for the city of Lisbon) tries to shed some light on the expressed needs of homeless women, comparing them with the types of responses given by the services. The data were collected from a representative sample of the users of the Misericórdia, from which we selected the homeless population.

According to Casanova et al (1998), the purpose of the initial study for which the information was collected was to directly reveal the sensibilities, evaluations and expectations expressed by the users of the different areas of Santa Casa da Misericórdia. The inquiry concerned only one institution and was not specifically addressed at homeless women – or even at homeless people in general. Nevertheless, given the lack of other types of information and the fact that the Misericórdia is the most important social welfare institution in the city of Lisbon, it seemed useful to analyse some data on expressed needs and the evaluation of the services by homeless (not necessarily roofless) women and men. The analysis performed here is specifically addressed to explore the dimensions relevant to the needs of homeless women.

The following table summarises the basic characteristics of the population sample.

Table 4.1: Main characteristics of the population sample

Gender	16 women 37 men
Age	16 women below 40 years of age; > 50% men above 45 years old
Family situation	> 50% women living with their children, almost three quarters living with their families; no men living with their children, 1 man living with his family
Housing	11 women living in rented room/guesthouse, 2 women sleeping rough; 12 men living in rented room/guesthouse, 11 sleeping rough, 11 sleeping in dormitories
Length of time as homeless	Women: average of 9 months; men: average of 27.6 months
Labour market situation	Women: 80% unemployed; men: 70% unemployed
Main source of living	Women: 88% dependent on social assistance; men: 50% dependent on social assistance, 50% dependent on income from 'work', unemployment benefits or pensions
Reasons for being homeless	Women: 50% employment, 25% family, 25% health; men: 40% employment, 26% family, 33% health

The initial comment that can be made on the first results of this secondary data analysis is that they present a view that is somewhat contrary to that image (or stereotype) of homeless women mentioned earlier in this chapter. Of course, the fact that women are comparatively younger has a bearing on some of these characteristics, namely, as far as the family situation and the length of time being homeless are concerned. Nevertheless, both the situation with respect to the labour market and the reasons for being homeless seem to stress the importance of a job in the lives of these women. This was precisely the area less focused by the provision of services targeted at women.

On the other hand, and although the fact that women have a much shorter time being homeless may be influenced by their younger age, this may also mean that women seek support when it is needed, in order to avoid dependency, but also to achieve autonomy sooner. This may explain the fact that among women the longest period of homelessness observed was for two years and refers to only one case, whereas more than three quarters of the men were homeless for more than three years.

Gender differences concerning the housing situation in the sample population once again confirm that women avoid as much as possible the alternative of 'sleeping rough'. Only two out of the 16 women were living on the street and one of them was living in an abandoned vehicle. The women in the study seem to prefer guesthouses, rented rooms and residential homes, where individual and family safety and privacy could be better safeguarded. Male 'choices' less frequently include these types of accommodation – this may also be influenced by the fact that shelters and dormitories are usually restricted to men.

The first interesting feature concerning the relationship between homeless people and the Misericórdia institution is the length of time that homeless people receive support. Here again women seem to experience shorter periods of time in receipt of support (see Figure 4.2). Their comparatively recent arrival to the services should be an important element to be taken into account by the services themselves in defining strategies and mobilising resources. In fact, the length of time can play a decisive role both in the resources mobilised or in the inevitability of their gradual exhaustion[3], and in the attitudes and methodologies adopted by the staff when working with the female homeless population. Very often duration has extremely negative effects both on users and on the relationship between users and staff. In this sense homeless women appear to be better placed to overcome their difficult situation.

Looking at the expressed needs of homeless men and women, it is possible to identify some interesting issues:

- women tend to express multi-dimensional needs (economic support, accommodation, child care equipment), whereas men more often refer to only one aspect (money, vouchers for meals or transport);
- only women refer to needs related to their children (child care facilities, 'opportunity for a new start' with their children);
- three out of the 16 women refer to their need to find a job/work together with other support; only one out of the 37 men refers to the need of a job/work;
- several men refer to very specific needs such as obtaining meal tickets for a particular institution, whereas women always mention support (money) for food and help (economic or other) to find accommodation.

Figure 4.2: Length of time receiving support

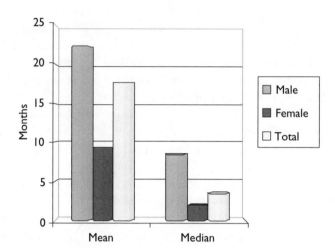

The results shown refer to a small number of people and the questionnaire used does not allow a better understanding of the needs expressed. Nevertheless, the results obtained seem to show that women search for a kind of help that not only aims at solving the actual problems they face, but expresses a better 'understanding' of the multidimensional nature of integration/exclusion; hence their request for a more comprehensive type of support. At the same time, they seem to seek a more 'autonomous path' of support, since they express their needs but wish to maintain a certain margin of choice in the way in which they solve their problems relating to food or accommodation.

The type of support given by an institution to both men and women is mainly based on monetary support (for food, accommodation, transport). Women made no mention of having received any type of job orientation, access to child care facilities or other kind of help. The inadequacy of the support received compared to the expressed needs of women certainly raises some important issues which deserve more in-depth attention and further study. No response seems to have been given to the need for multidimensional support and no help with a job or child-related care has been offered. It is difficult to assess whether the emphasis given by the services on providing monetary support aims at satisfying the apparently desired autonomy of women to choose their way(s) of solving their problems. Further investigation of this and other issues mentioned would certainly help in understanding the possibilities and the obstacles faced by both the excluded groups and the staff in coping with the problems and managing the available resources and solutions.

The users' opinions on 'what's missing' and on 'what can be improved' also revealed some different perspectives between homeless men and women. The first interesting point refers to the perception of time constraints felt by male individuals, which is translated either by the repeated reference to the need of quicker solutions, of different timetables (for certain equipment and services), of less pressure on people and of shorter waiting periods. Although women also expressed concern with getting quicker responses, the wide range of time constraints – as expressed by men – is not at all visible. However, different issues appeared: the need for more comprehensive support ("they should help people more, sometimes they only give money, transport tickets and little more"), earlier intervention ("people should be helped before they become homeless"), and quantitative and qualitative improvements of the support available ("more staff, more humanism, more kindness", "social workers should be more competent").

Once again, the priorities expressed by women concerning their expectations with regard to the way support services should be working reveal women's acute perception regarding vital dimensions of the fight against social exclusion: the complex and multi-dimensional nature of the phenomenon, preventive versus curative actions, the relationship between social services and their clients, and emergency measures versus medium/long-term intervention. One might even ask whether all these concerns are not pointing in the same direction: women's determination to engage in a one-way route out of social exclusion and dependency.

How women's and men's different perspectives reflect on the overall evaluation of the services is also worthy of attention, since their approaches present what, at first sight, appear to be some puzzling effects.

The general opinion homeless women have about an institution itself, as well as about the specific services they are receiving, is always more positive than that of men. The latter tend to express more negative and more 'extreme' opinions about the services. At the same time, women have a more positive appreciation of the way in which the support received has brought about a change in their situation and opened up new opportunities, and express higher motivation, than men, to participate in solving their own problems.

The fact that women express a higher level of needs, and therefore higher expectations, than men, could lead us to infer that they have a comparatively lower level of satisfaction with the support received. This, however, is not the case. It would be interesting to know whether the greater dissatisfaction expressed by men is linked to the urgency they attach to their needs, to a different perception of time, to different attitudes towards social workers – mainly women – or to other factors. A number of other questions remain unanswered, for example whether women have an understanding of the multi-dimensional nature of their problems and needs, and hence a different perception of the time needed to get a satisfactory response. However, the fact that women are more motivated and feel that new opportunities emerge and that the support received brings about changes in their situation is in itself important.

Although based on a limited number of cases, this first attempt to identify and understand the relationship between homeless women and the provision of services in Lisbon does not seem to correspond to with the earlier image of homeless women as totally vulnerable and dependent.

Coordination of services

The complexity of homelessness, taking into account the various dimensions of the problem (shelter and various forms of support), demands a high level of coordination between the services and institutions involved. The importance of partnership is increasingly being recognised in Portugal. However, actual practice has to make progress towards coherent and coordinated cooperation between the interested institutions. Lack of coordination between institutions – and sometimes between services of the same institution – has been widely recognised by staff as a major drawback.

Healthcare has been one of the areas in which the lack of coordination has caused more difficulties to the homeless, with respect to initial access as well as to continuous follow-up. The rules and proceedings of the National Health Service are usually not adjusted to the needs of this group of the population. 'Pulling' medical support into the services for the homeless has filled this gap. However, service providers for the homeless realise that this kind of support is not as complete as it would be if it was performed by, and within, the National Health Service itself. Furthermore, it is also recognised that social integration should also mean overcoming the ghettoisation of basic services such as the healthcare services. This will necessarily require more coherent and systematic coordination between social services and healthcare services.

Internal institutional organisation and networking basically rely on personal contacts. The importance and effectiveness of these contacts are not being questioned, since they prove themselves vital to the everyday life of the services and their users. What can be questioned is the actual scope of such a practice, bearing in mind that the ultimate aim of social support services is not the management of poverty and social exclusion but the eradication and prevention of such situations. Coordination should be more than the result of individual action. Cooperation at the institutional level would certainly have a positive impact on the use of the available resources, the assessment of the homeless women's needs and the definition of strategies to cope with their situations.

In short, the problems related to coordination belong basically to three different areas: policy, institutional organisation and networking, and resources.

Conclusions

In this chapter we focused on service provision for homeless women. The underlying philosophies of the different kinds of services (specialist services for women and generalist services for homeless people) have been discussed.

It has been argued that these philosophies have a direct impact on the type of provision available and that it reflects not the actual needs as expressed by homeless women, but rather the socially expected needs of homeless women, about whom specific social images have been built. The absence of training and job arrangements within the range of service provision targeted at women has been presented as an example of this 'divorce' between social images and the actual needs of homeless women.

In opposition to this victimised and fragile image of homeless women, arriving at the services usually at an older age and presenting severe psychological problems, we have argued that this represents only one of the profiles within the heterogeneity of the phenomenon of homelessness among women. Empirical findings presented in this chapter emphasise the existence of a younger group of homeless women whose expressed needs and evaluation of the services seem to translate to what seems to be an acute understanding of the multi-dimensional nature of homelessness.

Compared to men, women seem to express their needs in a more comprehensive way, not revealing, as men do, the sense of urgency in their responses, and are more concerned with the achievement of comprehensive support. We have further argued that the alleged female vulnerability to, and stigma of, dependency does not match with homeless women's desire for responses that allow a certain margin of personal decision within a range of solutions. The need for autonomy seems to underlie their options. Service providers should certainly consider women's views and evaluations when defining women's 'specific needs', rather than conforming to socially constructed images of homelessness and femininity.

Finally we have discussed coordination issues, namely the importance of enlarging the scope of coordination practices beyond the actual telephone-to-telephone contacts between technical staff, in order to also engage the institutions themselves in a process comprising the different levels of policy making and implementation needed to meet the needs of homeless women.

Notes

[1] The various studies refer to different figures. See Figueria et al (1995), Pereira and Silva (1999), Bento et al (1996) and Pereira et al (2000).

[2] According to the 2000 update of the survey of homeless people in the city of Lisbon, there has been a shift in the relative position of younger and older homeless people: in the last century around 70% of the homeless were also less than 40 years old (Pereira et al, 2000).

[3] On the effects of time on individual resources it has been argued that "the period of time during which the person exposed to vulnerability is likely to be crucial. For a limited period, the person may be able to resort to personal savings and family borrowing, but these are likely to be of limited duration. Social insurance benefits may suffice but many are time-limited and means-tested assistance then kicks in with its associated stigma tending to close off opportunities which depend on some degree of reputational respect" (Room, 2000, p 3).

FIVE

Homeless women in Spain[1]

Pedro José Cabrera

Introduction

An understanding of homelessness has traditionally been sought, on the one hand, through a macro, structural approach associated with the 'sociology of poverty' and, on the other, through a micro, individual approach linked to the 'sociology of deviance'. The call for social intervention by those who work with homeless groups demonstrates the inadequacies of such explanations. They point to the huge analytical gap between analysis at the macro level, which emphasises such structural issues as the magnitude of poverty in Spain (eight million people have less than 50% of the average national income), and micro level explanations, which focus on the description and analysis of 'exotic' individual behaviour.

The emergence of the theoretical framework of social exclusion (Paugam, 1996) offers the possibility of overcoming the limitations and inadequacies of previous approaches in that it gives priority to disentangling the process by which individuals and/or groups are excluded from social participation. Figure 5.1, drawing on the work of Castel (1993), and García Roca (1998), attempts to express graphically the analytical potential of the new paradigm in relation to the analysis of homelessness.

The process of social exclusion represented in the figure has three phases: integration (insertion), vulnerability (precariousness) and disaffiliation (exclusion), although the boundaries of these phases are more blurred than the figure itself suggests. This is important because it is in the process of transition from one phase to another that we can detect the structural connections between social marginality and the other 'worlds' of integration and welfare. The transition from one phase to another is an integral part of the process of social exclusion; it involves a process of 'distancing' in that it represents the cumulative move of citizens away from access to goods and scarce resources and from participation in society. This is the process that causes vulnerability/precariousness and disaffiliation/exclusion.

If vulnerability is marked by precarious access to employment, housing, and social and political participation, exclusion is defined by 'no access' to these facilities (Laparra et al, 1996). In this chapter we use the axes of Figure 5.1 to examine the issue of homelessness among women in Spain. This examination demonstrates the growing precariousness of the position of women and their increasing vulnerability to homelessness in the context of the changing social and economic structures of Spanish society in the last quarter of the 20th century.

Social relationships and exclusion

There is widespread opinion in Spain that the role of supporting family networks is crucial as a buffer to exclusion. These networks, although they do not resolve the fundamental problem, at least permit people to subsist in relatively decent conditions, even if some members of the

Figure 5.1: The process of social exclusion

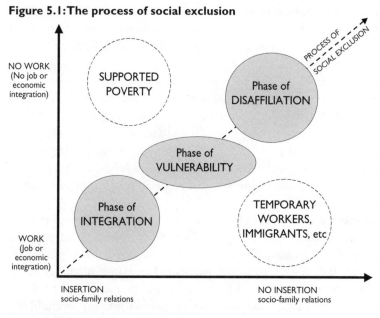

Source: Castel (1993); García Roca (1998)

family (particularly young people) are thereby caught in a situation of what is sometimes called "stable precariousness" (Tezanos, 1998, p 102).

However, there are indications that this supportive role of family networks may be declining. As De Miguel has observed: "[t]he Spanish family is gradually less of a school, less of a hospital and less a form of social security ... even if it still maintains many functions of caring, psychological and economic aid for the members" (De Miguel, 1993, p 443). There are a variety of factors which have created this situation. First, there has been an increase in women in the labour market; second, we are witnessing a change in opinion regarding housewives, who now have a more negative image; third, young women's attitudes have changed substantially (Tobío, 1996). Additionally, structural issues suggest that, in the future, the family will be less supportive. The reduction of family size is already apparent and is reflected in the lowest fertility rate (average number of children per woman) in Europe, which has decreased from 2.8 children in 1960 to 1.16 in 1997. At the same time, the number of people living alone has increased by 79% between 1970 and 1991 to two million (particularly older) people (De Miguel, 1993, p 450).

As in the rest of Europe during the 1990s, Spain saw an increase in the number of lone-parent households, particularly in the proportion headed by separated/divorced women (de Ussel, 1998). The number of households headed by women increased from 15.8% in 1981 to 20% in 1991 (Madruga Torremocha and Mota López, 2000, p 41). The cause of this increase lies, principally, in the break-up of couples. Over 90% of all lone-parent families have the mother as head of the family. Many of these families come from the most impoverished section of society. Additionally, many women, who were not poor in their original family, live in poverty after a process of family breakdown which often leaves them ill-equipped to compete in the job market.

We should remember that the homeless condition is inversely proportional to the number of active family ties (Cabrera, 1998, p 290). Such demographic changes have had a major impact on the position of women in Spanish society; in terms of our model (Figure 5.1), many women have passed from a situation of integration (within the traditional structures of Spanish society) to a position of vulnerability.

Economic dimensions of social exclusion

Social inclusion through employment is the most important social factor in enabling adults to build a life and achieve economic independence.

Because of this, it is important to highlight the special difficulties women have in obtaining an equal education or paid employment. Traditionally, women in Spain have had limited access to education. Because of the previous gender bias in education, 72% of the one million illiterate people in Spain are women. If we include women who did not complete their primary school education then there are almost three-and-a-half million women without substantial education or ability in literacy in a country of less than 40 million inhabitants.

Spain is one of the European countries with the lowest rate of female participation in the workforce. While the average female participation rate in the European Union in 1998 was 45.9%, the figure for Spain was 37% compared to nearly 60% in Denmark and other northern European countries. Also, since the mid-1980s, the female unemployment rate has been 10 points higher than the male unemployment rate. The labour crisis of the last 10 years has had detrimental effects which have disproportionately affected young people and women. Lastly, despite the end of the period of economic crisis, women still work in more precarious and unstable jobs than men, often receiving lower salaries, and usually, with temporary contracts. The average salary for women was two thirds of male earnings, while over a third had part-time contracts compared to 17% for men (Spanish Institute of Statistics, 1991). Hence, while in recent years women have been incorporated into the workforce in larger numbers, this has not always resulted in the achievement of greater personal independence.

The effect of a withdrawal of women from the workforce due to marriage is substantial; the activity rate of women changes significantly from 55% for single women to 37% for married women. This creates a situation of dependence on men, which can then be broken suddenly in case of separation or divorce.

All these factors suggest that women, with lower levels of education and with little work experience, are at risk in the housing market if their relationships break down. Often these women also have social integration problems as a result of domestic violence.

Poverty, exclusion and homelessness among women

The official definition in Spain of 'homelessness' differs from that used elsewhere in Europe. In Spain homelessness is defined not so much in terms of precarious accommodation but as the total or almost total lack of accommodation. Because of that, if we do not want to restrict our view to the institutional construction of the problem, derived from information provided by homeless organisations (most of which were designed to accept only men), we should begin our approach to homeless women in Spain from the analysis of the feminisation of poverty. Over 10 years ago the annual report of the charity Cáritas (1990) identified: "women living alone with family responsibilities and young long-term unemployed women" as the newly precarious group needing special attention. More recently, de Elejabeitia (1996) also points out that the female proportion of the poor has increased considerably in the past two decades.

According to recent research (de Elejabeita, 1996), around 54,000 Spanish families live in substandard conditions (squatter settlements, caves, etc), and a further 245,000 live in inadequate conditions. This low standard of living is especially serious among certain groups: while 13.7% of all families live below the poverty line in poor housing conditions, 31% of emigrant families and 43.9% of gypsy families live under these conditions (EDIS, 1998, p 280). In a country where the rate of owned housing is the highest in Europe (around 85%), poorer families have to resort to other ways of finding accommodation; 27.6% of the poor live in rented houses, and only 8.5% borrow money for a mortgage.

Bearing in mind the inflexibility in the Spanish housing market and the fact that those with less money are unlikely to own their home, it becomes doubly difficult for women with dependent children to secure housing. For instance, after separation or divorce it is normally the woman who leaves the home and seeks support from the family network (if it still exists or if they still have connections within it) or moves into a less expensive, rented house. One of the requirements for renting a house is proof of employment. In the case of separated or divorced women with small children who do not work, they are only able to keep their house as long as they are granted custody of the children and their ex-husband is prepared to pay maintenance. In the case of women who do work, after separation or divorce they often receive less income than during their marriage, which creates difficulties in taking care of the house and the children.

There are no recent studies, covering the whole of Spain, which would allow us to establish a national profile of homeless people. For this reason it is impossible to know the exact proportion of women among the total number of homeless. There are, however, several local studies which provide data from the annual reports of some particularly important centres and there are a few national studies available, although they were conducted some years ago. For instance, the Cáritas study of 1985 estimated the percentage of homeless women at 15.6%; a few years later the IOPE-ETMAR study for the Ministry of Social Affairs in 1991 found 10.6% of women homeless. It is important to note, however, that these figures were collected exclusively from transient shelters and did not include dining halls or other services. Hence, these figures do not provide a full or accurate picture of the proportion of homeless women in Spain; rather they record the number of places occupied in these shelters by each sex.

In 1996, in a survey of the homeless population in Madrid, Cabrera produced the figure of 13% for women (19% when confined to centres that claimed to cater exclusively for women). This information was obtained from sample data and from the files of providers of services for the homeless in Madrid. More or less in the same period, Vega González (1996), found the same proportion (13%) in a study carried out in Gijon in the north of Spain. In Barcelona, Lucas et al (1995) spoke of 14%. A year before, in 1994, Barroso and Martín Símon, using data on social intervention with transients in Extremadura (in the west of Spain) again reported 13%. Recent unpublished research, in the city of Seville (carried out by the Centro Andaluz de Prospectiva), interviewed people who came to social services centres, including the municipal and other shelters, dining halls, and clothing distribution centres, where a large number of the homeless use the facilities. The proportion of women among the interviewees was 16.2%.

Considering these data, albeit partial and limited, at present we can estimate that, today, women represent at present between 15% and 16% of the homeless population in Spain. This slight increase over previous counts (13% in the mid-1990s) could be due to both a larger percentage of women being excluded from housing and to better methods of detecting homeless women. If we accept the figure of 8,500 as the average number of homeless cared for daily in Spain, then the number of homeless women on any day would be around 1,300. In addition, we must take into account women who are not provided with shelter; on this basis it would not be an exaggeration to speak of 2,000 or 2,500 homeless women in Spain on an average day. However, this estimate is made using the narrowest definition of homelessness as 'rooflessness'. In the remainder of this chapter we therefore consider the housing situation and exclusionary processes affecting two groups of women who do not appear in the homelessness statistics in Spain: women suffering from domestic violence and single parents.

Homeless women and domestic violence

In 1980, the United Nations stated that violence within the family is the most frequently concealed crime in the world (Alberdi, 1993, p 245). In 1984, for the first time in Spain, the number of reports to national police stations of the ill-treatment of women in the previous year (16,070) was published. From that time awareness of the seriousness of the problem of domestic violence, suffered by many women, has developed in Spain. Yet women have received little help from government offices; their demands for access to social services, the police or the courts are often not heard.

In 1998, increased social awareness of this problem resulted in a report from the Ombudsman in Spain on 'Domestic violence against women'. Among its conclusions, it pointed out the lack of research that would provide reliable information and the shortage of existing social resources. This led to the recommendation that the Ministry of Work and the Ministry of Social Affairs, "increase, through the relevant Administrations, the number of Shelter Homes in our country, adapting, in this way, the number of places available to the European Parliament's recommendation".

In March 2000, the first results of a macro-survey on 'Violence against women', commissioned by the Women's Institute, were presented to the press. Although there is no chapter in which the connection between domestic violence and housing is dealt with explicitly, it is interesting to consider this report because it presents updated and reliable data on the extent of the problem in Spain. In the survey 22,552 telephone interviews with Spanish women over the age of 18 were carried out. The most important results showed that 4.2% of Spanish women over 17 stated that they had been victims of ill-treatment during the last year. This percentage represents a total of 640,000 women. A total of 12.4% of Spanish women can consider themselves 'technically' ill-treated (1,865,000).

As part of the same study, a more exhaustive survey was conducted on a sample made up of 395 women who, in the first stage of the research, had declared that they had been ill-treated, or claimed to know some women, close to them, who were being ill-treated. In terms of the social consequences suffered by the women, the following answers were collected: 48% stated that they were worried about the future for economic reasons because they had to face it alone; 13% said they have had to take sick leave; 11% said ill-treatment had led to the loss of their job; and 8% said that they had been driven to excessive drinking and/or taking drugs. After losing their jobs, the violence and the addictive behaviour, in many cases, creates instability in the home and leads women to go to women's shelters. To form an assessment of the entire problem we have only to recall the previous figure of 640,000 Spanish women, all of whom said they had suffered ill-treatment at some stage.

Nearly half of the interviewed women said they had looked for outside help, while the rest remained hidden and felt ashamed. Those who ask for help, turn, in the first place, to the family (64%) and to their friends (38%), then to a psychologist (37%), and just a minority look for the services of a lawyer (25%), a doctor (20%) or a social worker (16%). As a result of asking for help only 67% of the women who had been ill-treated said they took a decision one way or another, and of the suggestions received, only 20.3% were advised to leave their homes. In other words, in around one fifth of ill-treatment cases, the opinion of external observers, professional or just friends or relatives, was to advise them to look for another place to live.

Of course, this option is only viable for those who have sufficient economic and property resources. When women with few resources suffer ill-treatment, there is often no choice but to put up with it or to 'go out onto the streets'. When there are children involved, frequently the step forward is postponed and leads to a huge and understandable sensation of insecurity and fear. In fact, although 57% know that there are shelters available, they rarely use this kind of service. Seventeen per cent say they have turned to social services, 16% to services for legal information, 15% to the free telephone number at the Women's Institute, and 14% have turned to specific organisations and associations which deal with these matters. However, the fact is that shelters were used by only 4% of the interviewed women, and 3.1% went to live in supported flats under the protection of town halls and autonomous regions.

On the other hand, it is important to remember the nature and size of this referential sample. Applying this figure, of 3-4% of women living in alternative social accommodation, to the estimated figure of 640,000 women who declare that they have suffered ill-treatment in the last year, it would not be implausible to assume that around 25,000 female victims of domestic violence need temporary accommodation. Therefore we are faced with one of the largest homeless groups, who are in a prolonged or temporary situation, but who never usually appear in the statistics relating to the homeless in Spain.

Homelessness and lone parents

This section discusses the increased vulnerability in the housing market of single-parent families headed by women. Information for this section is obtained from a self-help discussion group of eight women run by the Association of Women with Non-Shared Family Responsibilities in Tetuán (a famous quarter of Madrid). Different aspects of life were dealt with during the discussion, including the following: economic difficulties; jobs; problems regarding housing; and the conditions of access to the services of social protection.

Almost inevitably any marriage break-up has a detrimental impact on the economic position of the partners, especially on that of women. In general, divorced people become poorer, but this has the greatest impact among marriages which, before their break-up, were in a low economic position. Among marriages with low incomes, the consequences of separation for women who are left alone with children can be particularly difficult. The reasons for this deterioration in the position of separated or divorced women include the failure of ex-husbands to pay the maintenance stipulated by the courts, or in cases where payments are made, it is not enough to maintain the previous standard of living; separated or divorced women usually have lower qualifications, abilities and/or experience for securing a job; and deficiencies in social policies regarding separated and divorced people. This latter reason is especially serious because, currently, those families who need more economic support are the ones most likely to be unprotected or not sufficiently protected.

Female lone parents also experience considerable difficulties in securing housing, partly reflecting their precarious employment situation. Current housing policies assume that everyone is able to access property ownership. In Spain, renting is considered an eccentricity, a choice which requires an explanation in comparison to property ownership which is 'natural'. Nevertheless, this 'unnatural' option is one of the few remaining for most of the single-mother families with a low income. Not having a stable job is an almost insurmountable obstacle to getting a mortgage. Even when job conditions improve, the lack of government housing forces people to waste money, which took so much effort to earn, on astronomically high rents. If there is a family dwelling, women with small children usually remain there, but often until the children reach an age of independence. As soon as they get older and leave the home, the woman loses the house and cannot rely on being re-accommodated in other supported accommodation.

In conclusion we could say that, although the situation of lone-parent families rarely becomes so bad that they are literally living on the street, it is nevertheless obvious that they run the risk of finding themselves living in a situation of extreme poverty. Female lone-parent families are headed by *tight-rope walking mothers* who balance all their economic, social and emotional needs without having the sufficient resources within their reach and without having the supportive net of any welfare system. Therefore, we have before us a *circle of poverty*. Lack of training leads to the lack of a good job. Wages are low, insecure and obtained through long hours of unsatisfying work. This insufficient salary does not allow for saving enough to buy a house and the money earned is consumed by the high rents which then go up every year. These women feel the threat of being homeless every day: any slip, any new loss (fundamentally of their job) ends up placing them directly in the centre of the homeless population in Spain.

Conclusions

Our understanding of extreme homelessness and poverty continues to be obscured by our image of the homeless throughout history. In Spain we still identify it with the 'tramp' and the nomadic life more or less related to the picaresque. All of this leads to a social and political neglect of the issue of homelessness in Spain, relegating it, symbolically at least, to the status of a marginal issue from a statistical, political and social point of view.

When the homeless population includes women, the difficulties society has in 'seeing' the problem become such that its existence is almost completely denied. To use the slogan from a famous TV commercial for cognac in the 1960s, we could say that for many people in Spain, being homeless is fundamentally 'a man's thing'.

However, the everyday experience of the people in charge of shelters, dining halls and centres that care for the homeless shows again and again that the number of homeless women (as with young people and immigrants) is growing. This is consistent with the accelerated changes experienced in Spanish society in the last 25 years: demographic changes and changes in family models that have led to a considerable increase in lone-parent families and women living alone. As the family becomes smaller, it loses its social function and becomes weaker as a basic mechanism for social protection, yet many aspects of the family (for example, in relation to expectations of role fulfilment) that discriminate against women remain. In spite of the fact that equality between men and women has progressed enormously, especially in the educational system, there continues to be important sexist biases in the job market. The percentage of female labour is still low and the unemployment rate for women is practically double that of men. In these conditions, buying a house is much more difficult for women. Instability in housing is particularly prevalent in family units headed by a working woman. If this does not lead to literal homelessness, it is largely due to the enormous capacity for daily survival that these women show in giving their children a good start in life and in keeping going.

In any case, the dependence of women on men makes them much more vulnerable from an economic and job perspective, as is shown in the case of many women who are the victims of mistreatment and for women whose relationships end. It is these women who are literally forced onto the street with nowhere to go when the crisis breaks. In Spain this problem is not reflected in the statistics of the homeless because, up until now, the institutions that helped mistreated women operated autonomously. The lack of an official definition of homelessness has prevented these women from being classified as homeless. This explains the fact that figures taken from organisations for the homeless show the proportion of women as relatively low, at around 13% of the total. The majority of women temporarily homeless do not have contact with these organisations and therefore are not counted as part of the homeless population. The problem of female homelessness has also been neglected, in part, because historically institutions dedicated to caring for the homeless have not been set up to deal with women and children. This leads to added difficulties for women who do not have easy access to the services such institutions offer. Our conviction is that homeless women will continue to grow in number and importance over the next few years. We hope that a greater social and political sensitivity will open the way to social research and that the official statistics concerning this area will increase, become more precise and up-to-date, so that the problem will no longer be hidden and will be recognised and dealt with in its true form.

Note

[1] Thanks to Ángeles Arechederra-Ortiz, Isabel Madruga-Torremocha and Eva Rubio-Guzmán for their collaboration.

SIX

Women, the welfare state and homelessness in the Republic of Ireland

Eoin O'Sullivan and Mary Higgins

Introduction

Homelessness in Ireland has been generally viewed as a phenomenon that has principally affected men. This is not to say that there are no homeless women; rather that they were conceptualised as something other than homeless. It is only in the 1980s and 1990s that homeless women have been recognised as homeless rather than as victims of domestic violence or inadequate or deviant. Both in ideology and practice a woman's place was seen as within the home. For those women who wished to escape from the home, options were severely limited and those who transgressed established norms by escaping the home were invariably stigmatised. Garrett and Bahr (1976), in their pioneering studies of homeless women, suggested that the pathways to homelessness differed between men and women and that "failure in marriage may very well be a key variable in explaining the 'skid careers' of women, while among homeless men it seems to play a relatively minor role" (p 380). This and other early research, in Stoner's (1983) view, "supported views of homeless women as derelict eccentrics who choose their lifestyle ... and ... consolidate[d] long held beliefs that homeless women are even more derelict and eccentric than homeless men, and thus the most socially undesirable of all marginal people" (p 570).

More recent studies have suggested that homelessness among women is growing and, rather than seeing homelessness resulting from their eccentricity, an examination of family structures, welfare systems, demographic change and legislative provision offers more insightful explanations. Wardhaugh (1999), for example, suggests that in modern society the home has been constructed as a source of identity and as an essential foundation of social order in which women have an identifiable place. Yet such order is based on the experiences of many women of the home as a prison. These 'homeless-at-home' women suffer abuse, violence and the suppression of self within the supposed safe haven of the domestic home. Passaro (1996) has argued that because homeless women are seen as the apotheosis of woman, that is 'dependent, vulnerable, frightened', they do not challenge dominant beliefs. As a consequence,

> ... homeless women quickly learn that to work their way through the system, from emergency shelter through transitional housing to, ultimately, an apartment – they need to behave in such a way as to appear 'worthy'. Many, therefore, act meek, don't cause trouble, and are grateful for help while in the sight of shelter officials or others who may decide their fates. The homeless women who do not play this game often find themselves having as few options as men. (Passaro, 1996, p 2)

Women and the welfare state in Ireland

Historically, in Ireland, the key social assumption underlying both social welfare (including housing) provision and the taxation code was that of a 'male breadwinner' household with dependent spouse and children in a lifelong marriage (Yeates, 1997a, 1997b, 1999; Cousins, 1995; Cook and McCashin, 1997; O'Connor, 1998). This policy in Article 41 of the 1937 Constitution, for example, states:

> The state recognises the Family as the natural primary and fundamental unit group of Society.... The state, therefore, guarantees to protect the Family in its constitution and authority, as the necessary basis of social order and as indispensable to the welfare of the Nation and the state. In particular, the state recognises that by her life within the home, woman gives to the state a support without which the common good cannot be achieved. The state shall, therefore, endeavour to ensure that mothers shall not be obliged by economic necessity to engage in labour to the neglect of their duties in the home. (Government of Ireland, 1937)

It has been argued that this fusion of familialism and subsidiarity[1] impeded the development of a state-based welfare system in Ireland resulting in a profusion of voluntary activity, generally on a sectarian basis, to meet the welfare needs of the Irish population. However, recent scholarship has suggested that while the state took a passive role in the provision of welfare services, it was highly interventionist, in collaboration with the Catholic Church, in regulating women and children (Fahey, 1992; Torode and O'Sullivan, 1999; Raftery and O'Sullivan, 1999).

Ireland is conventionally termed a strong male breadwinner state with strong familialistic tendencies, attributable to the pervasive influence of the Catholic Church and the agrarian foundations of the Irish welfare state (Fahey, 1992, 1998, 2000; Fahey and McLaughlin, 1999; Mahon, 1987, 1995). However, a number of key social, economic and demographic changes are forcing a reconsideration of these principles. These changes include the rise in the labour force participation rate of women, the increase in the number of women in part-time work, the decline in the fertility of marriage, the increase in the level of marital breakdown, the increasing numbers of those parenting alone, and the increase in cohabitation. These changes have challenged the existing policy framework; a coherent response to them, however, is far from fully articulated or translated into practice.

While the booming Irish economy has facilitated these social and demographic transformations (OECD, 1999), rapid economic growth has also coincided with an increase in inequality (Nolan, 1999). The incidence of low-paid employment increased between 1987 and 1994, as did the incidence of poverty (Callan, 1999). The increase in low pay reflects a growth in sectors with high demand for low-skilled workers. The growth in poverty is largely attributable to the failure of social welfare payments to keep pace with the growth in average incomes. Despite the dramatic increase in women's paid employment, married women and women with children face a series of interrelated obstacles to entering paid work. These include low wages, the lack of state support for child care, and disincentives in the taxation and welfare systems.

Ireland in comparative perspective

In his influential analysis of welfare regimes, Esping-Andersen (1990) encountered some considerable difficulty in locating Ireland within his tri-polar model. Depending on the measure used, Ireland is located both in the liberal and the conservative welfare regime. The regimes type analysis by Esping–Andersen has been subject to various critiques (Cousins, 1997; Abrahamson, 1999) arguing for more than the three ideal types and presenting more substantial criticisms based on the lack of analysis of the roles of families and women, a weakness readily acknowledged by Esping–Andersen in his recent work (1999). For Orloff (1996) Esping–Andersen's citizens are implicitly male workers; his dimensions tap into the impact of states on class relations and the relationship between states and markets without considering gender differences within classes or the relations between states and families; he leaves invisible women's work on behalf of societal welfare (that is, unpaid caring/domestic labour); and his framework fails to consider state effects on gender relations, inequalities and power.

Lewis (1992) has argued that the male breadwinner family model has historically cut across established typologies of welfare states and that the model has to be modified in different ways and to different degrees in different countries. She argues that, although the male breadwinner model is not found in its pure form anywhere, all countries reflect elements of this ideology and some countries adhere relatively strongly to the model. Britain and Ireland are characterised as strong breadwinner welfare states, France is a modified male breadwinner state and Sweden is a weak variant, with public policy being directed to facilitating women's labour force participation and the achievement of a dual-breadwinner society.

Strong male breadwinner regimes tend to have a firm dividing line between public and private responsibility with an absence, or scant availability, of services facilitating the labour force participation of women. The traditionally low level of female labour force participation in Ireland reflects this strong male breadwinner tenor of public policy. In recent years, rising levels of labour force participation by women, including those with young children, have put pressures on welfare states to adapt to this changing environment. Increasingly welfare states cannot assume the male breadwinner norm as the basis for social policy. However, as O'Connor et al argue in relation to the liberal welfare regimes,

> Despite convergence in male and female labour force participation over the past couple of decades, gender based stratification is still strongly evident.... This is evident not only in participation by family type and continuity of employment over the life cycle but also in part time work, which is predominantly female, and in occupation location and pay. (1999, p 224)

Esping-Andersen (1999) has argued that the family has become central in welfare state analysis in recent years for two reasons. First, a feminist critique of male-centred welfare state theory, although primarily concerned with the gender relations that are produced or reproduced by social policy, has led to reconsideration of the family. It has been argued that decommodification inaccurately describes women's relationship to the welfare state, because women's work is often unpaid family labour. Second, while the family may have become problematic – with the stable one-earner family now atypical and with cohabitation and single-person households growing – Esping-Andersen suggests that the family is still the lynchpin of policy. He notes that employment or career-based entitlement systems, such as social insurance or occupational benefits, implicitly favour the male breadwinner. Because women's attachment to paid employment is generally more tenuous, in such systems their entitlements tend to be derivative of the husband. As a consequence, when marriage becomes less stable, women's access to social protection may suffer, in particular if they are barred from a permanent employment relationship. Thus, lone-mother families, or women with interrupted careers, will easily find themselves in a welfare gap. On the other hand, individualised benefit systems – especially if they are citizenship-based – are more likely to grant women some degree of economic independence. This is particularly the case if transfers are coupled to affordable child care.

However, Esping-Andersen is not so much interested in gender relations in welfare state regimes; rather his key concern is the degree to which families absorb social risks. From this position, he prefers to discuss degrees of *familialisation* or *de-familialisation*. *De-familialisation* refers to the degree to which household welfare and caring responsibilities are relaxed – either via welfare state provision, or via the market. A familialistic system is one in which public policy assumes or insists that households must carry the principal responsibility for their members' welfare. A de-familialising welfare regime is one that seeks to unburden the household and the welfare dependence of individuals on kinship. Esping-Andersen argues that this concept parallels de-commodification, and for women, de-familialisation is a precondition for their capacity to commodify themselves. De-familialisation indicates the degree to which social policy (or markets) render women autonomous to become commodified or to set up independent households. Familialistic regimes are often influenced by Catholic social teaching and the principle of subsidiarity: limiting public interference to situations where primary social networks fail. As a consequence and paradoxically, active family policies are most undeveloped in the most familialistic regimes.

A key point of Esping-Andersen's analysis is that post-war welfare states did not absorb the family caring burden. The commitment of all post-war welfare states was narrowly confined to healthcare and income maintenance. He argues that most welfare states are still income transfer biased and only a handful pursue a de facto reduction of the families' welfare burden. Yeates has recently argued that Ireland has,

> ... historically pursued policies in the fields of taxation, social security, employment, social and health care, and reproductive health which have constructed women's social roles primarily as homemakers, wives, mothers, and carers and as economic dependants of their husbands and male partners. These policies have contributed to women's social and economic inequality by discouraging women's economic independence via the labour market, attributing women's economic security to their husbands or their male partners rather than the state, and devaluing the economic and social status of women's paid and unpaid work generally.... What is particularly notable about Ireland, though, is that women's social and reproductive rights have been the explicit focus of family law and social policy, unlike other similarly styled welfare regimes, such as Britain. (1999, p 608)

However, recent demographic and socio-economic changes in Ireland are placing considerable pressure on the maintenance of the regime described by Yeates, and it may be more accurate to now describe Ireland as a weak male breadwinner regime.

Housing has not featured to any significant degree in the feminist analyses of welfare regimes, which, by and large, have concentrated on the fiscal regimes of welfare states. A notable exception in relation to Ireland is Yeates' discussion of matrimonial property rights. She argues that housing as a particular type of resource is gendered in terms of access and control over such a resource and that this has consequences for women's autonomy and dependence. The ideology and fiscal policies that have resulted in Ireland's comparatively high rates of home ownership (in excess of 80%) can, according to Yeates, be seen as closely related to the Irish state's preference for the patriarchal family. Yeates concludes that the "contradiction between the constitutional preference for the marital family and the disregard for the rights of wives is stark, but is consistent with the Irish state's general unwillingness to intervene in matters of the distribution and redistribution of resources within the family" (1999, p 616). Thus, it may be argued that welfare states with a strong commitment to familialism in housing terms – the commitment to the nuclear family as the sole standard for housing – both in the private and public sector, operate to the major disadvantage of women.

Homeless women in Ireland

It was not until 1985 that the first dedicated study of homeless women in Ireland emerged. Written by Sister Stanislaus Kennedy (1985), the objectives of her study were to describe the needs of the visible homeless in Dublin and to identify the situations of hidden homeless women. Her research showed there to be 384 women in various hostels. The primary reason identified for women becoming homeless was severe family disruption, often involving violence and incest. The study also estimated, based on a range of secondary sources, that there were upwards of 9,000 'hidden' homeless women, the majority of them on housing waiting lists. As Kennedy notes: "The idea of women being homeless seems a paradox. Throughout history, the role of the woman has been as a homemaker, harbour, resting place" (1985, p 72). Describing homeless women as in the main the 'hidden homeless', Kennedy demonstrates that homeless women are less likely to be counted in surveys of the homeless, because of the lack of adequate facilities for them and their tendency to double up with friends and relations rather than approach emergency hostel accommodation.

A survey of hostels in Dublin in 1991 found that only just over 20% of all hostel residents were female (131 women without children and 75 with children) (Kelleher et al, 1992). The reasons for the relatively low number of women in the hostels were: first, that much of women's homeless remains hidden; second, that the availability of places does not match demand, particularly for women escaping domestic violence. The age profile of those in the women's hostels tended to be lower than the population in the male hostels and their usage of the hostels tended be of shorter duration than those in the male hostels. However the authors point out that "many women prefer to stay with friends or in dangerous and violent homes rather than to stay in hostels. This means that women's homelessness is often concealed or hidden and is therefore not reflected in hostel numbers" (Kelleher et al, 1992, p 58). Holohan's (1997) more recent study of hostel residents in Dublin confirms this pattern, with females accounting for less than 15% of his sample. Of these women,

77% were aged under 45 with 14.3% over the age of 65. The existing literature on homelessness in Ireland highlights the paucity of research on homeless women in their own right and the lack of knowledge on the underlying reasons for women's homelessness. It also highlights that methods of counting the extent of homelessness by utilising hostels or counting rough sleepers seriously underestimates the extent of women's homelessness. Implicit in the literature and discourses on homeless women is that poverty, domestic violence, sexual abuse, lone parenthood and psychiatric illness are the key factors which result in women becoming homeless.

The 1999 statutory assessment of homelessness provided, for the first time, a breakdown by gender of homeless adults assessed[2]. Of those 5,234 assessed as homeless, virtually half were male adults (49.5%), 26.7% were female adults and the remaining 27% were children[3].

In addition to the statutory assessment of homelessness, a separate assessment of the extent of homelessness was also conducted in the greater Dublin region in 1999 (by the Economic and Social Research Institute and the Homeless Initiative). This survey is the most sophisticated attempt to ascertain the extent of homelessness to date in Ireland (Williams and O'Connor, 1999). Based on a survey of users of homeless services in the Dublin region for a period of a week, two separate groups of homeless people were identified in the research: first, those who utilised homeless services during the week in question and second, those recorded on the local authority lists as homeless. Of the hostel users, 1,550 were identified as being on the local authority lists only (710 females and 840 males) and 1,350 had utilised homeless services (1,010 males and 340 females), giving a total of 2,900. The former group predominantly consists of families or single females usually with children who tend to find accommodation with friends, family or specific services such as refuges. Those in the latter group are predominantly male, sleep rough or stay in hostels.

Considerable divergences in terms of gender were evident between and within the two categories. Of the males who utilised homeless services nearly 94% were single compared to 68% of females. Of those on the local authority waiting lists, nearly 65% of females had child dependants compared to less than 14% of males.

In terms of age, of those who used homeless services, over 44% of females were aged under 25 compared to just over 20% of males. A similar pattern emerged for those on the local authority waiting lists, with nearly 44% of females under 25, compared to 18.6% of males. For both categories, the average age of males was 39.3 years and 31.9 for females. In addition, males experienced a greater duration of homelessness over the previous five years for all age cohorts, except for the under-20s and those over 65.

The data also shows that males are more likely to sleep rough or use hostels than females, with females more likely to access bed and breakfast accommodation or refuges.

Women, poverty and housing

The most recent analysis of the extent and risk of poverty in Ireland suggests that during the 1990s there has been a reduction of the risk of poverty for two-parent households with children, but an increase in the risk of poverty for single-person households, households headed by a retired person and those headed by females (Callan, 1999).

In a recent detailed study of women and poverty in Ireland, it was estimated that the risk of poverty at the 50% relative poverty line for women who live alone rose from 4% to 24% between 1987 and 1994. The risk for lone-mother households rose from 17% to 32% over the same period (Nolan and Watson, 1999)[4]. The risk of poverty for these two groups was higher than all of the other household types. The reasons for this were attributed to the level of welfare payments on which many lone parents and households headed by a single woman depend. Nolan and Watson argue that the growing number of women living alone and heading lone-parent households are the key factors leading to an increase in the risk of poverty for women.

The report also suggests that women experience a degree of protection from poverty by living in a household in which they are not the household head, and this is closely related to economic status (Callan, 1999, p xvi). The authors are at pains to point out that the policy implications of this finding are not that single adults and lone parents should be encouraged to remain in or return to their family home, but that the transition to independent accommodation should not result in increased poverty. They note, however, that given the substantial rise in new house prices, increased rents in the private rented sector and reduced opportunities to access social rented housing limit this possibility.

Domestic violence

Violent breakdown of a relationship does not appear as a category for those seeking local authority housing in Ireland, but international studies would suggest that many women, in some studies as many as half, become homeless because of the need to escape violence from their husbands or partners (Thomas and Dittmar, 1995; Passaro, 1996; Malos and Hague, 1997). There were 8,448 domestic violence incidents recorded by the Garda (Police Force) in 1998, representing an increase of 102% since 1997. The offenders were predominantly male (91%) and the complainants were predominantly female (189%) (Annual Report of An Garda Siochana, 1999, p106). In a national survey of the extent of domestic violence, it was found that 7% of women who responded stated that they had been abused in the previous year by a partner or ex-partner; 18% had been subjected to violence at some time by a partner or former partner; and 4% had experienced sexual violence (Kelleher et al, 1995). Despite the extent of domestic violence in Ireland, the Report of the Task Force on Violence against Women noted that only 13 refuges were operating in Ireland, with the majority run by voluntary agencies. The report argued that all refuges have more women seeking space than they can accommodate and stressed the need for additional places (Office of an Tanaiste, 1997, p 66). The Task Force noted that when refuge space was unavailable, victims of domestic violence were often placed in bed and breakfast accommodation. They argued that while such accommodation was necessary at times, it should only be used as crisis accommodation and that refuges and other agencies should provide advice and support to women in such accommodation. The report also argued that local authorities give special consideration to women who are victims of domestic violence in their scheme of letting priorities. Despite the development of refuges for victims of domestic violence, a recent survey showed that 88% of women said a key reason why they did not leave violent partners is that they had nowhere to go and could not afford alternative accommodation (Kelleher et al, 1995, p 22).

Women, homelessness and addiction

In a survey of users of the Merchant's Quay service for drug users during one week in early 1999, it was found that 63% of those who participated in the survey were found to be currently homeless; 38% of the participants were female. While the mean age of these homeless drug users was 24.4 years, females were on average younger, at 22.8 years. Females were reported to have first experienced homelessness at a younger age than males (18.4 years compared to 19.6 years) and had been homeless for longer than males (an average of 2.5 years compared to 2 years).

Strong divergences in accommodation were noted by gender, with 36% of males compared to 15% of females sleeping rough and 30% of females in bed and breakfast accommodation compared to no males. Thirty-seven per cent of respondents were in their current accommodation for more than one year, but 43% of males compared to 26% of females. Conversely, 42% of females had been in their current accommodation for less than one month, compared to 24% of males. When asked what they considered to be the primary reason for their homelessness, equal numbers of males and females attributed it to their drug use, but females were more likely to also cite physical/sexual abuse and family conflict than males (Cox and Lawless, 1999).

Conclusions

The limited literature and data on women and homelessness in Ireland suggest that existing methodologies for ascertaining the extent of homelessness are flawed in respect to women. However, the existing studies do highlight a number of distinct characteristics of those homeless women enumerated.

First, it appears that women become homeless at a slightly earlier age than men, but are more successful at making the transition from homelessness to permanent accommodation. Second, we find a cluster of older homeless women, often sleeping rough or using hostels. Third, women utilise a greater range of accommodation options than men. In some cases this reflects the presenting reasons for homelessness (domestic violence, for example) and the fact that a limited range of emergency accommodation is available for such women, or in other cases, a tendency by local authorities to prioritise certain emergency accommodation, such as bed and breakfast accommodation for women, particularly women with children. Fourth, while males remain over-represented in counts of homelessness, the number of females appears to be growing. However, given the limitations of existing data, we cannot state whether this represents a real increase in women's homelessness or that it reflects more accurate recording techniques and methodologies or broader societal changes.

It can be argued that the familialistic nature of the Irish welfare state rendered homelessness among women a hidden phenomenon, with those who needed to escape the family home, due to violence and abuse, offered few options. The options that did exist, certainly up until the late 1970s, were the punitive outposts of a retreating morality, in the form of magdalen homes and other stigmatising institutions (Luddy, 1995). With the dismantling of the institutions that catered for these 'fallen women', a small number have found themselves homeless and due to prolonged institutionalisation, without any of the networks or supports that would allow for their resettlement.

The Irish 'home' was, and in some cases is still, a site of incarceration for women, given the lack of options for those who need to escape from it. Recent changes in the Irish welfare state and the decline of the familialistic tenor of Irish public policy have emancipated many women, but the range of services required to adequately accommodate their needs has lagged behind. Simultaneously, and somewhat contradictorily, those women who do become homeless appear, albeit on very limited evidence, to find it easier to escape homelessness than men. Parenthood, in particular, would appear to give women an advantage in securing local authority accommodation. While lone parenthood may lead initially to homelessness (for example, following rejection by family or eviction from private rented accommodation), due to the scheme of lettings operated by local authorities, it may also prove to be a way out of homelessness.

The greater range of accommodation options, however inadequate to their needs, for women once homeless, results in a relatively low level of visibility in terms of their homelessness. Rather than be labelled as homeless, they are recategorised as victims of domestic violence, or as parents who require more support than those labelled as homeless would necessarily receive.

While we cannot confidently state whether a real increase in the numbers of women experiencing homelessness is occurring in Ireland, it is fair to say that a greater awareness of needs of homeless women is evident. More importantly, transformations in both the Irish welfare state and in the country's social, economic and demographic structures are changing the status of women in Ireland. While much of these changes have had a liberating effect, they have also increased income inequality and created problems of access to low-cost housing which cumulatively may result in increasing homelessness.

Notes

[1] That is that a community of a higher order should not interfere in the internal life of a community of a lower order, depriving the latter of its functions, but rather should support it in case of need and help to coordinate its activity with the activities of the rest of society always with a view to the common good. This principle was first articulated by Pope Leo XIII in 1891 in the papal encyclical *Rerum Novarum*.

[2] See O'Sullivan (1996) for a critique of the methodology utilised in these assessments.

[3] In their analysis of the 1993 assessment of homelessness, Fahey and Watson (1995, p 107) sampled 181 homeless households and found that over half were single males, 11% single females, 21% lone parents, 9% couples with children and 3% couples with no children.

[4] The relative poverty line is calculated by quantifying the proportion of mean household income, taking differences in household size and composition into account, and ascertaining the number of households falling below 40, 50 or 60% of that mean equivalent income. For further details, see Nolan and Whelan (1996).

SEVEN

Women and homelessness in the United Kingdom

Robert Aldridge

The findings of much homelessness research in the United Kingdom suggests that homelessness is predominantly a male experience. Detailed analytical research on homelessness in Britain has tended to concentrate on hostels and rough sleepers, where women are in the minority. Consequently the picture of women's homelessness in the UK is largely derived from disjointed anecdotal and statistical evidence in which the experience, extent and scale of homelessness among women has not been fully recognised. However, while the limited research which is available does not address fully the health needs, housing history or social circumstances of homeless women, it does suggest a growing awareness in the UK of the increasing incidence of female homelessness and also suggests that women are likely to manage their homelessness in a different way from men.

Women's vulnerability to homelessness

As long ago as 1981 Watson and Austerberry argued that recognising the position of women in a patriarchal society and the barriers such a society creates for women is essential to understanding the distinctive factors which affect and exacerbate women's housing problems. What is clear from this and later research is that women face distinctive barriers which increase their vulnerability to homelessness, and that they have distinctive ways of responding to homelessness, particularly in relation to sleeping rough and hidden homelessness.

Although women constitute a growing proportion of the workforce in the UK – well over 40% – they are more likely than men to be employed in low-status or part-time jobs, with low wages. Thus, while there is legislation to ensure that women receive equal pay for equal work, the concentration of women's employment in the low-paid end of the labour market means that women still earn less than men on average. Among the unemployed, the UK benefits system privileges the nuclear family, and benefits for lone parents, for example, are so low that it has been found that lone mothers reliant on benefits sometimes go without food to meet the needs of their children (Middleton et al, 1997).

Women are still the primary carers for children and older people in their families. Women may therefore have interrupted careers and have taken work in low-paid employment to allow them to cope with their family commitments. Many women caught in this situation are financially dependent on their male partner such that if a relationship breaks down the woman's poverty is brought into sharp focus. Many women are fearful of leaving unacceptable relationships because of the financial impact and the possibility of homelessness.

Housing policies in the UK throughout the 1980s and 1990s have focused on promoting home ownership. In a society where freedom of access to housing is directly related to ability to purchase, the relatively weak financial position of women places them at a clear disadvantage in the housing market. Indeed it could be argued that the structure of the housing market makes it very difficult for all single people, but single women in particular, to gain access to the wider housing market. This disadvantage is compounded when a relationship breaks down, and the options for women are extremely limited.

Attitudes and perceptions also make women's experience of homelessness distinctive. Traditionally, women spend a greater amount of time in the home than men, which may affect the decisions women make, for example, about whether to leave home, and, if threatened with the loss of their home, how they address their threatened homelessness. Similarly, single homeless women often face not only the problems of access and financial disadvantage referred to above, but also unjustified negative stereotypes of what it means to be homeless. These factors combine to persuade many women either to decline to describe themselves as homeless, or to conceal their homelessness. These factors make women especially susceptible to hidden homelessness.

Causes of homelessness: women's perspectives

Beyond the general structural disadvantages that women face in the housing market it is generally accepted that the underlying reasons for homelessness are varied, and homeless people's experiences extremely diverse. It is also very important to recognise that homelessness is rarely the result of a single event or individual characteristic. While destruction of a house by an earthquake would constitute such a circumstance, most people who become homeless do so for other reasons, and very often a combination of complex factors come into play.

Jones' (1999) research for the homelessness charity Crisis gives some insight into the varied reasons for homelessness among women. She carried out in-depth interviews with 77 homeless women to discover their experience of homelessness. By examining housing and social histories of the women, many of the underlying factors relating to homelessness were revealed. Many of the findings echo previous research (for example, Dibblin, 1991; Jones and Gilliland, 1993).

In the Crisis report, domestic violence was the single most quoted reason for having become homeless. This reason was primarily given by women aged 30 or over. It is therefore a reason given almost exclusively by older homeless women. Young women, with one exception, did not quote this as the cause of their homelessness.

For young women it was breakdown of family relationships which was the most quoted cause. More than half of those interviewed in the Crisis report (Jones, 1999) in the 16- to 19-year old age group gave this as the reason for leaving home. Sometimes a step parent was involved. This echoes Scottish Council for the Single Homeless (SCSH) research (Jones and Gilliland, 1993), which found that a risk factor among homeless young people was the existence of a step parent.

It was not solely young women who were thrown out by family or friends. In research on older homeless people (Wilson, 1996) there were instances of older women being thrown out of their former home by their grown-up children who had offered to buy the home on their parents' behalf. There were also instances where the older person had moved in to stay with the family, but the stresses had become too much. Sometimes women were given a lengthy period of notice by family or friends, and the need to move out was expected. In other cases there was virtually no notice given and the women were in shock.

Women who live as carers for another person may have very little security of housing when the caring arrangement comes to an end. Eight per cent of the women in Webb's 1994 study were carers, and only one of the women said she would definitely be able to remain once her caring ended. A significant number were in the position of wanting to leave their accommodation very soon, but had nowhere to go.

Eviction was the third most common reason in the Crisis report

(Jones, 1999) given for loss of home. Sometimes this was due to financial difficulties. Sometimes it was due to a complex combination of factors, which on occasion involved the behaviour of the woman's partner. Although women gave 'eviction' as the reason, many had left the tenancy before the eviction was actually carried out.

Ten of the 77 women in the Crisis study reported that they had become homeless after illness or discharge from hospital, even though homelessness legislation gives priority to people who are vulnerable due to illness, and health authorities are supposed to have protocols which ensure that no one is discharged to homelessness. Research for SCSH (Taylor, 1992) showed that there was a problem in ensuring short stay patients at psychiatric hospitals were discharged to appropriate accommodation. It appeared that the position for longer stay patients was relatively well managed. It may be that the results of the Crisis report point to continuing problems in liaison between health authorities and housing and support providers for short stay patients.

On release from prison many women end up homeless, although the true extent of this is largely concealed. One of the reasons for homelessness arising while a woman is in prison is that she may not have informed the housing provider of the situation and the house may be regarded as abandoned. Rent subsidy via Housing Benefit may cease, and rent arrears can build up. Similarly, women who are owner-occupiers are very unlikely to be able to maintain their accommodation while in prison. Alternatively, many women are told by friends, relatives or partners that they are not welcome back from prison to their previous accommodation. According to CHAR (Campaign for Homeless and Roofless, now the National Homeless Alliance) it is more common for a woman to wait for a man to get out of prison than for a man to wait for a woman. One woman interviewed by Webb (1994) indicated that prison was better than some of the hostels she had lived in previously. There was even a case of a woman who asked the judge to send her to prison because she had nowhere else to go.

There is evidence that ethnic origin is another factor affecting women's experience of homelessness in distinctive ways. There are a number of issues which arise in this regard and which vary considerably in different parts of the country. For example, in most of Scotland minority ethnic communities form a very small proportion of the population – mostly less than 2%. If a woman becomes homeless and has to leave a relationship in such circumstances there are problems relating to estrangement from the local minority community. If violence has occurred it is difficult for her to remain hidden from friends and relatives of the abuser.

In contrast, in London, and in a number of other areas in England, where there is a large population comprising a broad range of minority ethnic communities, the problem is one of access to accommodation. It is commonly reported that women from ethnic minorities comprise a higher proportion of hostel residents than their proportion in the population at large would suggest (that is, they are overrepresented in hostel accommodation). Overall men and women from ethnic minorities are overrepresented in hostel and bed and breakfast accommodation, but it appears that the situation with women is even more acute.

A study of young black and minority ethnic homeless people in England found some results which are different from the general trends among homeless women. For example, among minority ethnic young people, young men were twice as likely as young women to have been in institutional care. In the population as a whole, according to a Department of the Environment (DoE) report into single homeless people in England, homeless women were more likely to have spent time in care than men (Anderson et al, 1993).

Although the actual numbers of ethnic minority women interviewed were small, a high proportion of women from ethnic minorities had left home due to violence or abuse, which appeared particularly prevalent among Indian and Pakistani women, of whom one in three left home due to physical or sexual violence.

For women who are also refugees or asylum-seekers the above factors apply, but are aggravated by severe legislative constraints. There is little recent research available into the housing needs of women asylum-seekers. It is noticeable, however, that in the DoE study of single homeless people in England, a significant proportion of women interviewed in hostels were fleeing the political situation in another country. Indeed it was the single most cited reason by women in hostels – and that was in 1991. Since then numbers have increased greatly.

The extent of homelessness among women

A comparison of surveys of homeless women in hostels in England shows that while in 1972, 24% of women in hostels were under 30 years old, in 1991 the figure had risen to 67%. The clear trend is that there is an increase in younger homeless women using services, and a greater proportion of homeless women are young, compared to homeless men using such services. Some caution must be exercised since the statistics for these surveys relate to specific forms of emergency accommodation which were largely designed to accommodate a middle-aged white male population. However, anecdotal evidence from other agencies shows a trend towards greater numbers of young homeless women becoming visibly homeless and making use of emergency shelters. Among newly homeless young people arriving in London, around 25% were women. Recent surveys in London show a rise in the numbers of young women aged under 21 using emergency shelters. It is not clear to what extent this reflects younger women who are homeless being more prepared to make use of emergency services designed for homeless people than in the past; or to what extent it is a reflection of a general rise in homelessness among women; or whether it is reflection of options for accommodation of homeless women becoming more restricted.

Women's Aid, which operates refuges for women who have experienced domestic violence, reports growing numbers of women approaching them for assistance. Shelter (1999) has reported that in 1996/97 more than 36,000 women approached its network of advice centres in England. Of that number 21,000 were homeless, either living rough or in temporary accommodation. Around 80% of that number were in London. Women represented one third of people seeking assistance from the advice centres.

As far as young women are concerned, over a ten-year period Centrepoint projects offering emergency accommodation to young people in London show that the proportion of young women admitted to projects rose from 25% in 1987 to 44% in 1997; and among that group proportionally more young women had no income and less access to benefits than young men.

Rough sleeping

The 1993 DoE study (Anderson et al, 1993) found that women constituted a small minority of people who sleep rough, and that their characteristics were markedly different to men. Typically, according to the DoE study, less than 15% of people who sleep rough are women. This estimate is reinforced by a more recent study of Scottish rough sleepers (Shaw et al, 1996), which showed that 14% of Scottish rough sleepers were women. Both studies show that the age profile of men and women who sleep rough is also very different: over 40% of women rough sleepers were aged under 25 compared to around 15% of men.

The report also indicated that 16- and 17-year-olds living in hostels and bed and breakfasts in England were more likely to be women than men. At the other end of the age spectrum, research by Crisis and Help the Aged (Crane, 1997) showed that 21% of older homeless women were in the age group 75 and over, compared to just 6% of older homeless men. In all other age groups the number of men was greater than the number of women. Many of the respondents in the DoE study had experienced more than one episode of homelessness.

A study of winter shelter residents in England, Scotland and Wales (Gill et al, 1996) showed far more men making use of night shelters than women: 89% compared to just 11% who were women. A further study of people in London winter shelters (CRASH, 1995, 1996) showed that more women had been staying with friends and family in the previous month (18%) than men (10%), and a lower proportion of women (50%) than men (63%) had slept rough. This was, to some extent, reflected in the accommodation people moved on to when departing from the shelter. Of those leaving winter shelters, a slightly higher proportion of women (8%) than men (6%) went to friends and family, and a slightly lower proportion of women (5%) than men (7%) went back to the streets. However, given that by far the largest number went to unknown destinations or other shelters (around 66%), and the relatively low number of women in the survey in comparison to men, these statistics should be interpreted with some caution.

The political and media agenda concerning homelessness is dominated by those at the most visible end of the homelessness continuum. In particular the government at UK level is seeking to reduce rough sleeping significantly by the year 2003, while in Scotland the new Scottish Executive from the Scottish Parliament has stated that it intends that no one should need to sleep rough after the year 2003. The effect of this political priority is to focus attention even more on those whose homelessness is visible, while hidden homelessness slips down the political agenda.

Hidden homelessness

Hidden homelessness has been found to be a feature of homelessness among women, and also among vulnerable minority groups such as people from minority ethnic communities and gay men and lesbians. This is partly because of their increased vulnerability to violence and discrimination if they are visibly on the streets.

As a term, hidden homelessness is well used and widely recognised in the UK, although it is often used to mean different things in different circumstances. Indeed the term 'hidden' homelessness to some extent has a broad range of possible interpretations precisely because it was invented to cover all those situations which are not covered by the equally vague term: 'visible' homelessness. Existing definitions are related largely to current homelessness legislation which categorises certain groups of homeless people, but conceals others.

Homelessness legislation in the UK is aimed at assisting people 'in priority need', and in the process operates as a means of rationing accommodation offers by effectively excluding a large number of single people who are homeless. Because of its rigid structure, it also excludes many whose homelessness is hidden. In effect the legislation creates some of the problems of hidden homelessness, not least through a degree of discretion within local authorities which is open to abuse and often leads to the exclusion of women whose homelessness, although very real, remains hidden. It is therefore important not to base assumptions about homelessness solely on tenure or physical condition. As Webb writes in a SCSH study (described by Fitzpatrick et al (2000) as the most systematic study of hidden homelessness to date):

> Hidden homelessness is not about single women who need to move because their garden is too big or too small.... It is about women who are stressed and depressed, who lose sleep, friends and jobs, who have no means of claiming any benefits, who cannot eat a proper healthy diet, who have no privacy or space, who suffer violence, harassment or abuse, who lose their dignity and self-respect, who form relationships to secure a roof over their head, who must constantly move from address to address or face a seemingly endless wait trapped in an unsatisfactory situation, who see living in an institution as a better alternative to a job outside. (Webb, 1994, p 5)

Four main pathways into hidden homelessness for women were identified by Webb:

- the *homeless pathway*: where a woman actually presents as homeless but is not recognised as such by staff;
- the *allocations pathway*: when homelessness is presented simply as a housing need and is not recorded as homelessness;
- the *non-presentation pathway*: when a woman does not present to any organisation, but puts up with intolerable conditions;

- the *institutional pathway*: when a woman remains in an institution because there is no housing for her;

Webb further identifies a number of situations in which women are 'unwillingly living' and which potentially constitute hidden homelessness:

- staying 'care of' parents, relatives or friends;
- living in 'tied' accommodation (linked with employment);
- living with someone for whom they act as a carer;
- living in insecure rented accommodation (sometimes suffering harassment);
- remaining in or having to return to an institution;
- unable to leave a relationship (this includes abuse and/or violence);
- unable to live in their own house – perhaps due to violence, harassment or lack of support;
- forming a relationship simply to secure housing;
- sleeping rough other than in known sites;
- living in a hostel, emergency or temporary accommodation.

Women become homeless through a variety of pathways and circumstances and it would appear that many of them are likely to be more hidden than male homeless people. Some stay in the care of friends or relatives, some are 'trapped' in caring roles or in institutions, while others may be in insecure privately rented accommodation. Often they will have a roof over their heads, but will not be able to consider their accommodation as their home. Some women live a nomadic existence, 'sofa surfing' from one friend to another. Some endure abuse or harassment. Many live under the constant insecurity and stress of not knowing when they will have to move on to somewhere else, having no housing rights whatsoever in their precarious living arrangements.

It is of course extremely difficult to quantify a phenomenon which is by its very definition 'hidden'. Quantifying visible homelessness is the subject of great debate, and its complexity and the unreliability of statistics well documented. Hidden homelessness is even more complex. It is important therefore to identify a number of indicators of the scale of the problem.

Some of the most significant indicators of housing need, and pointers towards hidden homelessness, are the housing lists maintained by local authorities in Britain, and by the Northern Ireland Housing Executive in Northern Ireland. There has been no UK-wide analysis carried out examining the factors which might indicate hidden homelessness. Webb (1994), in examining just four local authority areas in Scotland, looked at hidden homelessness among single women. She found over 8,500 single women in such circumstances. There were at the time 56 local authority areas in Scotland.

The housing lists do contain valuable information about the number of households applying for housing who are sharing with other households, or who are living 'care of' another household. They also identify the numbers living in insecure or temporary accommodation.

In order to understand the specific circumstances of hidden homelessness it is important to look in greater detail at individual examples, which illustrate both the great extent of hidden homelessness and the variety of circumstances which categorisation in a statistical grouping can disguise.

Statistics from advice telephone lines give a similar picture of unmet need relating to women and homelessness. Despite the general picture of homelessness in its visible form relating mainly to men, the Housing Advice Switchboard in London in the 1980s reported that a majority of inquirers for housing advice were women. More recently a nation-wide housing advice line, 'Shelterline', has been set up, which shows an extremely high proportion of women callers (around 35%).

Conclusions

It is clear that women's experience of homelessness is distinctive, pronounced and often hidden. It is also clear that the research available is patchy and the statistical data scant – yet sufficient to indicate a serious problem begging attention. The general risk factors relating to homelessness are aggravated in the case of women by structural disadvantages in the housing and labour market suffered and the experience of violence and harassment. Among ethnic minorities the problem escalates through issues of racism and social isolation, becoming even more limiting in the case of asylum-seekers burdened with severe legislative constraints.

Fitzpatrick in the most authoritative survey of research into single homelessness in the UK to date, summarised the consensus on women and homelessness as follows:

> Principal findings ... include that homeless women are, on average, younger than homeless men; that they will take extreme measures to

avoid sleeping rough; and that homelessness among women is closely related to personal relationship problems, with a very high proportion having suffered physical or sexual abuse. (Fitzpatrick et al, 2000, p 8)

More research, both quantitative and qualitative, is needed into this entire area, and policy drives such as the Rough Sleepers Initiative need to be complemented with creative policy responses to the issue of hidden homelessness. In particular, the systemic (including legislative) factors working to conceal homelessness among women need to be tackled. To make assumptions solely on the basis of tenure or physical condition is problematic.

Finally, it is crucial to keep in mind, in responding to women's homelessness, that not all homeless women are the same, differing by gender, age, un/employment, and so on. Wide-ranging and targeted approaches are needed at the micro and macro levels to tackle the causes and effects of homelessness among women.

EIGHT

Poverty, housing problems and homelessness among women in Belgium

Pascal De Decker[1]

Introduction

Research has persistently found that homeless people and people at risk of homelessness are very poor (De Decker and Raes, 1996; De Decker, 1998). Poverty is thus considered as a macro condition in the production of homelessness. This chapter explores the nature of women's poverty in Belgium, and the relationship between poverty and homelessness for women.

Poverty is relative; numbers and causes change over time and differ for different groups. The relationship between poverty, housing and homelessness for women in Belgium is often problematic. To deal with this complex relationship, the chapter begins with a discussion of the debate on 'the feminisation of poverty' in which different perspectives have emerged. The second section looks at the profile of poor women in Belgium and argues that the traditional focus on female-headed households fails to recognise poverty among housewives. In the third part, we consider housing conditions with particular reference to affordability, tenure and amenities for groups living in poverty. The fourth part presents a profile of homeless women with some tentative comments about the relationship between their homelessness and poverty. The chapter then concludes with a brief examination of the current political climate.

This chapter is based on a review of available literature and on an analysis of existing data on poverty and housing conditions drawn from both Belgian and European level statistics. The results of a survey of services for homeless women in Flanders form the basis of the section on service provision.

The feminisation of poverty

In an introduction to a publication on women's poverty, Van Haegendoren (1996) comments on the high level of equality between men and women as evidenced by Belgium's score of 14 on the Gender Development Index. According to Vranken et al (1997), neither quantitative research nor data on women's rising participation in social benefits corroborate the perception of the feminisation of poverty. They suggest that the emerging debate is based on a stream of publications and their coverage by the media rather than a representation of the actual situation. Vranken et al argue that poverty is not feminine, but that it also does affect women. Being a woman is not the most important feature of their poverty; other features such as low levels of education and long-term unemployment are more decisive. The production of poverty is not gender neutral, but it cannot be explained solely with reference to gender.

Cantillon (1999) offers a somewhat different perspective. Using data on subsistence incomes and the empirical results of the Centre for Social Policy (CSB: *Centrum voor Sociaal Beleid*) surveys[1], Cantillon (1999[2]) argues that women cannot be seen as an homogeneous group. Risks of poverty are differentiated according to age, educational attainment and earning power such that some groups of women are increasingly more susceptible to poverty while the position of others has steadily been improving. Between 1976 and 1985, the increased risk of poverty for younger women was compensated for by the strengthened position of older women. The stagnation of the position of retired women during the following decade (1985-92) changed the balance, with a rising proportion of female heads of households in the poor population. This is true for both active poor households and retired (inactive) households. Using the EU poverty standard, Cantillon finds that the share of female-headed households living in poverty rose from 26% in 1985 to 38% in 1992, dropping to 28% between 1992 and 1997.

Cantillon (1999) draws two tentative conclusions from this analysis. First, within the active population there is a tendency in the direction of an increasing share of female-headed households in the poor population. This can be explained with reference to the rising destabilisation of the family, often linked to economic and policy conditions, enforced by the ever-weakening position of single mothers with children. Second, the analysis shows that retired women are still the most significant risk group.

Profile of women's poverty

According to Cantillon (1999) it is a paradox that, for women, the risk of poverty continues to rise despite the fact that, overall, women's educational level and level of economic activity have improved. This is explained, first, by what she calls 'the unfinished emancipation'. Because the growth in the labour market has not met women's increasing demand for work and because the labour market has not adequately adjusted to women's needs to combine work and family, the economic autonomy of women can only be partial. Especially among women with low socio-economic positions, a typical labour market participation pattern has emerged dominated by part-time work, unemployment, periods of working and periods of not working at all. The second explanation Cantillon offers is that women's emancipation functions as a boomerang for some groups and especially for the weaker groups. In an unbalanced labour market, rising economic autonomy reinforces inequalities, thereby discriminating against poorly educated women and single parents in general, and poorly educated single women and housewives in particular.

Analyses of the feminisation of poverty have almost exclusively focused on single women (Cantillon, 1999). Rarely does the position of married housewives figure in the statistics since the male is counted as the head of household. Besides single mothers and retired women, a growing group of housewives of active age has to be counted as a group at risk (see also Driessen and Smekens, 1996).

Single older women remain an important risk group. This is due to the very slow growth of women's pensions. The poverty risk of pensioned women households (80% of whom are single widowed women) rose from 9% in 1985 to 17% in 1992. This is nearly twice as high as that for pensioned male households (80% of whom are married couples).

It is well known that lone parents (among whom 80% are single mothers) have a high poverty risk. Cantillon (1999) estimates that approximately 8% of lone-parent households in Belgium have an income below the minimum EU standard, which is more than twice the figure for two-parent households. As the number of single mothers increases at a steady speed, their percentage in the poor population also increases (from 3.7% in 1985 to 4.6% in 1992[2]). Single parents are adversely affected by the cumulative effects of living on a single income, certain gender-related socio-economic features, and the insufficiency of private and collective protection mechanisms.

Between 1975 and 1985, the position of single parents was strengthened by two interrelated policy measures. The first saw the upgrading of the status of lone mothers from 'single' to 'head of household', leading to higher subsistence incomes. The second policy change gave lone mothers higher levels of child benefit. Since then, however, no further strengthening policy measures have been introduced. Nevertheless, their risk of poverty has not increased[3], a fact which can largely be attributed to their rising labour market participation (from 50% to 69%), an increase in the number in receipt of alimony (from 32% to 52%), a rise in the level of minimum allowances and the decrease in the average number of children per household.

Married/cohabiting housewives with children comprise an even larger group living in poverty. Approximately 42% of all poor households are this type of single earner[4]. Moreover, their risk of poverty is greater than that of single parents: 13.5% of housewives live in a household with an income lower than the EU poverty standard as compared with 8% of single parents.

Housewives' higher risk of poverty is directly and indirectly linked to the general trend towards dual-income families: directly because two incomes are becoming the standard; indirectly because the shrinking number of non-earning housewives is concentrated among women with low levels of education and above-average numbers of children.

Particularly for poorly educated women with (several) children, the benefits of working do not adequately compensate the problems of working out of the home. The likelihood of women participating in the labour market decreases as the number of children increases. Among all households with children under the age of 12, the proportion of two-income households drops from 90% when there is one child, to 81% when there are two children and 64% when there are three or more children. This general pattern is even more pronounced for women with low levels of education: for whom the proportion who are economically active decreases from 80% when there is one child to 50% when there are three or more children.

In 60% of cases, the partners of poorly educated women themselves have a low level of educational attainment. The, often forced, choice of households to rely on a single earner leads to a weakened economic position and poverty. Not only can one talk of an accumulation of weak professional positions, but one can also speak of reinforcing effects. Studies have shown that the employment chances of women drop with educational level, especially when their partners are poorly educated (CSB, 1985-92, in Cantillon, 1999). The chances of unemployment mirror this pattern. Household configuration has a profound impact on the labour position of women.

Somewhat contrary to Cantillon (1999), other authors have argued that the feminisation of poverty is not a clear trend (for example, Driessen and Smekens, 1996; Vranken et al, 1997). Data on applicants and recipients of subsistence incomes during the 1990s show a decreasing share of women and a growing share of men in receipt of subsistence incomes (Vranken et al, 1997). Nevertheless, it is important to note that the overall number of applications for subsistence incomes rose substantially during the 1990s and that, consequently, the number of women in receipt of subsistence incomes also rose from 29,885 in 1990 to 45,739 in 1999. These figures indicate a general rise in official poverty.

Within this overall picture, it is interesting to note that the proportion of single parents (predominantly women with children) in receipt of subsistence incomes dropped while that of single people (both men and women) rose. This can, at least partially, be explained with reference to a policy measure which augmented and differentiated subsistence incomes. The gain for single parents developed in two stages. In 1988, single parents were accepted as a distinct category. Initially, they received less money than couples, but more than other categories. The second stage saw the gradual increase of benefit levels to match that received by couples (reached in 1992).

Women and housing

Using available data, we compared the housing situation of single people[5] for the following housing indicators: tenure, amenities and housing costs. The picture differs for each indicator.

Single women of active age and single mothers are less likely to be homeowners. By contrast, single women and single mothers fare better in terms of amenities. Single men and especially single older men and women score worst on amenities. There are no significant affordability problems among home owners. On the other hand, tenants in all categories pay more than average for housing. This is particularly the case among older people and single women of active age. Interestingly, single people and single parents are paying less than average and even less than what in Flanders is taken as the affordability threshold of 20%. There are no conclusive explanations for this finding, but it is reasonable to assume that this is linked to their overrepresentation in social renting. The initial results of a study on the profile of the tenants of social housing, by Antwerp University (Pannecoucke et al, 2001), reveals an overrepresentation of single-person households (43% compared to 27% in the society as a whole) and single-parent households (15% compared to 3% in the society as a whole). Nevertheless, EuroSurvey data for 1995 reveal that, more so than other households, single women of active age and single parents report that their housing places a heavy financial burden on them and, as a consequence, they often face arrears.

Housing in Belgium is dominantly market-led, with only meagre subsidy schemes organised to counter market forces. In other words, very few households who cannot afford to buy their own home are actually helped by existing subsidy schemes to access secure, affordable housing in good condition. Home ownership is both the social norm in Belgium and the major structural housing 'solution'.

More than ever, home ownership is connected to dual-income earning households. Only those with two incomes – and those with high single incomes or financial support from families – can easily afford owner-occupation (Meulemans, et al, 1996; De Decker and Geurts, 2000). Single-income households are forced to rely on social or private renting. Lack of regulation in private renting makes this a very problematic option for such households. Within this sector, older, poorly educated, unemployed and single-parent households often live in poor and expensive housing conditions (Meulemans et al, 1996; De Decker et al, 1997). Although, in practice, discrimination is illegal, there is evidence to suggest that it is widespread. The chair of the AES (*Algemeen Eigenaarssyndicaat* [General Landlords Association]), H. Moriau, recently admitted in an interview that single women and single parents in particular are considered a high risk tenant group. 'Risk' is defined as non-payment of rent and/or early abandonment of tenancy (because of new relationships).

With only 5 to 6% of stock (10% in the larger cities), the social rental sector is too small to adequately meet needs. On the other hand, its means-tested nature means that rents are affordable and provide a buffer against poverty. With respect to women, three further points are worth noting. First, since 1991 single parents have been recognised as a separate category. Eligibility rules for social dwellings allow single parents to have a higher income than single people in general. This differentiation may explain the observed overrepresentation of single parents in the sector. Second, in Belgium, there has been a growing debate about the residualisation of social renting with concern about the increasing concentration of very poor people in the sector. This discussion will inevitably lead to the enlargement of the target groups. On the other hand, the broadening of target groups will not be complemented with an increase in stock. By implication, people with low incomes may face greater difficulty in entering social housing. Third, within current regulations, there is no specific priority of access accorded to homeless people. Thus, people living in a homeless reception house – even women with children – have no priority access to social housing.

Homeless women in profile

In Belgium, as in most countries, data on the profile of homeless women are largely collected from service providers. However, the administrative and legislative basis for provision differs between each of the three regions: Flanders, Wallonia and Brussels Capital. Most of the data below is based on information gathered from service providers in Flanders over two periods (1988–93 and 1995–98). The two data sets allow for some comparisons to be made over time.

The number of homeless women and children in residential care has changed little since the late 1980s. In fact, comparing figures from 1995–97 and older data from 1988–93, we find that the number of women and children in residential care has dropped slightly (De Decker, 2000). So one can conclude that fewer women (with children) enter residential care today than in the early 1990s.

The profile of homeless women can be summarised under a range of indicator variables.

Age

Somewhat contradictory to poor women in general, women in reception centres are young: half are under the age of 30, a further 28% are between the ages of 30 and 39 while 16% are between 40 and 49 years.

Parental status

There have been no significant changes in household type of women entering residential care since the late 1980s. In 1997, 59.1% of all women entering residential care were single people (compared with

96% of men). Single women and single mothers make up 94.1% of the women applying. Whereas men tend to enter residential care unaccompanied, just over a third (34.7%) of women entered residential care with at least one child. Sixteen per cent of women had one child with them, 13% had two children and 10% entered with at least three children. These children are young: 80% under the age of 10.

Ethnic status

Of all the women who stayed in residential centres in 1997, 83% were Belgian nationals, approximately 4% came from other EU countries, while 13% came from outside the EU. There is no increase in this last category if we compare the figures with those from the end of the 1980s or the beginning of the 1990s.

Marital status

The largest group of women entering homelessness services are married: in 1997, 42% were married, implying that they face severe relational problems. Unmarried women account for 35.2% of service users, while divorced women account for 19.8% and widows 2.2%.

Educational attainment

The education level of homeless women remains low: approximately 40% of the women had at best finished primary education, or denominational education, or received training on the basis of a learning contract ('articles of apprenticeship'). Among those who had finished secondary education, the majority stopped at the lowest levels: 45% went on to lower technical education. Of the clients who are still in secondary school (children and young homeless women), 70% are either in technical or in lower technical education (indicating a reproduction of the low education level of the parents).

The low educational levels of homeless women entering services mirrors the low educational level of poor women in general. This finding supports the now broadly accepted view that education has become a major social cleavage and a root to marginalisation (see, for example, Marx et al, 1999).

Income level

Figures from 1997 show that, at time of entry into reception centres, 35% of women had no income at all. This figure drops significantly during the stay such that at the time of departure, only 16% still have no income. The limited proportion of women who had a wage income rose slightly: from 12.4% at entry to 13.8% when leaving. Generally speaking, the overwhelming majority of women have no 'regular' wage income, neither at intake nor when leaving.

Besides wages, other important sources of income are: unemployment benefit (20.6% at entry; 21.7% when leaving) and social benefits (12.8% at entry; 28% when leaving). One can conclude that the economic position of women entering and leaving residential care remains vulnerable. Any observed improvements in income situations can largely be attributed to social benefits.

The high incidence of no income among women entering services is undoubtedly linked with their marital status (42% of women were married but fleeing from the family home due to relationship problems). We can expect that the majority are housewives dependent on their spouse's income. Often these women are caught in a cycle of dependence: they are doomed either to a lengthy stay in services or to return to their partner. So far only a small minority of women leave the reception centres to live independently (De Decker, 2000).

Presenting problems

At entry a wide range of problems is reported; in particular: relationship problems (24% of the women), housing problems (16%) and financial problems (11%) dominate. Relationship problems often coincide with housing problems (women leaving the family home where they lived with a partner) and financial problems (many women have no income of their own). This picture differs substantially from that of men for whom the dominant contributing problem is lack of housing (25%), coinciding with financial difficulties (16%). Few men become homeless as a result of relationship problems (5%).

It is somewhat surprising that 9% of women enter homelessness services because of problems in the parental home. Why this is happening remains unclear, although a tentative explanation may be found in the reorganisation and restructuring of welfare work responsibilities. Blurred lines of responsibility within the sector may be contributing to younger homeless people's entry into residential care as opposed to youth care.

Conclusions

In this chapter we have developed some ideas about the relationship between poverty, housing problems and homelessness among women. The debate on the feminisation of poverty is inconclusive with respect to the rising number of poor women and the rising proportion of women in the poor population. Echoing Vranken et al (1997) we conclude that poverty is not specifically feminine but that it does affect women. Among women, some risk groups have been clearly detected. Following from research by Cantillon (1999) it is evident that single older women, lone mothers and married, particularly (but not exclusively) poorly educated housewives with children, are at a higher risk of poverty.

Our analysis of the profile of women who entered a homeless reception house shows that the poverty profile is largely reproduced. Homeless women have a low socio-economic level and their application is linked to a lack of material resources – a lack of income or a lack of housing (or a combination of both). However, this general picture needs at least two caveats. First, older lone women are almost wholly absent from the homeless population (partly because they live in the family home and partly because they do not flee domestic problems). Second, for women, and this is very different from male homelessness, the single largest reason for admission into a reception centre is relationship problems. Thus, the largest group of women in reception houses combines the risks of poverty with relationship problems, leading to the hypothesis that middle and upper class women – even if they are housewives – have other alternatives available when relationship problems occur.

A number of positive measures have been introduced at different times, by different governments and different ministries to improve the position of some groups of women in poverty. Single women with children have benefited from improved conditions. First, social benefit levels were increased and, second, entry into social housing has been facilitated. In relative terms, the combined effects of these measures has been a decreased risk of poverty and an amelioration of housing conditions. Unfortunately, the conclusions cannot be as positive with respect to the functioning of homeless reception houses. Research has shown, first, that homeless reception houses have a very negative and paternalistic view of their clients, and second, that for women who leave the family home the most common outcome is a return to that spousal home. This is criticised on two grounds: it does not empower the women and it does not enhance their economic independence. To be sure, these are the unintended side-effects of a case-loaded sector, which is nevertheless aware of the need for change.

Notes

[1] CSB = *Centrum voor Sociaal Beleid* (Centre for Social Policy), Antwerp University – the centre regularly organises a large-scale socio-economic survey in Belgium.

[2] 4.8% for all single people in 1997 (author's own calculation based on Cantillon et al, 1999).

[3] This dropped slightly to 6% in 1997 (author's own calculations based on Cantillon, 1999).

[4] That is, couples with or without children, where the wife stays at home and has no income from social security.

[5] That is, single retired men, single retired women, single men of active age, single women of active age, one-parent households (either male- or female-headed).

NINE

Women, homelessness and the welfare state in Denmark

Anders Munk, Inger Koch-Nielsen and Mette Raun

Introduction

Much of the literature on women and homelessness suggests that it is a growing problem in the European arena. The reasons typically cited for this are related to the perceived vulnerability of women given the demographic, social and economic changes taking place across Europe. The underlying assumption seems to be that without male support women are at risk of social exclusion from society. In the Danish context there is some research which supports aspects of this assumption (for example, Kristensen, 1994), but other, and in our view more convincing, research (for example, Järvinen, 1992), which challenges the assumption. It is the argument of this chapter that, in the Danish context, the relationship between social and economic changes and the increasing vulnerability of women to homelessness is not well established. Our analysis is based on the existence of an elaborate Danish welfare state that can be said to counteract exclusion and provide protection for potentially vulnerable women. We would claim that for most women the availability of paid work, contraceptives, abortion, child care services and welfare benefits have altered the traditional patterns of male dominance. However, importantly we would also stress that, while the structural and legal conditions of the welfare state provide protection for women under threat from homelessness, this does not mean that there is no female homelessness in Denmark. Rather we would argue that an understanding of female homelessness and social exclusion requires us to identify the exceptional nature of the problem and the exceptional pathways and routes into homelessness.

The chapter is divided into four sections: first, we examine key aspects of the Danish legal system which are designed to protect women and ensure their equal place in Danish society; second, we examine social demographic, and economic changes in Denmark and evaluate their impact on the vulnerability of women to exclusion and homelessness; third, we examine, briefly, the nature of the housing market and the manner in which it caters for women on the margins; and fourth, citing evidence from interviews conducted in three homelessness shelters, we identify those factors which contribute to the social exclusion and homelessness among some women in present-day Denmark.

Social policy and the status of women

The fundamentals of Danish social policy related to the status of women pre-date the reforms of the 1960s. As early as the 1920s women had obtained the right to earn an independent income, to own property, to inheritance and to child custody. Family law from the 1920s considered domestic work as contributing to the income of the household and introduced the idea of compensation for the division of labour in the family. During the course of the last century, starting in the 1920s and accelerating from the 1970s, family law and family policy changed from a focus on married couples to a focus on children and parents. Marriage as a legal construct lost much of its meaning as cohabitation and homosexual partnerships were incorporated under the same legislation. Since 1987, in a further significant development, legislation has moved away from a focus on the position of women within the family to a focus on what is called the 'principle of individuality'[1]. In relation to most benefits the principle of individuality has replaced the principle of the household, that is, access to sickness benefit, unemployment and other benefits is unrelated to the family or household status of claimants and is made available on an individual basis. However, the operation of this principle very much reflects the assumption that individuals are attached to the labour market (currently Denmark has the second highest percentage of employed women in the EU).

Social and demographic changes

There has been a relative as well as an absolute increase in one-person households since the 1960s (16% in 1960, 35.8% in 1997). These increases are mainly accounted for by more young people (including women) living on their own after moving away from the family home (Christensen and Koch-Nielsen, 1992) and a larger group of older people living in their own homes. The majority of single households are younger people, both female and male. Among older people the number of single households is greatest among women reflecting, in Denmark as elsewhere, female longevity. Demographic trends in Denmark suggest that the number of older lone-female households will continue to increase. The majority of lone-parent households with children are headed by women; mostly single due to divorce – only a small percentage belong to the group of unmarried mothers.

Regarding the number of divorces, approximately three quarters of marriages contracted in the 1950s and 1960s still existed 20 years later. This is only true for approximately two thirds of the marriages contracted in the1970s. The likelihood of divorce is even greater if one considers marriages contracted in 1980 or 1985, but there might be a tendency towards a declining number of divorces in marriages contracted in 1990: after five years of marriage 14% were dissolved; the last time such a low rate of divorce was recorded was in 1975.

What do these trends tell us? Certainly that family patterns have changed, but we cannot conclude from these changes that there has been, necessarily, a decline in the role of the family. Among those aged 25 to 75, living in a relationship is still the dominant household form (Christensen and Koch-Nielsen, 1992; Thomsen, 1997) and most children grow up with two parents. Gundelach and Riis (1992) have described the intimate relations in modern society as consisting of several monogamous relationships – serial monogamy – throughout a person's lifetime. Danes still strive for a traditional family and still feel moral obligations towards family members. Recent empirical studies by Juul (1998) on the solidarity between family members provides empirical evidence for this interpretation of the intimate relations in modern Danish society (see also Arnmark and Raun, 1998).

Economic change

Danish women's affiliation to the labour market is characterised by a high activity rate. Compared to other European countries Danish women have the second highest employment rate (European Commission, 1997), although it is still lower than among Danish men. Danish women have a higher rate of part-time employment than men, but this gap has narrowed considerably over the past 10 years. The number of women employed part time has fallen every year since 1988. Since the late 1970s more women than men have been unemployed, but men tend to be out of work for longer periods. When we look at Danish women's income we find that women in the same labour market position as men earn less. However, women as a whole have a smaller personal income than men mainly because of their larger share of part-time employment and unemployment. If we only look at full-time employed men and women the differences have reduced since 1988 and are now small (Christensen and Koch-Nielsen, 1992). Danish women's activity rates suggest that dependency on a male breadwinner is a somewhat outdated concept (Kristensen, 1994); this is not to say that men and women have equal positions in the labour market, but it shows that women's provision is not closely linked with marriage – the majority of Danish women can provide for themselves and legislation further facilitates this.

Impact on the vulnerability of women in Danish society

The question is, then, do these social demographic and economic developments constitute a potential problem in Danish society regarding social exclusion of women? Is it mainly elderly single women and the single mother we find in the shelters and the refuges for battered women? Do older people and single mothers pose a potential problem in regard to hidden homelessness?

When we examine the use of institutions for socially excluded people our findings do not support a positive answer to the above questions. In our interviews at three kinds of homeless shelters[2] staff did not consider older women or single mothers to be a significant group of users. When asked what constituted the biggest problem for the socially excluded women none of the people interviewed mentioned lack of financial aid from the government. The single mothers in the refuges for battered women had all experienced violence in their relationships. We would suggest that in the Danish welfare state today, the fact that you are a single mother is not considered a particular problem since the social legislation ensures the right to governmental, needs-based support such as rent subsidy, child benefit, free child care, and maternity leave.

In relation to the extent to which older women are at risk of homelessness, our interviews suggest that there were very few older women at the shelters or at the refuges for battered women. Sundholm is the only institution where they had a few older women, and they are all, without exception, suffering from mental illness. These findings suggest that the older single women are not a large user group. Again this must be understood in the context of the provision of generous universal pensions in Denmark which are not occupationally linked.

Defamilialisation has proceeded apace in Denmark, perhaps more than anywhere else in Europe (see Sainsbury, 1999), freeing women from dependence on male breadwinners and in providing a degree of financial independence. The women who experience periods of potential vulnerability to homelessness as a consequence of divorce, single parenthood or insecure employment, are in most cases well provided for by legislation and benefits. They are also, by and large, well catered for by the operation of the socially regulated housing market. However, while access to housing with security of tenure and right of occupancy is no problem, the condition and location of such housing may be problematic.

The regulation of the housing market and the socially excluded

In Denmark today, a general housing shortage is claimed to be non-existent (Ministry of Housing and Urban Environment, 1999a), but there is a politically accepted shortage of housing for young and older people, and there is a need for alternative housing for the socially marginalised (Ministry of Housing and Urban Environment, 1999b). This last aspect was emphasised at the institutions where we conducted our interviews. Here we were told that the municipality currently has almost no dwellings to which the socially excluded can move.

The majority of social housing is for families; however, it is not reserved for specific groups of families. There is, for instance, in contrast to most other countries, no income limit for eligibility to social housing. However, households with children are given priority access to larger dwellings. Most social housing is assigned according to a waiting list. In addition to the normal waiting list there are certain groups that can be prioritised in the different housing associations. One such group is single parents with children, which provides an advantage for single mothers in that it operates as a protection against homelessness. There is, furthermore, the possibility of obtaining priority access to social housing through the municipality; until recently the local authorities had the right to use every fourth vacant flat for housing people that they consider in acute need. The municipality can also make agreements with housing associations allowing them access to a further proportion of municipal housing for those in need. While the public subsidised social housing sector in general secures good housing quality for the low-income sections of the population, there are additional and important laws and regulations that enable a higher housing consumption among the people with lowest income than would otherwise have been the case, especially through the provision of individual rent support and rent control. The housing legislation furthermore secures tenants against eviction and against rapidly increasing rent (Munk, 1998).

However, there exists a series of tendencies in the housing market that strengthens the concentration of socially marginalised groups and nurtures the development of 'distressed' neighbourhoods; this is especially apparent in the private rental market. Most of the dwellings in this sector pre-date 1940 and they are concentrated in the older neighbourhoods of the larger cities. Approximately 60% of these dwellings are in need of refurbishment.

Although the process of urban renewal is running at a slow pace, the result is a reduction in the number of low-priced dwellings, especially in the larger cities (Skifter Andersen and Als, 1986; Munk, 1998). This results in fewer cheap private dwellings for low-income groups who are thus forced into social housing, and the municipalities' obligation to assign dwellings to social clients produces a concentration of the marginalised groups in social housing estates. For example, the concentration of single women with children is high in social housing estates; however, as a group, they are not considered a social problem, nor a group in need for special treatment (Christiansen, 1993; Munk, 1999).

There are no specific regulations in relation to housing for women. Women are legal subjects with no restraint. The social incidents that will traditionally leave women in a vulnerable position are that of a break up of a marriage due to divorce or death and that of being an unwed mother. During marriage a spouse cannot re-let a rented flat or sell a house that is a jointly owned property (the normal case), without consent from the other spouse. After separation or divorce the couple has to decide who is to move to rented accommodation. If they cannot agree on this, a decision has to be made by the authorities – either the county or the court. The decision from the authorities will be in favour of the parent who is granted custody of any children (which will tend to favour the woman), and who is expected to be able to pay the expenses (which tends to favour the man). A study of divorces from the beginning of the 1980s shows that more men than women move out of the home due to the fact that more women than men had custody of the children. However, if we compare only women with custody to men with custody, a much higher proportion of the women had to move out. On the other hand, the relative proportion of those experiencing worsened housing conditions after the divorce did not reveal any differences between men and women: one third of both sexes experienced worsened conditions (Koch-Nielsen, 1996).

After the death of a spouse, the other partner is entitled to continue the rent contract. In relation to owner-occupation, the surviving spouse is entitled to about three quarters of the estate. The most important rule, however, is the right of the surviving spouse to retain the estate undivided. Furthermore, the municipality does not claim property taxes from pensioners – it will remain as a debt to be paid out when the house is sold, which is most often after the death of the surviving spouse.

One important scheme with regard to securing and keeping housing is rent subsidy and housing benefit. Generally rent subsidy is given to non-pensioners whereas housing benefit is paid out to pensioners. There are, however, a few pensioners who receive rent subsidy since this provides them with more financial aid than housing benefit. A household cannot receive both housing benefit and rent subsidy. In order to receive rent subsidy a person must live in a rented dwelling. This is not the case with regard to housing benefit which is also provided to dwellers in cooperative and privately owned housing. In both of these categories the dwelling needs to have its own kitchen and sewer system; rented rooms, dormitories, and so on therefore do not qualify for benefit. The important variables when deciding the amount that an individual can receive in support – if any – are the income of the household and the amount paid in rent.

Homeless women in Denmark

We have argued that, while Denmark is experiencing demographic changes similar to those elsewhere in Europe, they have not had the same consequences as are sometimes claimed in other countries. Such consequences are forestalled through the operation of a welfare state based on the 'principle of individuality', and through the operation of a housing market which protects the interests of lone parents and divorced and separated women. This is, however, not the same as stating that female homelessness or social exclusion is not an issue in Denmark.

Rather, it is an argument for understanding social exclusion through some less general causes and more concrete aspects than the general societal development of the housing stock or changing family structures. We are not arguing here for an understanding in a medical/psychological discourse; rather we are focusing on societal understanding and categorisation, not trying to present the excluded as lacking certain significant capabilities. For example, one more immediate factor would be violence in the family. These issues are elaborated in the evidence from our survey of the use of three institutions that provide accommodation for homeless women.

We interviewed staff at three different Copenhagen institutions: one a refuge for battered women (*Dannerhuset*); an institution that shelters families (*Garvergården*); and an institution that traditionally is said to take 'the rest' (those that do not fit in anywhere else) (*Sundholm*). The aim of the interviews was to get an impression of the women who used these facilities, through the eyes of the staff. What is clear from all the interviews is that the most excluded women – people using drugs and those suffering from mental illness – have the fewest choices regarding places to stay. Institutions like Sundholm (an institution run by the regional authorities under Section 94 of the 1998 Act on Social Services), that cater for very vulnerable people tend to be larger and have the least resources with regard to staff and finance per user. The living environments are rougher and male dominated. In such environments it is often difficult to take care of oneself – particularly to be able to defend oneself physically. It was also said that the women carry knives which gives a hint of the quality of life in these institutions. Other women know of this situation and they attempt to find other places to stay, meaning that the institutions become refuges of last resort. Approximately 20% of the residents in Sundholm were women, mostly Danish, but the number of 'foreigners' (mainly from European countries and from Greenland) is growing. Many of the women are addicted to drugs and quite a few are or have been prostitutes. There is a small group of older women defined as suffering from mental illness who have lived at the institute for several years. To the extent that staff differentiated between the problems of male and female residents, it was to identify for women the predominance of issues to do with relationship problems, sexual abuse, and mother–child relations. According to the social workers at Sundholm, many of the women residents had male friends whom they relied on for protection from the dangers of street life.

A very significant element in deciding what provisions are available to women is whether they have children. At the institutions such as Garvergården (an independent institution run under licence from the regional authority), where children are staying, the criteria for acceptance are more exclusive, meaning that the institutions where children are allowed will be more appealing to women but not all the women can stay there. The staff at Garvergården portray their clients has having a wide range of social problems. First and foremost among these is domestic violence. The women residents are seen as extremely vulnerable, having a troubled history from childhood, poor education, severe financial problems as well as violent adult relationships.

The third institute that we visited, Dannerhuset, caters for battered women. The first figures about domestic violence in Denmark were provided in studies of divorces. Koch-Nielsen (1984) found that 25% of divorced women claimed that a violent spouse was one cause, among others, for seeking divorce. During marriage one fifth of the women had been subject to severe physical violence. After divorce 6% were still subject to assaults from the former spouse. A follow-up study three years later showed that most women had managed to get into a non-violent relationship. In a more recent national survey on violence 1% of the women were reported to have been victims of violence from their present partner – and 8% from a previous partner (Christensen and Koch-Nielsen, 1992).

The women's movement has encouraged the development of refuges for battered women where the main criterion of acceptance is whether the woman has been exposed to violence. At Dannerhuset a large proportion of the available resources are spent on dealing with psychological problems and trying to build up self-confidence. Immigrant women are introduced to a support network.

Our intention in providing information on the residents of three homeless institutions is not comprehensively to describe 'the types of women' that are socially excluded in Denmark – there are plenty of other 'types' that could be shown. Rather our intention has been to demonstrate that the social and personal histories of women who are most at risk of social exclusion are not easily captured through a process of analysis focusing on a broad, structural understanding of social exclusion. Such an approach, in placing an emphasis on changing demographic, social and economic conditions, risks missing the true nature of the problems facing the most vulnerable in society.

Conclusions

In Denmark, the debate on social exclusion and homelessness has tended to neglect women, traditionally seeing homelessness as a male problem. This not the case; as Järvinen (1992) has shown, women have historically made up at least a part of the excluded in Danish society. The reasons why they are excluded varies through time. Analysis based on interpretation of those present at institutions (although ignoring the hidden homeless: those who exhaust other strategies before being forced into institutional living) suggests that women who experience homelessness are not easily categorised within the structural (demographic, social, economic) changes previously identified. This is not an argument against a focus on what might be structural differences between men and women and on what might be causing insecurity for women in Danish society; such analyses have to be carried out and such discussions have to be made. However, we would argue, in the context of a defamilialised and decommodified welfare state (while again stressing that we do not want to recall past medical/psychological explanations), that an understanding of homelessness and social exclusion requires us to identify the exceptional nature of the problem and the exceptional pathways and routes to homelessness.

Notes

[1] The principle was laid down in a parliamentary decision of that year in the following way:

Parliament requests the government to: (i) elaborate a plan on how to implement, gradually but decisively, rules concerning the independence of spouses and equal rights of cohabiting partners (the principle of individuality) in social legislation and all other areas of legislation, in accordance with a report from a Committee set up by the Ministry of Social Affairs on equal treatment of marriage and cohabitation and (ii) to ensure a constant automatic checking of the rules in the future legislative work related to the family in order to introduce the principle of individuality, and in those cases where exceptions are made to argue for those.

[2] Interviews were conducted at: a refuge for battered women, *Dannerhuset*; an institution that offers shelter to families, *Garvergården*; and an institution

Sundholm, designed to take those who do not qualify for entrance to other designated institutions.

SERVICES

TEN

Poverty, social exclusion and homelessness among women in Austria

Klaudia Novak and Heinz Schoibl

Introduction

Women's homelessness in Austria may be considered on two levels: manifest (that is, visible either on the street – rare – or within service provision) or hidden (for example, living with family/friends, remaining within an unsatisfactory relationship due to lack of housing options). In the absence of any national data collection on homelessness, information on the homeless population is drawn from local surveys (in the main cities of Vienna, Linz and Salzburg) and from the practical experiences of service providers. This data suggests that women account for about a quarter of homeless people using a range of services throughout the country.

Fragmentation and lack of coordination are key characteristics of service provision in Austria. Such segmentation is mirrored in the multi-tier social welfare system. While this situation has implications for all homeless people, for homeless women the implications may be more pronounced. This chapter deals specifically with issues of coordination of both services and social welfare provision and their implications for women's access to services and resources.

The chapter starts by exploring the causes and trajectories of women's homelessness based on a review of existing literature. The causes of women's homelessness are complex and include both structural and personal factors. Equally, women's trajectory into homelessness is heterogeneous, with some women experiencing a gradual process of homelessness while for others, homelessness is sudden. Second, the chapter describes Austria's multi-tiered social security system and briefly comments on the implications for women. Finally, we consider the nature of services for homeless women in Austria. Service provision remains dominantly male-centred with limited awareness of the specific needs of homeless women. Although specific women-centred services do exist, their focus and approach tend to largely marginalise issues of homelessness. Lack of coordination between services, whether within the homelessness sector or between the sector and the women-specific sector, is a major factor limiting women's access to services.

The chapter is based on an analysis of existing knowledge on women's homelessness and an interpretation of service providers' annual reports. These were supplemented by some additional investigations which included interviews with homeless women and staff from different service providers.

Homelessness among women

This section draws on the only empirical study of women's homelessness in Austria (Planer et al, 1994). It is evident that homelessness in its manifest forms is more visible among men – despite the fact that the risk of becoming poor is higher for women, who make up a disproportionate share of the poor population in Austria. Planer et al suggest that this low visibility among women may be explained with reference to the coping strategies that women develop when faced with poverty, acute housing problems or even homelessness.

The study (Planer et al, 1994) argues that the reasons and causes for female homelessness are multi-dimensional. Neither structural aspects and circumstances (for example, housing market, women-specific chances and disadvantages in the labour market) nor social or personal aspects (for example, women's socialisation, family backgrounds, relationship problems) can offer an adequate explanation for the development of women's homelessness (p 31).

Through narrative interviews with homeless women, the study demonstrates these complex dynamics and concludes that there are at least two different kinds of female 'careers' into homelessness. Some women have never been able to build up an autonomous secure existence due to a combination of factors such as persistent poverty (often starting in childhood) and individual deficits, such as lack of education. This type of trajectory is likely to be characterised by a gradual progression towards homelessness, housing insecurity and difficulties in maintaining housing. The second type of trajectory is more sudden and commonly occurs as a result of rupture in individual biography (for example, separation or divorce).

In the biographies of some homeless women, crucial deficits, caused by failed socialisation and poverty, appear to contribute to the process of becoming homeless. These include:

- structural deficits such as poverty, inadequate housing, inadequate vocational training, unemployment;
- deficits in social resources – few or no supportive relationships with friends, family members and the respective neighbourhood;
- deficits in personal resources – health and mental health problems, low resistance against problems and stress, unfit strategies to cope with crisis.

The childhood experiences of women in this category are characterised by concentrated misery, neglect and an early start into a deviant career. Interviews with women in this group revealed disturbed family backgrounds, early experiences of violence and/or sexual abuse, identity problems, difficulties in building up and sustaining personal relations, running away or being excluded from the family home, institutional care and custody, and self-destructive strategies such as prostitution, drug addiction and criminality.

> Women in this group develop a life-style almost without continuity in the dimensions of personal relations, employment and/or housing. Hidden or manifest homelessness is – in a sense – just one of their problems, but it is the obvious sign of a far-reaching and gradual devastation of life-perspectives. In the biographies of these women long phases of hidden homelessness occur – sometimes beginning with early departure from family or institutional care. (Planer et al, 1994, pp 35f)

Women who have lived for long periods in traditional and commonly accepted gender-specific roles as mothers, wives or employees experience homelessness as a result of a break in their female biography. A complete breakdown of their social and economic foundations (income, social security, social status and, last but not least, housing) is usually precipitated by separation or divorce.

Nevertheless, separation and sudden loss of economic security are not, in themselves, sufficient explanations for the occurrence of manifest homelessness. The report finds that specific additional factors combine with separation/divorce to precipitate homelessness; otherwise it would have been a life crisis but not a complete breakdown. Interviews with homeless women in this category enabled the study authors to trace a number of typical contributory factors:

- strong identification with traditional female roles as married women and mothers;
- weak development of personal autonomy;
- protracted stays in unsatisfactory personal relationships, sometimes even despite domestic violence.

The loss of social status and role coincides with the temporary loss of housing but this is an accompanying and not a causal relationship. Social and personal factors are of higher and more immediate importance in the context of the trajectory into homelessness as are psychological dependence on relations, identity crises and a lack of a social net within or outside the family. These factors combine to build up the dynamics of the trajectory into homelessness (Planer et al, 1994, pp 36f).

Segmentation of social security

The Austrian welfare mix is characterised by a complete segmentation of benefit systems according to target groups, demands and life circumstances. Uppermost is the system of employment-oriented social insurance. For families, and especially those with children, there exists a separate family and child benefit system. At the lowest level and aimed at those who are excluded from the insurance-based system, is the *sozialhilfe*, a needs-oriented instrument of welfare benefits. Below, we examine more closely the implications of each of these systems for women, especially women with low or insecure incomes.

Employment-oriented social insurance forms the central part of the Austrian social security system – safeguarding against social risks and specific life cycle developments such as unemployment, invalidity, sickness and old age. These measures have been built around the conceptual male work biography – a proper education, full-time and continuous employment. As a consequence of changes in the labour market since the 1970s (deregulation, structural unemployment, long-term unemployment), this conceptual framework has become increasingly inadequate even for male workers. However, it was never relevant to the female work career biography in the first place. In reality, a large proportion of women work in the low-income sectors of the labour market which are characterised by inadequate labour conditions and high risks of unemployment. In the event of unemployment or retirement women are at a high risk of poverty since most of them will only be eligible for low transfer incomes. There is also the additional risk of dependency on their partners or husbands.

Austria's family- and child-oriented benefits system is built around the ideal of the small family prototype, consisting of father, mother and two children. These benefits aim at compensating the temporary loss of one family income during the period of child rearing. Its aim is to provide for families with children and to protect them from poverty. In Austria – as in other Western industrial countries – approximately 40% of marriages end in divorce. A growing number of households are either single-parent households (about 15%) or single-income households (due to unemployment, illness or invalidity). Thus, the assumptions that underlie the double-income model of family- and child-oriented benefits (*Familienbeihilfe*) no longer hold for these new types of families. Recent strategies such as granting supplementary support to single mothers are time limited and are not needs-oriented. Moreover, these benefits often fail to cover the real costs of living, leaving recipients dependent on further benefits.

A lack of child care provision further frustrates women's efforts to stay in employment during their children's early years. After a child caring career break, it is subsequently sometimes difficult for women to re-enter the job market. This is especially true for women with poor educational backgrounds.

The subsidiary welfare benefit system is neither strictly employment-oriented nor centred around the presence of young children. It provides monetary benefits to those people who do not have any or enough income to cover the real costs of living. Welfare benefits only cover the basic costs of survival. In many cases, reliance on welfare benefits is associated with continued dependency rather than recovering from poverty. Given the low income and transfer income perspective of women it is no surprise that welfare benefits in Austria are mainly used to support poor women.

Services for homeless women: segmentation and lack of coordination

Gender-specific services exist in Austria. However, the majority of provision is neither gender-specific nor gender-aware. There are three distinct groups of services for homeless women. The first group consists of family- and child-oriented services such as Mother and Child Homes and shelters for battered women. These services are aimed at women and families. Issues such as homelessness are only of secondary importance. Secondly, there are services specifically aimed at homeless women – still only few in number and located exclusively in some regional capitals of Austria. Third, there are mainstream services for homeless people – almost entirely lacking in gender-specific provision and seldom used by homeless women.

In general, then, there is a wide range of services and differentiated provision at the local level – especially for poor, excluded and homeless women. It is apparent that these services and provision are not adequately linked together. Consequently there is still the danger that homeless women (especially those with multi-dimensional needs) are excluded from professional support if they do not meet admission requirements or if they are unable to organise the support required themselves.

The most significant aspect of this situation is the fact that between these completely disparate system segments of individual support in Austria there are no interlinking structures that allow for systematic and meaningful cooperation. Furthermore, there are barriers to communication and cooperation between the different parts of the support system. For example, it is often difficult for services for homeless women to cooperate with 'gender-neutral' services for homeless people.

There remains a general lack of awareness of gender-specific issues and needs. Most services for homeless people are still based on conceptualisation of the needs of the homeless male. This lack of awareness of homeless women's specific needs and issues is evident in the low numbers of female service users. On average, services for homeless people are only able to reach a small number of homeless women (about 25% of the services' clients are female). Especially in maladjusted shelters and asylums without women-specific provision, women's attendance rates are minimal.

> In services which are not specifically shaped according to gender issues the female homeless will be almost neglected. They are clearly disadvantaged in attracting attention and keep in the shadow of

their male colleagues or partners. Usually adequate sensitivity to their specific needs and demands is missing. (Planer et al, 1994, p 13f)

The acceptability of services to women depends on their standards and adequacy. An increase in the percentage of female clients using services has been associated with improvements in service standards and greater gender awareness. In particular, guarantees of privacy (for example, in supported housing in single flats) is a factor in encouraging women to approach services. In some progressive services such as supported housing in single flats the percentage of homeless women has risen to 34%.

Looking at the strategies and tools of the services for homeless people we find evidence that service providers are slowly realising the extent of homelessness among women and their different needs. A broad acceptance of the need to develop adequate standards and provisions for this target group is emerging. Without such changes, women are less likely to seek professional or institutional care and may instead choose alternative paths such as hidden homelessness.

In addition to a general lack of awareness of women's homelessness, there is also a lack of awareness of homelessness among women-specific services. We will now look at a specific range of services such as Mother and Child Homes, homes for battered women (with or without children) and counselling services for women. In our interviews and workshops with staff from these services we found that, to a large extent, they are faced with problems and issues which are similar to those faced by other homelessness services. Nevertheless, most of these services do not see themselves as homelessness services and focus instead on psycho-social support. In these types of services, counselling in special cases of homelessness and/or individual support in housing are often either altogether missing or only offered alongside mainstream services.

While there is a lack of awareness of female homelessness, the effectiveness of services is also constrained by an overall lack of coordination of services at a regional level. The situation in many Austrian cities like Linz, the capital of Upper Austria, can be described as an elaborated system for poor and homeless people to guarantee their existential needs. There are sufficient supplies to cover existential demands (shelter, nutrition, clothes, day centres). These include low level access services as an entry point to the support system, street work and medical support. Nevertheless, there are many questions to be asked about how this elaborated system actually works.

Provision for homeless people is delivered by a large number of separate service providers, all with different standards of support, access conditions and degrees of gender-awareness. Low level access services exist alongside high level access services, all inadequately linked together. There is also a relatively wide range of women-specific services but the terms of cooperation between the different services are structurally inadequate.

Each of the services, at the local or regional level, focuses on a specific issue. As services develop a more narrow focus on a special target group and/or issue, the essence of the support scheme tends to get lost. With insufficient resources for networking, systematic cooperation between different parts of the support system is becoming the exception. Consequently clients are driven to manage the organisation of the types of support they need by themselves.

The different paradigms of support prevent structural cooperation between services. There are at least three different paradigms of support at local and regional levels:

- the subject-oriented approach – involving strategies for social support which are aimed at single clients, mainly restricted to specific issues and target groups;
- the institution-oriented approach – support is limited by the specific focus and the frequently restricted resources of the institutions;
- the regional-orientated approach – considers the regional impact of services. This applies in particular to the public office for children and youth affairs as well as to parts of the social infrastructure such as day care centres for young children and schools. In general, however, the core of social service provision lacks a regional focus.

The development of social services for homeless people as well as for women in Austria has been characterised by growing professionalism and specialisation. This tendency is still being extended and reinforces the segmentation of the individual support schemes into a patchwork of target group-oriented services. The distance and the differences between the single services are therefore growing and the services are turning farther away from assessment of regional impact. At the same time, the support and social security systems are becoming more complex. As mentioned above, the clients themselves are often forced to become experts on where to find the right type of support, a task which they sometimes cannot fulfil.

These different social services paradigms lead to a lack of cooperation. Actual cooperation between the different services, especially between those from different parts of the local social network (for example, women- or homeless-specific services) is not based on any sound structural foundation. Furthermore, there is a marked absence of structural cooperation in the referral and follow-up process. Even among services whose purpose is to provide information, arrange contact between follow-up services and clients and provide follow-up support, such lack of coordination and communication is evident.

Women-specific barriers to accessing social services

The availability and nature of information about services can either facilitate or hinder women's access to them. Two important sources of information have been identified. First, the reputation of the service in public opinion as well as among the target group is of particular importance to women. Second, knowledge and recognition of services by the public offices (for example, office for housing affairs, welfare benefits, child and family affairs, labour market issues) are critical in terms of the referral process.

A number of barriers to access can be identified in relation to each of these sources of information. The bureaucratic organisation of public institutions in Austria requires clients to fulfil many prerequisites before they can request the support needed. For example, set procedures for claimants have to be systematically followed in order to qualify for support. Furthermore, the complexity of the social security system as well as its segmentation can frustrate women's efforts to access both benefits and services. In this context, it is no surprise that the number of people who do not claim welfare benefits is at least as high as the number of successful claimants. The experience of services dealing with the prevention of eviction suggests an even higher rate of non-take-up with only 20% of clients facing rent arrears and eviction action making contact with social services.

The second barrier to access is women's traditional preference of informal support and their possible lack of experience with or confidence in approaching public institutions. This factor may also be linked to what female staff members of services for homeless women refer to as 'a women-specific shame barrier'. It is more difficult for women to admit that they have problems with housing, money, their children or in their personal relationships. This shame barrier may coincide with a fear of intervention, especially if this might affect their children, their way of living and their personal relations. In public opinion, social work is still identified with social control and intervention. To seek help from social services therefore carries with it the potential stigma of failure.

Finally, the reputation of services is a key factor facilitating or hindering women's access to them. Traditionally women–specific services are run by women. But most services are still managed by men. These male-dominated services not only tend to be the larger ones but also tend to have more influence in the public sphere in relation to social policy, social administration and social planning. It is thus reasonable to suggest that there is a gender-specific hierarchy in the awareness of social problems which prohibits women-specific adjustment of services.

Fear of stigma and of public intervention into their private spheres may be a contributory factor in women's more defensive attitude towards both publicly and privately organised social support. Hidden homelessness may therefore be understood as an active strategy to prevent an intervention into one's personal affairs.

Women's experiences of homelessness

Drawing on Planer, Stelzer–Orthofer and Weitzer's (1994) findings about the causes of and trajectories into homelessness for women, it is possible to identify two main streams of demand in relation to access to social services.

Planer et al identify a first group of women whose trajectory is characterised by protracted experiences of poverty and deprivation, suggesting a socialisation into poverty conditions of life. These women perceive homelessness as a temporary break between phases of more or less mainstream housing and living – mainly near the poverty line. For them, homelessness is not exceptional in any way but just a hard time to get through. In times of particular hardship, they may turn to strategies such as prostitution to secure their survival and re-establish mainstream living conditions. For this group of women, hidden homelessness may be more common while, at the same time, their coping strategies may be better developed.

The second group consists of women whose experience of homelessness is characterised by sudden rupture and who, to a large extent, identify themselves with traditional female roles as mothers and married women. Such sudden rupture is likely to mean that women are confronted with radical changes in their lives. For these women, guilt, shame and a sense of failure are likely to be strong barriers to seeking professional help. Unlike women in the first group, these homeless women are less likely to have the resources to manage homelessness without support. Their need for professional support may be more acute. At the same time, shame and a sense of failure may be powerful barriers to seeking that support. At the first sign of intervention into their life-style and/or of stigmatisation as women who failed against the social norms, they are likely to disappear out of the range of public or individual support and stay in substandard and provisional conditions.

Tendencies, perspectives and proposals

The national conference on poverty, held in Salzburg in 1995, launched a public discourse on poverty in Austria. Having been started by non-governmental organisations, this discourse has now been taken up by the federal ministries for women, family and social affairs. This debate has resulted in a rapid increase in the production of data about the distribution of wealth and the risks of poverty. In 1999, this extended public discourse about poverty issues was reinforced by a debate at the political level about the development and implementation of an alternative model of needs-oriented social security. The proposed model envisages a minimum wage (*Mindestlohn*) combined with a fixed level of transfer incomes independent of social insurance contributions, payable regardless of employment or claimant status. This fundamental alternative instrument of social security would particularly help women. Women are less likely than men to earn adequate wages and receive adequate transfer incomes. An alternative model of needs-oriented social security should decrease women's disproportional high risk of poverty and/or dependence on male incomes.

This model of needs-oriented low standard security is aimed at the reduction of women-specific disadvantages in income perspectives and the prevention of risks of poverty. However, the model's exclusive focus on monetary support is unlikely to adequately meet the individual and social needs of women in poverty and those experiencing exclusion and homelessness. An appropriate approach to meeting these needs would have to consider female life conditions holistically and should end segmentation. Models neglecting these imperatives might have the opposite effect and may increase the potential for hidden poverty.

The new Austrian government, a coalition between the conservative ÖVP (Christian Democratic Austrian People's Party) and the right-wing FPÖ (right wing Freedom Party of Austria), has yet to indicate whether or not it is prepared to implement the anti-poverty strategies developed under its predecessor. Indeed, its recent political measures and announcements suggest that, on the contrary, its priority is to consolidate the federal budget. Furthermore, there are alarming signs of a decreasing political will to improve social security for disadvantaged people and/or households. In this political climate, it is reasonable to assume that poverty will increase.

This chapter has shown that despite the availability of a wide range of services for different groups of vulnerable women in Austria, segmentation and lack of coordination between services create access barriers. Access to the different available support schemes is increasingly complicated and it is incumbent on the clients to manage access to the services they require. In order to provide adequate social security for women on the local and regional level the different services should build up systematic structures of cooperation to improve accessiblity to available services.

An integrated reintegration and support chain in the sense of a network does not exist in Austria. The different segments of social welfare do not link up as they should, beginning with low level access to the support schemes, needs-oriented individual support, preventive monetary benefit to secure the conditions of life, and provisions of subsequent support in follow-up arrangements of self-sustained mainstream housing and living. On the contrary, the Austrian welfare mix can be characterised by barriers against access, segmentation into different parts of the support scheme and negligent withholding of sufficient provisions against poverty, social exclusion and homelessness.

ELEVEN

Homeless women in France

Amy Mina-Coull and Stéphane Tartinville[1]

Introduction

In France, the causes of women's homelessness, their experience of homelessness and their experience of service provision differ from men's experiences in several ways. Yet there has been no systematic research which has sought to understand and examine these differences. This chapter is a preliminary attempt, based on the limited available data and literature, to identify the gender-specific characteristics of women's homelessness.

The chapter argues that the key difference between men's and women's homelessness in France can be understood in terms of perceptions of women's role in society and women's own socialisation within that society. In this respect, women's position as mothers and wives/partners is central. Relationship breakdown and particularly breakdown due to domestic violence is one of the key causes of women's homelessness. Relationship formation while homeless may prevent women's access to appropriate services since few services cater for couples. As mothers, women are able to access more specialised services with support as well as higher levels of social security, whereas single women have fewer options and lower benefit levels. The chapter argues that it is this relationship context (to partners and to their children) which distinguishes women's homelessness from that of men.

The chapter starts by examining the extent of women's homelessness in France drawing on available data. It then considers the risk factors which lead to homelessness. The third part looks at women's role as mothers, the services and benefits available to them, as well as the difficulties which they may encounter in their efforts to maintain family integrity. In the fourth part, we discuss the conceptualisation of homeless women as either single women or lone parents without a partner and show how this artificial notion limits couples' access to services and fails to recognise the importance of relationships in women's lives. Our conclusions bring together these discussions and highlight both the gender-specific aspects of women's homelessness and the gaps in current services to meet them.

The extent and profile of women's homelessness

In general, there is little data on homelessness in France and even less on homelessness among women. Available data may not be representative for two reasons. First, most data are too narrowly focused on the situation in the Ile de France area, itself not representative of the national picture. To address this geographic imbalance, INSEE (National Institute for Statistics) has launched a national study on homelessness whose findings were published in 2001.

Second, data is drawn from service providers rather than from the homeless population itself thus often reflecting both changes within and limitations of service provision rather than actual need. Nevertheless, figures from service providers and data on callers to the national homeless helpline (known as 115) show that:

- women account for between one quarter and one third of all service users; and
- the proportion of women among service users appears to be increasing.

Specifically, the data show that nearly a quarter of users of reception centres in the Paris area are women[2]. The proportion of women in long-term provision for the homeless is higher, at just over a third[3] (CHRS: Centre d'Hébergement et de Réadaptation Sociale). Data from reception centres in Paris show an increase in the proportion of women clients from 21% in 1998 to 23% in 1999. Evidence over a longer time period shows an even more marked increase in the feminisation of long-term homelessness (CHRS) provision.

Two observations can be made from these figures. First, the higher proportion of women in long-term accommodation as compared with reception centres suggests a preference for these forms of provision which are more specifically targeted at women with children. A recent study of homeless people in Paris (Marpsat and Firdion, 1998) confirms this preference and shows that 66% of homeless women stayed in CHRS provision as compared with only 29% of homeless men. Unlike reception centres, CHRS provision offers stability and an individualised support package, including support for children. As a result of this support, residents are often in better health, have more secure incomes and are less marginalised than roofless women or women using reception centres.

The second observation to be drawn from the data above relates to the growing number of homeless women. This evidence may be interpreted in two ways. The figures may suggest an increased risk of homelessness among women, or they may suggest a greater awareness of women's needs among service providers who, in turn, adjust their provision to better meet these needs. Under the latter scenario, growing proportions of women among service users may simply be a reflection of improved service standards. At any rate, in the absence of systematic and comparative study, it is not possible to clearly interpret the data.

Data from a study of service providers' records in the Paris region show that homeless women are generally younger than homeless men and that many are immigrants. More than 31% of women in CHRS accommodation are under the age of 25 as compared with less than 24% of men. In Paris, 17% of homeless women are under the age of 25 whereas the equivalent figure for men is just 9% (Marpsat and Firdion, 1998). In the provinces, 45% of callers to 115 (the national homeless helpline) are under the age of 25 (35% of men). One possible explanation for this trend may be that older women are more likely to have children; women with children are able to access a wider range of housing solutions and social security benefits which may prevent them from sliding into homelessness.

Immigrant women account for a large proportion of the female homeless population. In Paris, half of all homeless women are of immigrant origin (Marpsat and Firdion, 1998). The evidence suggests, however, that this is primarily an urban phenomenon. Immigration policy clearly plays a role. In France, economic in-migration has been superseded by immigration for family reunification. Today, it is primarily women who are entering as immigrants to join their husbands and families. In theory, these women are unlikely to join the homeless population since family economic and housing stability are conditions of entry. However, should family breakdown occur before the woman gains full citizenship rights, she would find herself without rights and with limited access to any benefits. In these circumstances, women would have no right to work and would be denied social assistance although they would have access to housing allowance, child benefit and medical assistance.

Risk factors

Women face several risks which increase their vulnerability to homelessness. Lower rates of economic activity, higher rates of unemployment and lower incomes when in work are barriers to accessing and maintaining housing in good condition. Changing family structures and particularly higher rates of divorce and the growth in lone parenthood mean that women are increasingly dependent on their own income alone to make ends meet for themselves and their children. Finally, difficulties in accessing affordable housing and lack of prioritisation in social housing allocation leaves women vulnerable in the private housing sector.

Among economically active women, unemployment rates are higher than those for men (14% for women compared to 11% for men). The growth in part-time employment in France has primarily been a feminine phenomenon: 30% of women in work are working part time as compared with just over 5% of men. Studies have shown that 40% of women working part time would like to work more hours, possibly even full time. Thus, it seems reasonable to question whether women are in part-time employment or part-time unemployment. Moreover, women in full-time employment earn, on average, less than their male counterparts. Lower education levels, occupational segregation as well as sex discrimination all contribute to this gendered wage disparity. The DARES report concludes that "the conjuncture of the two phenomena [part-time employment and lower full-time wages] leads to an income gap between women and men of, on average, 25%" (DARES, 1999).

Women's economic vulnerability is increasingly placing them in precarious financial situations and may be contributing to their risk of homelessness. In addition, changes in family structures are complicating the situation for many women.

As in many European countries, the incidence of marriage in France has been falling while the rate of divorce has been climbing, despite a range of incentives introduced over the years by successive governments in support of marriage. In 1990, 87% of newly formed couples were cohabiting compared to a mere 20% 20 years earlier. Studies have shown that the risk of relationship breakdown is greater for cohabiting couples as opposed to married couples. Among new relationships formed during the 1970s, the risk of dissolution for couples without children was six times higher in the case of cohabiting couples while among couples with children the risk was five times greater (INSEE, 1995).

However, the risks of relationship breakdown are not restricted to cohabiting couples. The divorce rate in France, in common with other European countries, has risen consistently in recent decades. The vast majority (85%) of lone-parent families are headed by a woman. Lone-parent families are at greater risk of poverty than other household types. In 1989, 19% of female-headed lone-parent families lived below the poverty line (defined as household income below half median equivalised household income). In the population as a whole, 10% of households lived below the poverty line in the same year (INSEE, 1995).

The 'advantages' of the traditional family structure in terms of protection against homelessness, however, are only relative and can often be gained at a high price. In exchange for a roof over her head, a woman may find her choices, freedom and sometimes even her own physical well-being compromised. Indeed, women living with domestic violence may be considered homeless within their own home. Figures from callers to the 115 helpline as well as data on CHRS clients show that domestic violence is the immediate cause of homelessness for 35% of women.

Legislation in France has yet to fully recognise these demographic changes. The rights of the family and, in particular, rights to social security provision remain largely based on the stable two-parent family model. In 1999, consultation on the PACS (Pacte Civil de Solidarité) legislation engendered a new debate. The legislation, which was finally passed in 1999, will give some rights to cohabiting couples.

A similar lag between legislation and changing demographics has been identified in relation to housing, both in terms of access to the rental sector (including social housing) and access to owner-occupation. The National Agency for Information on Housing (ANIL) has criticised this growing gap: "Faced with the transformation of family structures which is one of the key changes in the evolution of our society over the past thirty years, the legal and financial framework for housing remains largely focused on the model of the stable couple" (Habitat Actualité, 2000). Lone-parent families are overrepresented in social housing HLM (Habitations à Loyer Modéré). Census data from 1990 show that lone-parent families account for 15% of HLM tenants as compared with 6.6% in the population as a whole. Although there is no legal right to housing, in practice, priority in HLM allocation is often given to families (couples) and lone parents over single people.

This section has shown that women are likely to be at higher risk than men of homelessness due to their economic vulnerability as well as to changes in their family structures. Low incomes, higher unemployment, changing family structures and lack of legal rights to housing all contribute to women's risk of homelessness. In the next section, we examine the characteristics of homeless women in order to identify specific groups who are most vulnerable.

Homeless mothers or homeless women?

Traditional perceptions of women's role in French society play an important part in the development of services for homeless women. Seen as 'victims' rather than 'agents' of their own circumstances, homeless women, whether with or without children, are offered greater protection than homeless men (Svahnstrom, 1996). This impulse towards protection is significantly more pronounced in the case of women with children. A clear distinction exists between women with children and women without children in terms of access to services, appropriateness of services and access to adequate social security measures. While this traditional protectionist approach may offer homeless mothers a number of 'advantages', the same gender stereotyping often excludes women from labour market reinsertion programmes. Moreover, such traditional images may disadvantage women without children.

This section examines the availability, accessibility and appropriateness of services and benefits for homeless mothers and contrasts these with the situation for homeless women without children. It then considers the impact of traditional perceptions of women's role on their access to the labour market.

In France, the majority of services for homeless people are gender-neutral. There is no legal framework for gender-specific service provision. Nevertheless, associations can target their services at particular groups within the homeless population. Targeting may be aimed at homeless women in general or it may be focused on specific groups of homeless women such as mothers or women escaping domestic violence. Decisions on the specific target group for the service are coordinated through departmental planning in order to ensure adequate coverage for all vulnerable groups. Service provider and local authority awareness of the needs of specific groups is crucial to the development of services for the groups. Equally, public perception of particular groups within the homeless population tends to influence choices in so far as public opinion distinguishes between the 'deserving' and 'undeserving' homeless.

It has been argued that perceptions of homeless people are combined with race and gender stereotypes to produce a discriminatory system perpetuated by social legislation and social work assessment practices (Passaro, 1996). In particular, women with children are able to access subsidised housing whereas other homeless people, especially men, without children, may remain homeless for several years, if not for the rest of their lives (Passaro, 1996).

By contrast, homeless women without children may be the subject of disapproval and criticism particularly if their behaviour (alcohol abuse, vulgarity, violence) challenges gender stereotypes. In this respect, it is important to underline the fact that it is the presence of children rather than the status of motherhood which differentiates access to services. Research (Marpsat and Firdion, 1998) has shown that two thirds of homeless women under the age of 45 staying at reception centres are in fact mothers of young children, even if these children are not living with them. Stigmatised by both their behaviour and the 'bad mother' label, these single homeless women face marginalisation and inadequate service provision.

Hence, access to services is differentiated between women with children and women without children. Two types of services exist for homeless women with children: CHRS provision (housing and support) and Mother and Child Homes. In the former, support is individualised for both the mother and the child(ren). Mother and Child centres are open to mothers of very young children (under the age of three). Their principal aim is the protection of the child (Rollet et al, 1995). By contrast, single homeless women have few options other than reception centres, usually mixed gender. The fact that a high proportion of women living in reception centres are mothers without their children also suggests that this type of provision is inappropriate for families and may be contributing to family break-up.

The presence of children can often prevent a slide into situations of extreme precariousness. Two advantages can be identified in relation to the presence of children:

- First, as mothers, women may be motivated to actively seek out and participate in reinsertion programmes. The fear of having children taken into care may act as a strong impetus in the search for housing solutions.

- Second, social assistance programmes for women with children are more generous. These include: family allowance and higher levels of minimum income (RMI: revenu mimimum d'insertion). In addition, lone-parent families benefit from means-tested allowance (API). Finally, women with children can claim family support allowance (ASF).

For homeless women living in poverty, often without qualifications or work, social assistance usually represents the sole means of income. More generous benefit levels linked to the presence of the child create a significant difference between homeless women and homeless mothers.

The same gender stereotyping which is placing homeless women with children in a more privileged position vis-à-vis other homeless groups is also responsible for enclosing these women within their maternal role. The result is that women as mothers benefit from greater access to accommodation, while at the same time they may find themselves dually disadvantaged in relation to labour market reinsertion. Higher benefit levels linked to the presence of children may be a disincentive to work while the focus on psycho-social support rather than labour market reinsertion perpetuates the cycle of poverty and dependency.

For example, the API has until recently been based on the assumption that mothers are economically inactive and, as a consequence, there is less incentive to seek employment.

Most services for homeless women with children focus on psycho-social support. This can be compared with services for homeless men where the focus is firmly on labour market reinsertion. Few services for homeless women offer labour market reinsertion. Among those that do, there is evidence of gender stereotyping in relation to employment sectors.

A study of Mother and Child Homes found that some centres are supporting women into the labour market through training or sheltered workshops. It is still the case that most such provision is grounded in an ethos of psycho-social support where the woman's role as mother is paramount (Corbillon and Dulery, 1996). In Brittany, FNARS (Fédération Nationale des Associations d'Accueil et de Réadaptation Sociale) found a marked absence of labour market reinsertion programmes for homeless women. To fill this gap, a European-funded project 'Employ Now' has been introduced with several protected workshops aimed specifically at homeless women.

These initiatives, however, appear to replicate gender-biased labour market segregation. A study of employment policy shows that labour market reinsertion projects for men are geared towards work in the private or business sector whereas similar projects for women are geared towards the service sector or other non-business oriented training (DARES, 1999). At the end of the training period, women may still experience greater difficulty in gaining employment.

The question of women's role as mothers or workers is a complex one. Labour market reinsertion is not necessarily a priority for homeless women. Homeless women themselves have criticised the structures which push them into the labour market at a time when their priority is to gain emotional stability and moral reconstruction[6].

The image of the woman as mother is clearly advantageous in terms of accessing services. On the other hand, homeless women may find themselves entrapped in the role of mother with limited opportunities for breaking the cycle of dependency.

Single women or women in couples?

The guidelines which underpinned the research for this chapter specifically indicated that identification of target groups should focus on single homeless women with or without children to the exclusion of women living as part of a couple. It is reasonable to question this arbitrary division of women into these groups. Unlike homeless men the majority of whom are single, a large number of homeless women are either in a relationship at the time they lose their home or are likely to form a new relationship while homeless. Creating artificial boundaries between women with a partner and women without a partner ignores the reality of women's lives.

In France service provision in general has a tendency to separate men and women. Mixed gender reception centres have few, if any, facilities for couples. CHRS provision and Mother and Child Homes are single sex only. The physical separation of couples has been criticised by many women for preventing them from forming or maintaining relationships. Women with partners may be reluctant to enter reception centres due to concerns over privacy and violence. On the other hand, more private and safer accommodation offered in CHRS provision discourages women from maintaining contact with their partners:

> "You cannot receive guests in your room.... There is no private life in the foyer."

"The children's father could only come to my room for two weeks after the birth of the baby. After that, no more."

"They [staff] don't like you to spend time with your boyfriend outside the foyer. They say it makes us look like street girls." (Rollet et al, 1995, pp 210, 216)

Recent legislation to combat social exclusion includes an article intended to encourage provision for couples and their children: "... in order to respect couples' rights to a family life [service providers] ... are required to seek solutions to avoid the separation of families, or if such solutions cannot be identified, to establish ... new projects which would enable families to remain together" (article 27). In practice, lack of resources will inevitably delay the implementation of such directives.

The importance of both children and partners in women's lives clearly reflects traditional perceptions of women's role in society. However, it seems equally important to recognise that many homeless women have been socialised within that model and thus are likely to view maintaining and developing their role within the family as critical to their social integration within society. It is clear from the last two sections above that service provision in France, while on the one hand prioritising the needs of women with children, nevertheless ignores the importance of relationships in women's lives and fails to take into account the fact that many seemingly 'single' homeless women, are in fact mothers.

Conclusions

This chapter has shown that the gender-specific dimensions of women's homelessness are closely correlated to societal and personal perceptions of women's role as mothers and partners. The importance of the family for homeless women may be contrasted to the importance of work for homeless men. Whereas many men's homelessness may be linked to loss of work, women's homelessness is more often caused by family breakdown.

Homeless women are less often in very precarious situations. As mothers they are eligible to higher benefit levels and have better chances of accessing supported accommodation to meet their individual needs.

The chapter has also identified a number of difficulties experienced by homeless women. First, homeless women without children have fewer options both in terms of accessing appropriate services and in terms of rehousing. Second, gender stereotyping is evident in the emphasis on psycho-social support and the limited opportunities for training and labour market insertion. Finally, the importance of relationships in women's lives is largely neglected by service providers (as well as researchers) who may be arbitrarily defining women as single.

Single men seeking work, women with their children: these are traditional and enduring representations which are clearly shaping public opinion, perceptions among social actors as well as the views of homeless people themselves. While it is important to raise awareness of the relevance of family life and family structures for homeless women, these traditional images should not limit women's opportunities. Society is gradually working towards greater equality of the sexes both in terms of employment and within the home. This evolution should be extended to the world of homeless people.

Notes

[1] This chapter is based on the National Report for the European Observatory on Homelessness written by Stéphane Tartinville (2000).

[2] Result of DRASSIF (Direction Régionale des Affaires Sanitaires et Sociale d'Ile de France) count conducted on a single winter night in 1999. This comprehensive study counted all homeless people accommodated in emergency reception centres in the Paris region.

[3] Centre d'Hébergement et de Réadaptation Sociale (CHRS).

[4] Epidemiological study based on records of callers to the Homeless Helpline (115), Observatoire du SAMU Social de Paris, 1998.

[5] Emergency Number *"115 - Homeless Helpline"*, Data and documents n° 3, FNARS, September 1999. These results integrate calls and callers. Anonymity is guaranteed.

[6] Video cassette of women living in CHRS, produced by l'Association Moderniser sans Exclure.

[7] *L'accueil en urgence des personnes en difficulté sociale*, Recueils et documents, n° 1, FNARS - CREDOC, February 1999.

TWELVE

Access to housing for women in Greece

Aristides Sapounakis and Vasiliki Gamagari

Introduction

State intervention in housing in Greece has always been too modest to cope effectively with the level of need. As housing integration is an important component, if not a prerequisite, for social integration, a growing section of the population is becoming socially excluded.

Homelessness has only recently been considered a social problem in Greece. Family and community networks have generally provided adequate safety nets for people in need, and there is very little public awareness of homelessness. By the end of the 1990s, however, homelessness in Greece had grown to reach visible dimensions due, in large part, to the influx of large numbers of immigrants from south eastern Europe and the Middle East. This increased visibility has attracted publicity and slowly raised awareness both among the public and within statutory authorities.

Although the Greek Constitution states that housing is a special task for the state and a legal framework for the provision of social housing to low-income groups does exist, there is no statutory obligation on local authorities or central government to provide accommodation or support to any individuals or social groups defined as vulnerable. Hence this growing awareness has not led to an ordered approach to tackling the problem. There is no proper research concerning the extent of homelessness (including the extent of women's homelessness) while service provision and preventative policies remain insufficient and fragmented.

Women constitute a vulnerable group that presents a higher incidence of poverty and unemployment than men. The overarching aim of this chapter is to assess women's access to housing in an attempt to understand the gender dimensions of homelessness. In this context, we identify the specific groups of women who either experience homelessness or are in danger of losing their homes.

There are two significant issues which affect women's access to housing in Greece. The first is women's position in the labour market. With subsidised housing in Greece available only to those in employment, and rising housing costs outside this sector, it is reasonable to assume that women's ability to access employment will affect their ability to access housing. Women's position in the labour market is affected by three factors: the impact of equal opportunities policies, women's continued child care responsibilities and perceptions of women's position in Greek society. These three issues form the subject of the discussion in the first section of the chapter.

The second significant issue affecting women's access to housing is the changing role of traditional family structures. Until recently, Greek women's active inclusion in traditional family life has acted as a buffer against poverty and housing difficulties. The second part of this chapter examines the extent to which this pattern of living remains as dominant today and the effects of recent changes in Greek family structures on women's housing vulnerability and their risk of homelessness. It considers the role of the dowry system in safeguarding women's access to housing as well as reproducing gender stereotypes.

The third part examines the extent of homelessness among women in Greece, drawing on what limited data is available. Specific target groups who may be vulnerable are identified, along with a brief description of available provision for each target group.

The absence of gendered data on homelessness raises the danger of jumping to conclusions that are only relevant to part of the total population. For this reason, data on homelessness is paired with demographic data as well as social and economic trends relating to the female population. It is expected that such data will produce an adequate conceptualisation of the relative difficulty that women have in gaining access to proper housing.

National population and housing surveys have not been much help due to the nature of the issue and the state's indifference to the dimensions of homelessness. Research conducted on housing is, to a certain extent, outdated. The studies used for this chapter are: the EKKE (National Centre of Social Research) survey conducted in 1986-87 (Maloutas, 1990; Kouveli, 1991a, 1991b, 1993), the DEPOS (Public Corporation for Housing and Urban Development) survey (DEPOS, 1989, 1990) and the survey of the EOP which took place in 1991-92 (EOP, 1992).

Data on homelessness are in fact mostly estimates collected on a first-hand basis for the European Observatory on Homelessness. As there are only a few service providers in Greece, this was a relatively easy task. On the other hand, the lack of a proper overview of service providers by statutory authorities is certainly obscuring the scene. Moreover, the lack of sufficient data on the characteristics of service users is a definite drawback.

Women's position in the labour market

Greek women have traditionally faced a number of barriers in the labour market, many of which coincide with perceptions of the role of women in Greek society. After a long period of inequality, women now legally have equal opportunities in education and employment. They keep full property rights after their marriage and they are treated as equal to men for the same work (equality of payment, equal work opportunities).

It has become apparent, however, that the legal system alone is incapable of enforcing the principle of equality in real life situations. Prevailing modes of social and personal behaviour in contemporary Greek society have been governed by a long tradition of distinct differences in the roles of the two sexes. Although the situation is steadily balancing for some groups of women, unemployment figures show that a certain period of time is still needed before existing trends subside. Moreover, legal provisions are not particularly relevant for women who are already marginalised.

Women's participation in the labour market is relevant to our discussion on women's homelessness for two reasons. First, access to social housing in Greece (provided by the Workers Housing Association, OEK) is restricted to those either in employment or with strong employment records. Second, to access owner-occupied or private rental housing women would need either adequate family support or an adequate income which, in the absence of a well developed state benefit system, would have to come from employment.

A review of employment statistics reveals that although women constitute the majority of the working-age population, their contribution to the labour force and hence to employment is much lower than the equivalent of males. With the notable exception of Spain, Greek women's labour market activity rate is the lowest recorded in the European Union.

ESYE (National Statistical Service, 1994) statistics show that unemployment among women is at a much higher level than among men. Women in Greece represent 52.5% of the working-age population but only 39.2% of the labour force. Moreover, 60.7% of the unemployed and 67.2% of the long-term unemployed are women. Another disturbing feature of the employment–unemployment nexus in Greece is that long-term unemployment affects women to a greater extent than men. According to statistical evidence, 65.3% of all unemployed women were classified as long-term unemployed as opposed to 36.4% of men.

Furthermore, female activity rates vary considerably with age with activity rates starting at very low levels for young girls, increasing thereafter until the age of 25-29, where they achieve their highest value (63.4%). Older women and younger women appear to be most vulnerable to unemployment.

A great part of the difficulties that women face in the labour market can be attributed to structural factors that have a persistent character and lie largely outside labour market planning and management. Support to this conclusion is the overview of the evolution of the male–female unemployment differential for the last 12 years: female unemployment rates have consistently been more than double those of males in every single year during the 1990s.

To summarise, over the past 10 to 15 years women have made considerable progress in entering the labour market. But unemployment and long-term unemployment rates remain persistently high, especially for some groups of women. For those women who lack family support, a weak position in the labour market is likely to increase their vulnerability to homelessness.

Women's position in Greek society

Since the late 1970s women's emancipation has had a significant impact on Greek society. Women used to be in an inferior position to men, a role reproduced through a strict dowry system. In rural areas, women helped their husbands in the fields while in urban areas they were expected to work in the, usually small, family businesses without their own income or insurance. During the 1980s and 1990s this position has been changing as women gain greater access to work while at the same time traditional family structures are weakening.

Governmental policy in Greece has generally followed the pattern of other southern European countries in that social welfare has been treated as the responsibility of the family rather than the state. In other words, family solidarity has been filling the gaps left by insufficient welfare provision. It is therefore a widespread and accepted feature of Greek society that accommodation problems are dealt with within families and reliance on services is usually a last resort for those who lack family support.

Cohabitation of parents and adult children, and even other family members, is still fairly common in Greece. It is partly dictated by financial incapacity; to some extent, however, it is also due to the fact that the extended, as opposed to the nuclear family, is still the most dominant form of family organisation. In most Greek families adult children stay in the family home until marriage while elderly relatives live with the younger generation, especially after the death of one spouse.

Women in Greece have traditionally developed a tight interdependency with the concept 'family' as, indeed, they find themselves at the core of the Greek family system. Reliance on family support for their survival needs, including housing needs, is still common. It is particularly interesting to note the way family support mechanisms function in Greece and especially how their contribution is differentiated between men and women.

In the traditional Greek family, the husband would be responsible for the family's income while the wife would care for the house and children. In fact, very often the house would initially have belonged to the wife's family and been donated to the new household through the traditional system of 'dowry'. This very common form of housing provision in Greece concerns the allowance granted to the majority of married couples throughout the country by the bride's family; in most cases this allowance is a house or flat.

The institution of the dowry was legally abolished in the early 1980s. Nevertheless it has remained a strong element in Greek tradition, as most families, and especially the bride's side, continue to provide a house or flat for a newly married couple, whenever financially possible.

The system of dowry is indeed a 'key issue' in a number of ways. First, it constitutes a measure through which young married couples gain access to housing. Given the lack of state subsidy or provision for housing coupled with high rates of unemployment among younger age groups, such family support in housing is critical.

Second, the dowry system has inadvertently reproduced and reinforced the idea of the wife as the person incapable of working, whose only contribution to the household comes in the form of housework and child bearing/caring. This image forms the basis for the offer of property by the bride's family in exchange for the groom's acceptance of the marriage contract. Thus, the dowry system has had a double-sided effect. On the one hand, it has enabled women, as part of a couple, to access housing. On the other hand, the dowry system has not only resulted in the alienation of the bride in respect of her property, since the groom retained legal rights over it, but also in underlining differences in status between families depending on the dowry they can afford to offer.

As family bonds slacken and women start to experience the benefits and difficulties of emancipation, they gradually tend to question their reliance on family support. Increased employment opportunities, paired with the recent development of supportive mechanisms, such as child care institutions, have allowed a growing number of women to pursue an independent living. Women with low levels of education and/or limited experience in the labour market are likely to face greater barriers in accessing and maintaining housing. National statistics reveal that lone parents account for nearly 5% of the total population, most headed by a woman often with a low educational background. In the absence of a sound statutory scheme of policies and services, women who choose to live independently tend to rely on the development of their own life-sustaining mechanisms.

This section has shown that traditional family structures in Greece have, until now, acted as buffers to women's homelessness. Family solidarity and responsibility coupled with dowry systems have effectively minimised women's risks of housing vulnerability. On the other hand, dowry systems have reinforced women's dependence on their spouses and denied them access to housing in their own right. Moreover, there is evidence to suggest that economic and demographic changes are weakening family bonds and increasing women's sense of independence and reluctance to rely exclusively on family support. These changes may, in future, increase women's vulnerability in the housing market.

Women at risk of homelessness

Before identifying risk groups, we present an overview of the extent of homelessness among women in Greece. As noted earlier, the lack of data on rough sleepers or the characteristics of service users limits us to estimates.

According to such estimates, there are approximately 3,000 homeless women in Greece. This figure represents roughly 35 to 40% of the total homeless population. The figure includes an estimate of 500 squatters and rough sleepers, 50 users of statutory emergency hostels, 200 users of de-institutionalisation services and 300 occasional residents of cheap hotels and boarding houses.

Women constitute 50% of users of homeless hostels and shelters for older people in Greece. Data collected for the European Observatory on Homelessness reveal that nearly 1,300 older people in this type of provision are women. This phenomenon highlights the particular problems faced by older women who, on the one hand, experience severe financial difficulties while, on the other hand, may also lack proper family support.

There is evidence to suggest that although older women still find it hard to gain access or even manage to keep their homes, a growing number of younger women are currently experiencing similar problems in life. As yet, these women do not fall into specific categories so as to constitute a distinct target group.

In view of the above one can distinguish the following groups of women who experience exceptional difficulty in accessing proper housing. These target groups usually face additional problems, such as poverty, inability to work and social prejudice, which act as reinforcing barriers to social inclusion.

The first group of women who suffer from severe housing conditions are lone, older women. Women in this group usually live alone in owner-occupied houses and are very poor, often solely dependent on a small pension. Dwellings are small and usually comprise of one or two rooms in a detached one-story dwelling over 30 years old with serious lighting, ventilation, heating and noise pollution problems. Most of the women are widows, divorced or unmarried, the first category being the largest (87.4%). A high proportion (44.3%) have had no proper education. Income levels are minimal, and they often have to live on family support. It should also be noted that, in Greece, divorced women are not entitled to receive any part of their former husband's pension after he dies.

The second risk group is single-parent families who, in Greece, represent nearly 5% of the total population. Most single-parent families are female-led. There is little evidence as to the kind of housing problems faced by lone mothers, yet it is reasonable to suggest that they are bound to rely heavily on state or family support in order to be able to combine child rearing with employment. As both housing and child care costs steadily increase, the slightest disturbance of this usually unstable equilibrium may prove particularly dangerous to the household's living standard and may even lead to the loss of home. The situation may become even worse in the case of unmarried mothers who usually face wider problems of social prejudice.

The last group of homeless women are women who experience domestic violence. There is no statistical data about the incidence of domestic violence. Women seldom talk about it and usually avoid reporting it. In the majority of cases they are afraid of social rejection and stigma. Domestic violence appears to occur in families of low educational level although there is no conclusive evidence on its prevalence within different socio-economic classes. Faced with low family income and no property in their own right, women experiencing domestic violence may have few options. They have nowhere to go and they feel insecure and vulnerable. In other words they could be characterised as 'homeless in their own homes'.

Provision for women at risk of homelessness

In the case of lone, older women, housing standards are generally low and statutory provision non-existent. Limitations of income sources often force older women to move into shelters for older people, a solution that is not easily welcomed. Older women who have generally lived in poorer quality housing most of their lives are likely to have lower incomes and limited choices. In view of this, the expectations of this group of women concerning their housing remain remarkably low. This tendency is usually reflected in their contentment with their low standard housing conditions.

Insofar as single-parent families are concerned, there are significant allowances in respect to access to housing granted by OEK. Thus a lone mother with a fairly consistent working record may achieve access to proper housing through the Association's programmes easier than a couple with children. Nevertheless, beneficiaries have to prove a consistent working record.

Lastly, provision for women experiencing domestic violence is not particularly well developed; the only service in operation is a hostel for battered women in Athens funded by the municipality and run in conjunction with the General Secretariat of Equality. The hostel shelters women with their children regardless of nationality. Women come from all over the country and there are no special criteria for admission. Ages usually range from 25 to 45. Battered women reach the shelter through the social services of hospitals or other institutions, the police or the courts of justice.

Conclusions

The historically low incidence of homelessness among women in Greece can be attributed to the operation of strong family networks. Women have traditionally gained access to housing through institutions such as the dowry system which, on the one hand, ensured a certain standard of living while, on the other hand, kept women in a permanent state of dependence and, hence, prevented them from leading an independent living should the need arise. Apart from their household duties, women were often obliged to work in the family business with no income or insurance.

This situation has now changed as women increasingly join the labour force and evolve non-traditional roles within Greek society. Nevertheless, unemployment among women is at a much higher level than among men. Poverty of the late 1990s differs from the past as new causes are added to traditional ones. Demographic changes have resulted in the increase of the proportion of older people and dependent people in the total population, while unemployment is bound to increase within the following years.

In view of the above, it appears reasonable to argue that women face increased difficulties in accessing housing, with the danger of becoming homeless. For this reason, it is essential to ensure that the safety nets provided in order to safeguard society's homogeneity will be particularly effective in the case of women.

The three target groups listed seem to be in need of an elaborate system of support in order to cope with exclusion from the labour market and adverse housing conditions. In certain cases it is essential that specific measures such as the provision of a percentage of the ex-husband's pension to divorced women ought to be granted.

Increased interest is due for cases of women who belong simultaneously to more than one disadvantaged group. Furthermore, and as the legal framework in Greece has already been adjusted to European standards, the necessary instruments for its continual amendment must be in operation. Inevitably, it appears that the issue of equality of opportunities between women and men is a matter that essentially relies on the manner in which Greek society operates and surely needs a considerable amount of time before this is actually accomplished.

Finally, the need for a national scale body dealing with homelessness including women's homelessness has to be stressed. Its absence is evident both in the analytical and the policy making phase of the issue. Homelessness in Greece has matured enough to convince central and local government officials of the need for more positive action to address it. The establishment of a body not necessarily belonging to the public sector, yet with the state's backing and support, appears to be essential towards this end.

THIRTEEN

Just looking for a home: immigrant women in Italy

Antonio Tosi

Women and poverty

According to recent estimates, women account for around 15% of those 'of no abode' in Italy. Local studies on specific services for the homeless typically record between 10 and 15% of women among total users. However, women constitute a much higher proportion (20-30%) of service users for people 'in poverty' or people 'in difficulty'. While we can certainly speak of an increase, in recent years, of situations of vulnerability and of the risk of homelessness among women, it is more difficult to say whether the absolute number of homeless women is increasing. However, change in the composition and profile of homeless women is clear. For example, this can be seen in the appearance of increased numbers of young women with drug addiction or psychiatric problems and, in some areas, an increase in the numbers of foreign immigrants; both these groups contribute to the numbers of street homeless or 'of no abode' women in the strict sense (Tosi, 2000a).

The available data suggests a specific structure to the problem of female poverty and social exclusion in Italy. Ruspini, for instance, argues that "from the viewpoint of European comparisons, our country seems to represent a paradoxical combination of high risks of social precariousness and, at the same time, of relatively little actual social exclusion" (1998, p50). Three interrelated reasons are given for this situation: women are less affected by extreme poverty (Meo, 1997); female poverty and homelessness are less visible (Meo, 1997; Ruspini, 1998) and women in conditions of hardship have different relationships with (state-provided) services (Tosi and Ranci, 1999).

Examination of the nature of the Italian welfare system (Ruspini,

1998) demonstrates both women's vulnerability and, simultaneously, the importance of the protection afforded to women by family and family networks. Taken together, these factors mean that women are very vulnerable yet, at the same time, not often visibly homeless: women are rarely 'of no abode' or affected by advanced stages of social marginalisation or exclusion. This vulnerable, but not visibly 'homeless', status also means, however, that there is a high percentage of latent marginalisation and latent homelessness among women in Italy, which is a characteristic not unique to Italy (Marpsat, 1999). It is apparent that relationships with family and family networks constitute a critical factor in the path towards female exclusion. Current explanations highlight the persistent capacity of the family to prevent women from becoming excluded, but at the same time they highlight the limits of its preventative capacity. Research on individual case histories indicates that the absence or failure of this resource is the main determining factor of (or risk of) marginalisation or exclusion. The increase in family and conjugal vulnerability in recent decades has increased the risk of exclusion for women.

The important role played by specific services in helping to prevent homelessness among women must also be recognised. Specific forms of provision (particularly temporary accommodation) have emerged to address the most common risks in the paths to female exclusion: those resulting from family break-up, violence and single parenthood. These services – sometimes provided by local administrations, but more often by voluntary organisations and religious bodies – perform important functions. Where and when these services are available, they help prevent exclusion or stop risk situations from progressing to extreme forms of hardship and marginalisation for women.

An analysis of homelessness among women immigrants and a comparison between indigenous and immigrant homeless women throws light on important elements of female homelessness. This analysis of the limits of provision for women immigrants also allows a discussion of problems concerning housing policies in particular. It also clearly shows the inappropriateness of concentrating all the attention in the debate on the extreme forms of homelessness – those characterised by extreme marginalisation, multiple deprivation, de-socialisation – with which the problem is often identified. An examination of the situation of women immigrants shows how, particularly in Italy, an understanding of the causes of homelessness, based on such processes, needs to be modified to provide a more adequate explanation.

Women immigrants

The nature of the social marginalisation and homelessness of immigrant women in Italy as compared to their Italian counterparts is clarified with reference to two basic types of protective/preventative factors. The first of these is the protective role of family networks. Critically, while many immigrant women are strongly integrated into informal networks, a significant proportion have, from the very start of their migratory path, no (or only weakly developed) family networks. The second protective/preventative factor is the role of services, where there is a considerable mismatch between needs of immigrant women and the services provided. This holds both for general services (targeted at the entire population of women in need) and for specific services targeted at immigrant women. For this reason, services are less likely to have a preventative effect; disadvantage for foreign women in Italy is inscribed in the history of provision.

The supply of services targeted at immigrant women who are at risk has traditionally been scarce, particularly as far as accommodation facilities are concerned. For a long period, local authority provision of services for immigrants was mainly targeted at single males. Immigrant demand for assistance and protection, particularly from women in possession of residence permits, has been met by non-specific services targeted at women at risk or already marginalised women. This form of service provision, however, was constructed without any reference to the specific problems of immigrant women; problems that are, to a large extent, different from those of non-immigrant women. Only recently has specifically targeted service provision for immigrant women started to be considered and established. Today, in most regions of the country, there is a supply of small accommodation centres, targeted at different types of need and with different objectives (emergency accommodation, support for the integration of women 'in difficulty', reintegration of marginalised people, accommodation for prostitutes, temporary accommodation for women with children). The supply, on the whole, is nevertheless still inadequate in quantitative terms, despite its range; and the approach adopted, as our analysis below demonstrates, is questionable from many viewpoints.

Women account for 46.6% of the total immigrant population in Italy, numbering 508,000 legal immigrants according to 1999 data (Caritas di Roma, 1999). Their average age is younger than that of their male counterparts. Fifty-two per cent of these women are in Italy for work and 42% for family reasons, while the respective percentages for men are 77% and 10%. Both the percentage of women immigrants and the reasons for immigration differ greatly between different nationalities and countries of origin. The percentage of women among immigrants is nearly 70% for some groups (Philippines: 67.1%; Peru: 68.6%; Poland: 69.1%; Brazil: 74.3%) while the percentage of women coming to Italy for family reasons rises to two thirds for North African women and to 60% for Albanian women (1997 data). The main area of entry into the labour market is that of services, working as domestic maids and assisting older people (Commissione per le politiche di integrazione degli immigrati, 2000).

In general, women immigrants are more integrated into society than immigrant men. A recent study carried out in the Milan area shows that immigrant women are more securely settled and more firmly rooted in family structures. A lower percentage of women live alone and a lower percentage are unemployed, while the proportion living in precarious accommodation and in hostels is negligible (Provincia di Milano and Ismu, 1999). The greater integration of women is also confirmed by national data which show that women have less experience of living as illegal immigrants (without documents) than men; almost two thirds of men have experienced this during the course of immigration as opposed to little more than one third of women. Women resort to crime more rarely than men and they are generally seen as more integrated into the neighbourhoods in which they live (Commissione per le politiche di integrazione degli immigrati, 2000).

However, by comparison with immigrant men, women are strongly disadvantaged with regard to finding work, particularly in finding secure, permanent employment (Commissione per le politiche di integrazione degli immigrati, 2000). The kind of work that they find most easily, that of domestic work and in service sector jobs, is very low skilled (for many immigrants it represents a step down compared to the work they did in their own countries or to the qualifications they possess), very insecure and often in the 'black market'. The Milan study cited earlier, found that:

> ... while it is true that the percentage of unemployed is greater among men (perhaps more easily motivated to immigrate without help or points of reference), it is also true that the contingent of employed women shows a higher level of job insecurity. Furthermore, from the viewpoint of financial resources, average female income is approximately 20% less than that for men, while average monthly

expenses are approximately 10% higher. (Provincia di Milano and
Ismu, 1999, p 40)

Female immigrant unemployment appears to be rising in many areas of
the country (Caritas di Roma, 1999). The difficulty immigrant women
have in finding secure employment has increased: the percentage of
those registered as unemployed rose from little more than 20% in 1992
to almost 37% in 1999; indeed 1999 marked a sharp widening of the
gap between men and women in relation to the probability of finding
permanent secure employment (Commissione per le politiche di
integrazione degli immigrati, 2000). In terms of family integration, in
1998, in the Milan area, there was an increase in the number of women
not living with their partners, presently about 21%, and the percentage
of female immigrants arriving in Italy for reasons other than to join
their family has also increased (Provincia di Milano and Ismu, 1999).

To summarise, there are important elements of protection that prevent
the large majority of immigrant women, even those living in precarious
conditions, from falling into conditions of marginality and homelessness:
relatively easy access to the labour market (household domestic work,
caring work), and relatively easy insertion into groups, which at times
provide very supportive communities (Tagliaferri, 1999). At the same
time, immigrant women are widely affected by insecurity factors: the
type of work they obtain, usually unskilled, difficulty in reconciling
work (often 'black market') with motherhood, widespread housing
problems and difficulties in relation to service provision.

This combination of factors contributing to protection, on the one
hand, and, on the other, to insecurity does not give rise to the same
level of homelessness among immigrant women as among immigrant
men (according to recent estimates, foreigners account for more than
40% of those 'of no abode': Tosi, 2000a). To see how, and in what
circumstances, the sum of different types of disadvantage translates into
situations of extreme hardship or homelessness, a closer look must be
taken at the specific factors that determine the vulnerability of immigrant
women.

Homeless immigrant women

Immigrant women experience problems which are very different from
those of Italian women, and they also face a larger range of difficulties.
For Italian women, the processes of marginalisation are caused, to a

great extent, by family problems and break-ups. For foreign women, an important role is also played by problems such as legal status (the condition of illegality, as with men, raises the costs of survival and exposes women to high risks of exploitation); difficulty in finding housing and work; and the scarcity of services specifically targeted at their needs. For immigrant women, vulnerability is also connected with the weakness or loss of family relations, such as isolation from the family or single parenthood. In Milan, in 1999 the proportion of women over the age of 14 who were single was 42.4%. The proportion increased, however, to 61% for African women (excluding those from North Africa) and to 65% for Eastern European women. Single-parent families are typically female-headed. Fifty-eight per cent of immigrant mothers bring children with them, compared to only 38% of immigrant men. This discrepancy is explained by the fact that a significant number of women were already separated or divorced before arriving in Italy, and also that there is a growing number of female-headed single-parent families (Provincia di Milano and Ismu, 1999; Caritas Italiana and Fondazione Zancan, 1997).

To understand those problems which are specific to immigrant women, we must consider both the marked incidence of isolation and loss of family relations and, within the wider range of difficulties they experience, the different meaning of the family. Attention must be paid to the interplay between family problems and other factors which may be material to successful integration.

The relationship of immigrant women with accommodation services appears to differ from that of Italian women. Immigrant women rarely make use of public dormitories: as noted by a service worker in Turin, "they [may] have no housing and no resources, but ... they are [nevertheless] frightened of living with drug addicts" (Tosi, 2000a). Women immigrants infrequently present problems of de-socialisation or 'maladjustment', and they rarely have problems of drug addiction or substance abuse. They simply find themselves in a condition of extreme poverty, with a transitory problem of not having a place to sleep, at least in the first stages of integration.

Immigrant women's use of *centri di accoglienza* (which translates as 'welcome/reception centres': emergency/transitional shelters or hostels), whether targeted towards women in general or in a small number of cases specifically towards immigrant women, is different to that of non-immigrant women. Because their problems relate mainly to a lack of housing and resources and because of their fear of living with drug addicts immigrant women rarely make use of emergency accommodation. This is one area in which efforts have been made to produce targeted provision that takes account of the specificity of the problems of women, and, to some extent, of women immigrants. In accommodation services for immigrant women the distinction between emergency and transitional accommodation is blurred; services are almost never limited to only shelter for the night. The terminology adopted – 'welcome centres' – is illuminating. Even when they are emergency hostels, the model is quite different from that of a dormitory.

> A stay in a community hostel can mean very different things according to the type of need: it may be understood as a temporary refuge that allows a bit of money to be saved while awaiting other accommodation, a secure source of support, a home of their own.... What some occupants lack is simply the chance to work – and consequently the ability to keep accommodation.... It is more difficult for foreign girls, who at times must face the prejudices of landlords to obtain accommodation. (Maselli, 1999, p 324)

The gap between the need and the purpose of the supply may have paradoxical consequences:

> The community of the *Missionarie della Carità* (Missionaries of Charity) of Bologna takes around twenty women aged between 20 and 40, both Italian and foreign. In a few cases the women in the hostel belong to families that, having arrived in Italy with no precise source of help or support, have been forced to separate in order to gain access to different accommodation services. In these unnatural conditions, family relations are subject to great stress ... husband and wife couples find themselves obliged to employ individual survival strategies. Families do not always manage to remain united in this type of situation, especially if the initial period of adaptation is prolonged. Paradoxically, it is their very condition of being in a family ..., the absence of which causes great suffering for the individual, that constitutes a disadvantage in attempts at integration or reintegration. The family that wants to escape from a homeless condition is in fact forced to face greater difficulties than an individual, and housing is not the least of these. (Maselli, 1999, p 320)

All this indicates the existence of a large number of immigrant women who are living in very insecure housing conditions, but who have not been exposed to those processes of extreme marginalisation that are usually associated with the image of the 'no abode'. In many cases, the precarious nature of their housing situation is temporary, and how it develops depends on the opportunities that they encounter in the route to social integration and therefore also on social policies. Essentially, two points are brought out by an examination of the network of service provision and its use by immigrant women. First, immigrant women need work and housing, and it is more difficult for foreign women to obtain accommodation. Moreover, although immigrant women live in poverty, often extreme poverty, this does not imply that they suffer from multiple deprivation or personal and social problems such as drug or alcohol dependency which is often associated with extreme forms of marginalisation. In many cases they simply require temporary assistance to help them overcome the precariousness typical of the first stages of immigration.

The problem for homeless Italian women is basically determined by an exit from society, the epilogue of a process of exclusion often associated with family problems and break-up. For immigrant women, on the other hand, problems of legal status, difficulty in finding housing and work, the language and scarcity of services targeted to their needs plays an important role. The problems of immigrant women are, to some extent, mediated by the presence of positive integration plans and of capabilities which can support their paths to integration. This observation leads to some more general policy questions regarding foreign immigrants. The fundamental point is that the homelessness of immigrants is different from the homelessness of non-immigrants. In this respect, two complementary aspects deserve attention.

On the one hand, the socially excluded and homeless immigrant – the 'no abode' immigrant – seems to have a specific profile. Individual case histories of immigrants suffering homelessness are quite different from those of the native population, and exclusion from the housing market plays an important role. For Italians today, paths leading to marginalisation do not tend to begin with the loss of a home; but for immigrants the paths to marginalisation often start with situations of housing exclusion. Continued exclusion from the housing market can accelerate the drift towards social exclusion (Tosi, 2000b). Compared to the native population, there is a greater probability that housing exclusion among immigrant women will occur without strong elements of marginalisation and even more frequently without those self-destructive traits – those traits of shattered personalities – that often characterise the 'no abode': they are simply poor people without housing. For immigrants the lack of housing may be nothing more than a phase in the path to settlement in society (Pollo, 1995).

This concept of transitory homelessness as part of an immigrant's settlement process is more easily understood if a 'process approach' is adopted. Research on homelessness recognises that the meaning of housing deprivation cannot be understood simply by recording the availability or unavailability of accommodation by itself or at a determined moment in time. The situation of homelessness is not necessarily a 'permanent state', but rather a 'point in time in a process' and a 'transitory situation in a career'. Being homeless at any given moment may mean different things; depending on the immigrant's stage in integration it may be a phase of initial precariousness common to many immigration case histories, or it may be the outcome of a process of marginalisation (exclusion that has become chronic) which indicates the failure of a migration plan (Carchedi et al, 1999).

Housing and social policy

The probability of both general and specific homeless services failing to match needs is higher for foreign women than for Italian women. As well as an overall relative lack of specific provision for immigrant women, homeless services do not deal with the circumstances that typically define the conditions of risk and vulnerability for immigrant women: the difficulties of finding housing and work at the time of arrival in Italy. The *centro di accoglienza* approach, which to date has been the main means of dealing with the needs of newly arrived immigrants, does not address the needs deriving from initial precariousness on entering the country and the search for housing and work. The *centro di accoglienza* are specialist resources, dominated by a welfare assistance approach, in which accommodation is provided in tandem with social support. The system of *centro di accoglienza* does not recognise that the problem of immigrants is related more to housing per se rather than the need for social work support. By providing special purpose accommodation and social support instead of ordinary housing, the *centro di accoglienza* run the risk of ignoring or neglecting the insertion needs of newly arrived immigrants.

This raises general questions about the adequacy of housing policies for immigrants in Italy. Housing difficulties represent a fundamental element of all the difficulties that immigrants encounter. Both at the arrival stage and at subsequent stages, the general picture is that of large numbers of immigrants suffering housing hardship and exclusion. As well as immigrants in poverty who are without housing, there are many immigrants who are not particularly poor but are nevertheless inadequately housed; precarious or substandard accommodation is not unusual even for immigrants with a job and an income (Tosi, 2000b). Their accommodation tends to be worse or more expensive than that of the native population with the same level of income. Housing hardship manifests itself for immigrants in the lack of affordable rented housing and in the relationship between their poverty and the processes of social exclusion. These are the areas in which there is a structural policy deficit in Italy, namely the extremely limited supply of affordable rented accommodation. This reflects insufficient attention being paid to the processes by which poverty of choice in the housing market intertwines with risks of marginalisation and social exclusion. Not only is housing supply at the cheaper end of the market scarce, but social housing policies are also poorly integrated with general social welfare programmes. In other words, the limitations of Italian housing policies exacerbate the vulnerability faced by immigrants in the housing market. The weakness of general social housing policies has constituted the main cause of housing problems for immigrants.

The needs of immigrant women for affordable housing cannot be satisfied by policies which are aimed specifically at immigrants; they can only be adequately addressed within the context of the mobilisation and improvement of policies aimed at rectifying the scarcity of social housing provision (Tosi, 2000b). What is required is a shift of emphasis from 'reception' policies to housing policies (even if the need for a supply of facilities for the new arrivals remains). This will require the adoption, at national level, of innovative social welfare policies in the field of housing, particularly of the type experimented in other countries. There should be the aim of producing affordable housing that is qualitatively consistent with the needs of the groups at risk of exclusion ('suitable' housing, close connections between public housing and social services, close integration between housing policies and policies against poverty).

The case of immigrant women thus illustrates both the points in favour of strong welfare housing policies and also the reasons for widening these policies beyond a focus only on those 'of no abode'. In Italy, the perception of homelessness – centred on the image of those 'of no abode' – leads to a primary focus on situations of particular gravity characterised by an advanced stage in the processes of marginalisation. This perception runs the risk of neglecting housing exclusion when it is not accompanied by strong traits of social marginalisation. The image of the marginalised and de-socialised homeless person which is so common in the debate on homelessness defines only one type of homelessness. The lack of housing constitutes one aspect of a wider syndrome of social exclusion. Housing exclusion, however, may occur without involving marginalisation and even less so disaffiliation or personal disabilities. There are people who are 'simply' excluded from housing: they may be just too poor to afford housing offered on the market, or they may lack (formal or de facto) qualification for access to social housing. As Haut Comité has observed, in providing housing for disadvantaged people,

> ... two categories of families are continually confused. This confusion tends to lump together in a single group families whose only difficulty is that of financial resources and whose only problem is of affordability with those who, having accumulated various handicaps, are in need of full social support. The case of the latter ... seems to be gradually becoming much better understood and treated, while families with no social integration problems but who have poor financial resources are more likely to remain with no solution to their problems. (Haut Comité pour le Logement des Personnes Défavorisées, 1997, p 41)

The distinction is important because housing exclusion without marginalisation is a widespread phenomenon and represents an important area for policy; an area in which the principles for dealing with marginalisation (for instance, social reintegration programmes) do not apply.

FOURTEEN

Homelessness and ethnicity in the Netherlands

Henk de Feijter

Introduction

This chapter focuses first on homelessness among women in the Netherlands, identifying recent changes in household composition, the increasing association of poverty with female-headed households and the problems of appropriate service delivery. Second, the chapter examines the relationship between ethnicity and homeless women. The issues need to be seen within the context of a level of homelessness in the Netherlands which, despite projections in the early 1990s that it would more than double (Avramov, 1995), has been fairly static since the mid-1990s and is low relative to other European countries. This situation has prevailed even though the Netherlands has experienced the largest population growth (12%) and household growth (33%) of any European Union (EU) country over the last 20 years. The growth in population, particularly during the 1990s, has been fuelled by immigration which reached a peak in the mid-1990s with a positive migration balance of 100,000 people (Boelhouwer et al, 1996). While the importance of the social rented sector in maintaining a state of equilibrium in the housing market during this period of rapid population growth should not be underestimated (McCrone and Stephens, 1995), the flow of migrants and asylum-seekers led to fears of a growing housing shortage and calls for more government intervention. Despite these fears and demands, government policies continued (and indeed continue) to pursue the decentralisation, deregulation and privatisation of the social rented sector.

The most recent 'Monitor on Homelessness' (Wolf et al, 2000) estimates the likely number of homeless people to be between 25,000 and 30,000, although these figures are based on the numbers registered in subsidised shelters. Within this relatively static position the Monitor identifies important and significant trends in the composition of the homeless population. In particular it identifies a rise in the number of illegal asylum-seekers who have exhausted their possibilities for legal status but are unwilling or unable to return to their own countries. In addition to the reported influx of people from Eastern Europe and the Balkans, the Monitor also identifies a rise in the number of ethnic youth and in under-age asylum-seekers who come to the country on their own. It is in this context that women's shelters report an increase in immigrants among the service users.

Women, poverty and family structure

The Netherlands is a relatively affluent country. On a range of social indicators it has more in common with the Nordic countries than with its other European neighbours. The Netherlands is comparable to Denmark, Sweden and Finland in terms of level of education, employment rate, unemployment rate, social protection expenditure, income distribution and proportion of households with a low income (see European Commission, 2001). Where it diverges from the Nordic countries is in relation to the relative position of women in the labour market as measured by their employment rate, part-time employment and relative earnings. In common with other northern European countries, there has been an overall growth in female employment during the 1990s, however, much of this employment relates to part-time jobs; the Netherlands also has the highest proportion of women in part-time employment in the EU. While the employment rate of women without children is comparable to other northern European countries, the rate for women with children is relatively low. In 1997 only 40% of single mothers were active in the labour market, one of the lowest participation rates in Europe (Van Solinge and Plomp, 1997, p 159).

Over the same period changes in family status have contributed to what some call the 'feminisation of poverty'. The growth in single-person households has been impressive, both in the younger and the older age groups. Together with the Nordic countries and Germany, the Netherlands has one of the highest proportions of people living in one-person households. The proportion of single-parent households in the population is among the lowest in Europe, however, the proportion of low-income households who are single parents rose from 7% to 14%

between 1977 and 1997. Taken together these trends have meant that the proportion of female-headed households within the total category of poor households has risen from one third in 1977 to 56% in 1997 (Sociaal en Cultureel Planbureau en Centraal Bureau voor de Statistiek, 1999, p 141). It follows also that there has been a growth in female-headed households dependent on welfare benefits. While welfare benefits have risen in line with inflation, during the 1990s, rents have risen much more rapidly.

Women and homelessness

Homeless people in the Netherlands are to be found on the streets, in shelters and in 'uncertain' housing situations, also called marginal housing. Marginal housing ranges from 'squats' and cheap boarding houses to living with friends and not staying at the same address for more than three months. The actual number of people sleeping rough can only be estimated: research indicates that the number may not be more than 2,000 (Deben et al, 1999). The number of women among those sleeping rough is relatively small, probably around 11% (Korf et al, 1999). The reason for this can be found in the different strategies, from men, which women use to survive. One important reason for women to employ different strategies is that, unless the Child Protection Agency has intervened, they nearly always have and take responsibility for their children. A second important reason is that most women have undergone negative experiences of violence on the streets; places frequented by homeless men are generally not safe for women. However, the Monitor on Homelessness (Wolf et al, 2000) shows that the proportion of women staying in homeless shelters has risen from 5% in 1994 to 26% in 1999.

In terms of its nature and magnitude, the problem of domestic violence can be described as a very pressing and relevant social problem and is closely associated with female homelessness. Research (Croes et al, 1990) shows that in the Netherlands one in every five women between 20 and 60 years of age is threatened with violence by a male partner at some point in their relationship. Annually, something in the region of 200,000 women between 15 and 60 years of age in the Netherlands fall victim to domestic violence; 50,000 of these cases involve serious or very serious violence. The close relationship between domestic violence and homelessness means that 90% of the homeless women in the Netherlands are received in special shelters for women. Women fleeing their homes are given shelter primarily in women's refuges known as

Blijf van mijn Lijfhuizen (literally translated as 'Hands-off Houses'). These centres were established in the 1970s to offer a safe haven for women who have become the victims of domestic violence. In addition, two other types of shelter for women can be distinguished. FIOM shelters (Netherland's Federation of Institutions for the Care of Unmarried Mothers), originally established in 1929 for unmarried mothers, now provide support for a wide range of women and operate on a self-help basis. Here, women are received with multiple and complex problems: pregnancy, sexual violence, single parenthood, financial, child raising, relational and borderline psychiatric problems. Another category of shelter aimed at women was established by social workers from care provider agencies. In addition, a small group of women have no privileged access to special facilities for women,.and are admitted into general shelters for both men and women.

The *Federatie Opvang* (the Netherlands Federation of Shelters), maintains a database on services provided by its member organisations (numbering some 300 in total). This database (known as the Klimop system) suggested that in 1999 there were about 73 shelters for women with a capacity of 2,041 places. *Federatie Opvang* estimates, from their registration system, that in 1998 some 5,500 clients with 4,000 children had to be refused admission to women's shelters because of a lack of capacity. Another 4,500 women were refused because of psychiatric or addiction problems. For these reasons it has been recognised (Bateman et al, 1999) that there is a need for low threshold shelters for women with less strict admission criteria than those set by the women's refuges and for more capacity for women with children.

The different services attract different client groups, although a significant overlap is also shown (see Table 14.1). In Amsterdam, for example, 61% of the women in the refuges came because of some sort of violence from their partner, while another 25% came for reasons to do with housing and financial debts.

This evidence suggests both support providers for the homeless and women's refuge centres have to deal with more complex problems of their clients than has been evident in the past; consequently, the transition to a situation of normal independent living becomes difficult to achieve for many clients since the average length of time required for support will be longer.

It has been noted that, in recent years, the population of women's shelters is changing, with other target groups now seeking shelter and support. According to Van Gils (1994) and Croes et al (1990) more young 'teenage' mothers or pregnant women are now seeking help.

Table 14.1: Main problems of clients that left care provisions (1998) (%)

	Blijf shelters refuges	FIOM women's shelters	General crisis shelters	Shelters for the homeless	Total
Structural sexual violence	84.0	52.1	7.4	1.3	29.5
Incidental sexual violence	4.9	5.3	3.0	1.0	3.5
Violence	22.8	22.6	15.3	8.8	17.0
Relations	39.1	49.1	46.1	23.6	41.2
Psycho-social problems	23.5	30.1	30.2	15.0	26.1
Psycho-social deficiences	4.7	5.7	8.1	8.7	7.1
Financial	5.8	9.9	14.5	10.4	11.1
Housing	4.3	20.2	41.7	68.8	35.8
Addiction	3.5	7.5	13.2	20.6	11.7
Pregnancy	2.2	6.9	1.8	0.3	2.9
Culture	3.5	4.2	2.5	1.4	2.8
Residence permit	4.2	5.5	2.6	2.9	3.7
Justice	0.3	0.8	2.5	4.3	2.1
Life	0.1	0.1	0.0	0.1	0.1
Medical	1.5	2.7	2.8	5.2	3.0
Total	205.4	229.9	191.8	172.3	197.5

Note: Sum exceeds 100.0 since more than one reason may apply. All clients, both men and women, figure in the table.
Source: Federatie Opvang (2000)

The Monitor on Homelessness estimates that, in 1999, almost half of the clients of women's shelters were aged 18 to 30 years. While the duration of stay at the shelters is relatively short – three quarters of clients left within six weeks – two thirds of clients had been admitted to another women's shelter within the previous year ('revolving-door' clients). At the same time there are now more women who were formerly on the street and who need long lasting support. A growth in the number of women who are in debt and women who have psychiatric and/or addiction problems also plays a role in making the service provision much more complicated than was foreseen when these services were first established in the 1970s and 1980s.

One of the new groups coming to the shelters is women from ethnic minority groups and, in particular, illegal immigrants. In 1998 almost 60% of those admitted to women's shelters and 40% of women in shelters for the homeless were born in another country or had at least one of their parents born in another country. As a result of a change in legislation in 1998, the number of illegal immigrants (former asylum-seekers) without a residence permit has increased. It is a fact of life that there are people living in the Netherlands without a valid residence permit. If a female immigrant applies for help at a women's shelter, it is often very difficult to find the financial means to pay for her stay. This is especially so for women applying for shelter who remain in the Netherlands without a residence permit, or who have exhausted all asylum seeking procedures: they are generally admitted, but with dim prospects. In 1999, this applied to 1,200 illegal immigrants out of the total number of 1,600 women asylum-seekers staying in shelters.

Ethnic origin of homeless women[1]

There are significant differences in the household and labour market positions of women from different ethnic groups. Turkish and Moroccan women are rarely seen to head a one-parent family, only 6 to 7 % of all Turkish or Moroccan households are one-parent families, a percentage equivalent to that for the Dutch population as a whole. Most women have children and the labour market participation of women between 15- and 65-years-old amounts to 25%, much lower than that for Dutch women and other ethnic groups.

Among Surinamese and Antillean women, on the other hand, one-parent households are quite common. Almost a quarter of the households belong to this category, and almost all of these households are female-headed. It is part of the Caribbean marriage pattern, in which women are much more independent from men and take care of their children themselves. Labour force participation among Surinamese and Antillean women is also much higher than among Moroccan and Turkish women, reaching almost 60% (Martens, 1999).

This would suggest that women from Turkish and Moroccan cultures are in a relatively worse situation and are more dependent on their husbands. Should a divorce or separation take place their chances of earning an independent living are low. Culturally women from these groups rely on support from an extended family. On arrival in the Netherlands, their networks are broken and many face isolation especially if they do not speak Dutch. Often their residence permit is dependent on their husbands. According to the 1994 Immigration Act (*Vreemdelingenwet*), women only qualify for an independent residency permit after three years. Without this a woman will be seen as an 'illegal alien' and not entitled to welfare benefits or housing.

Faced with a growing ethnic population, service providers are continually confronted with new problems for which no specific services are available. As a consequence, these women turn to available services even though these may not be suited to their problems. By way of illustration, we will look at some of the new phenomena with which service providers are confronted. For example, there are young Antillean women, often teenage mothers with children, who have often just arrived in the country from the Antilles and who are accommodated by relatives for only a short time. After their short stay with relatives, they are often completely dependent on social services. Another very different problem is posed by some of the second-generation Islamic women from Morocco and Turkey who were born in the Netherlands, but resist having arranged marriages or rebel against a strict Muslim upbringing. They sometimes have to be protected against male family members. New groups that arrive also mean that new methods of care and help have to be developed. Shelters have to adapt to women that are not as emancipated as Dutch women are likely to be. This easily leads to problems inside the shelters and feelings of superiority on the part of those who feel they know how to behave, how to raise children and how to handle violent husbands (Sijses and Bekkers, 1990; Fest, 1996).

It is not only the traditional migrant women who are in a difficult situation. New groups have come into the picture: women imported for prostitution, illegal immigrants, asylum-seekers whose application for residence is denied and refugees are all part of a growing problem. A large number of these women have turned to shelters for the homeless, who in turn do not know what to do with them. They cannot afford to keep them for a long time. On the other hand, abused women in particular are entitled to assistance as is laid down in United Nations Treaties. In 1998 a law was introduced by central government (*Koppelingswet*), in which social benefits and healthcare were explicitly denied to illegal aliens (*Koppeling* means the administrative linking of data-files in order to be able to identify individuals and it is used here to identify those that have a legal permit to be in the country). The Secretary of State for Care and Health, while acknowledging their rights, has refused to allocate additional funding. Care has thus been decentralised to municipalities. The larger cities are willing to pay, the smaller ones are reluctant.

Since that date, it has therefore been difficult for service providers to provide care to those who do not have a legal residence permit. A special fund has been established from which hospitals and medical care in general can be paid. *Federatie Opvang* has suggested that the fund for medical assistance to illegal people could be extended to shelters. Until the *Koppelingswet* came into force, shelters used to treat victims of domestic violence who had become illegal aliens in the normal way. Now, this is much more difficult. Since 1998 some 1,200 women asylum-seekers who are denied access to the Netherlands have sought assistance.

Conclusions

Despite the enormous growth in the number of households, the level of homelessness in the Netherlands appears to have remained relatively stable in recent years. The level of homelessness among women reflects this general situation. However, in the context where 90% of homeless women are received in either women's refuges or women's shelters, there is currently a lack of capacity at the present time to meet the known need. This may, in part, account for the fact that there has been an increase in women using 'general' homeless shelters. The evidence also points to the fact that women's refuges and women's shelters have had to cope with a wider range of target groups and a wider range of problems from those for which they were originally intended. This is particularly evident in relation to women from ethnic minority groups. This chapter has shown that services may not be attuned to the needs of women from different ethnic backgrounds. The effect of the introduction of the *Koppelingswet* law has meant that, since 1998, there has additionally been an increase in demand for the services of women's shelters from asylum-seekers whose rights have been restricted under the legislation. This has created added pressures of demand and funding dilemmas for service providers. This overview also suggests that the recent budget increase of 20% for women's refuges is probably not sufficient to cope with the more varied nature of the demands that these new groups of women place on existing services.

Note

[1] In the Netherlands, the four main ethnic minority groups that are normally distinguished are Surinamese, Turks, Moroccans and Antilleans. Including the first generation immigrants and those that were born in the Netherlands from at least one parent from the foreign country there were about 900,000 people from these ethnic groups in 1997.

FIFTEEN

Substance abuse problems and women's homelessness in Finland

Sirkka-Liisa Kärkkäinen

Introduction

This chapter focuses on one specific aspect of female homelessness in Finland. Using previous research, information collected by previous surveys, as well as interviews conducted for the national report of the European Observatory on Homelessness (Kärkkäinen, 2000), this chapter considers the issue of substance abuse as a factor in homelessness among women in Finland. It begins by examining the image of a homeless person and a homeless woman in the public debate and presents evidence about the extent of female homelessness in Finland. Within this context, it proceeds to discuss the nature of women as clients of substance abuse services, how the numbers are changing, the typical processes leading to homelessness and how the services for these women are changing. A key concern of the chapter is the structure, relevance and effectiveness of service provision both in relation to the prevention of homelessness and reintegration. In this respect social welfare and health services, as well as housing services, are considered.

The image of homelessness

In Finland homelessness has usually been considered to be a male problem. Four fifths of single homeless people are men. A man's downward spiral usually begins with family problems, alcohol abuse, unemployment and divorce. After leaving the family home a single man faces great difficulties. The shortage of small and reasonably priced dwellings makes it difficult for a single man, especially if his income is low or he is unemployed, to find a dwelling. Unemployment, alcohol abuse and homelessness are a vicious circle from which the homeless man has difficulty freeing himself. Furthermore, the typical Finnish man is not used to talking about his problems; he may not even be able to seek help.

The woman, especially if she has children, is usually the one who stays in the family home after separation or divorce. However, a single mother has priority in social housing allocation and social welfare support is relatively generous. A single woman, or a woman who has lost her family status, is in a much worse position than a mother on the housing market and in the social welfare system.

Perhaps because of this, the official image of the homeless man and the homeless woman differs in the media. Jokinen (1996) analysed the gender-bound cultural interpretations of homelessness in television programmes about homelessness. The title of the article written on the basis of her research indicates the main difference: 'Men without accommodation and women without a home'. The word 'home' reflects a distinctive image or perception of homeless women. The image of homeless or 'houseless' men consists, according to Jokinen,

> ... of men who swear to mutual friendship, drink together and are free from family obligations and whose substructure is tinged on the one hand with humour and bragging and on the other hand the hopelessness of life. Men do not generally give reasons for their situation and they do not mirror themselves in the role of a father or a husband. Women, on the other hand, are obliged to account for their own situation, use of alcohol or family relations, or they do so on their own initiative. Homeless women seem to stand on a kind of divide: they either succeed in explaining themselves 'morally out of the woods' or their destiny is to be defined as truly dubious and deviant. (pp 206-7)

Women's homelessness has, hitherto, been a neglected area of study. During the 1990s, as new generations of homeless women have emerged on the streets and as service users, interest in the lives of homeless women has increased, and researchers, authorities and service providers have begun to pay more attention to the needs of women. Some research reports on interviews with women living in hostels for homeless women were carried out in the early 1990s (Granfelt, 1992; Maunuksela and Salminen, 1994). More recently, research has turned the interest and debate from purely structural problems of the welfare society to the experiences of homeless women (Granfelt, 1998), more than has been usual in the Finnish debate on homelessness. The purpose of these reports seems to be primarily to improve understanding of the lives of homeless women and of their needs and, in doing so, they have provided basic material for the development of services (Granfelt, 1998; Mecklin and Sonninen, 1998; Viljamaa, 1999).

Latent, hidden and open homelessness: when does the path to homelessness begin?

After the recession of the early 1990s the welfare state has become less generous. Changes in the economy, and in social protection, have been more dramatic for those households whose income is based on one person's earnings or on unemployment benefits or labour market support. The subsistence of low-income people living alone, of lone mothers and other low-income families with children has fluctuated mostly because of the cuts and changes made in the housing allowances and family benefits (Heikkilä and Uusitalo 1997).

According to a study of clients seeking help from the Lutheran Church's aid centres, more than 40% of people seeking help are women, both married and single mothers and single women. One of the most significant problems among these women was rent arrears (Iivari and Karjalainen, 1999). Thus the crisis leading to homelessness usually has economic reasons at its roots. Many people may only face one more problem, often a substance abuse problem, and the network will snap.

Attempts are being made, however, to prevent the evictions of multi-problem families. As part of a study in Helsinki this researcher interviewed the managers and other staff of the city council housing department and social workers in the same housing areas. The managers were willing to discuss rent arrears with tenants and to arrange new time schedules for their payment. The municipal social welfare authorities were apt to pay the arrears of families in order to avoid eviction (Söderholm, 2000). The 1983 Child Welfare Act obliges the municipalities to provide housing for child welfare clients. This obligation means that a new dwelling can be allocated to families with children even in cases where the family has been evicted from the previous dwelling due to rent arrears or anti-social behaviour (Asukasvalintatyöryhmän muistio, 1999). If living in mainstream housing does not succeed, due to substance abuse problems, the social welfare authorities will provide the tenant and her family with supported accommodation. However, when the problems caused by substance abuse, among other things, have recurred over a long time, the eviction is put into effect without any further negotiations. If there are any children, they are then taken into custody or placed in foster homes. The adult(s) often becomes homeless (Söderholm, 2000).

Forssén (1998) has studied the outcomes of Finnish family policy. She has seen signs of a new culture and lifestyle with which the welfare system often has difficulty coping. Long-term exclusion may also cause families to become excluded on the basis of criteria set by the service system for the clients. Forssén (1998) questions whether the welfare society has failed in determining and responding to the needs of different groups of clients.

There remains a difference between women, depending on their parental status. The measures by which evictions are being prevented are mostly designed for families and for women with children. Shelters or temporary homes for women fleeing domestic violence are also provided for mothers with children. A hostel for homeless women may be the only option for single women or women who no longer take care of dependent children (Eeva-Maria Home, interview). Granfelt (1998) has asked, after interviewing women living in hostels, why there is not a place in social work's image of a woman for women who do not have children and who live alone?

A fifth of homeless people are women

According to the housing market survey of the National Housing Fund, municipal authorities estimated that there was a total of 10,000 homeless single people in November 1999. Both open and hidden homelessness in municipalities are included in this figure, insofar as the municipal authorities have knowledge of or can estimate the number of people. In addition to single homeless people, the municipalities estimated that there were 800 homeless or houseless households with more than one person, the majority of which are immigrant households waiting for ordinary housing in some temporary accommodation. As a result of preventative measures, families of Finnish origin are seldom homeless, or then usually for only a short period (Tiitinen, 2000; Ikonen et al, 2000).

While the total level of homelessness has remained static in recent years, the geography of homelessness has changed. It has increased in the Helsinki region and in some other growth centres while it has decreased in other parts of the country. More than half of the estimated number of homeless people live in the Helsinki region. The number of households queuing for social housing has increased in precisely the same cities where homelessness has increased (Tiitinen, 2000). Quite recently, the housing market situation has compelled the housing and social authorities in Helsinki to house even families with children in temporary accommodation.

Of the total number of homeless people, little more than 1,800 are estimated as being women, according to the housing market survey. The total number of homeless women has remained static in recent years. However, nearly 1,200 of these homeless women live in the Helsinki region (Tiitinen, 2000).

Who are these homeless women, where are they staying?

According to some qualitative studies and interviews conducted with service providers, the majority of homeless women have children. The children had been taken into custody and/or they were living in foster homes or institutions due to problems in the family. Alcohol and other substance abuse, along with mental health problems, seem to be the most common problems (Granfelt, 1998; Mecklin and Sonninen, 1998; Viljamaa 1999; Eeva-Maria Home, interview).

Homelessness often begins with divorce or a cohabitation break-up. When the woman, left alone in the dwelling, does not pay the rent (or is left with rent arrears) she is evicted. Some women or couples lose the dwelling because of anti-social behaviour. Young women leave their parents' home and thus become homeless, are forced out of their family house because of a drug habit. Whatever the trigger, homelessness is a consequence of a long and hard process during which the women have gradually lost their hold on life.

Homeless women solve their accommodation problems in different ways. However, staying on a temporary basis with relatives and friends is usual for homeless women. Staying with someone or moving from one male partner to another is a common way of avoiding open homelessness among female substance abusers. Of all the single homeless people, in November 1999 about 60% stayed temporarily with relatives and friends (estimated by the housing market survey, Tiitinen, 2000). If this pattern also holds true for women, then some 1,100 homeless women would belong to this category.

The status of excluded woman with substance abuse problems is poor and the women often experience both violence and sexual abuse, which causes them to feel shame. Research has shown (Mecklin and Sonninen, 1998) that, as a result of such experience, there is a high barrier for women to overcome in using services which cater for men. We know, for example, that women try to avoid using hostels and night shelters because of fear of abuse.

A common problem facing managers of housing estates all over the country is that once one person is allocated a flat, other people come and stay, until the tenant is evicted due to disturbances. A young drug abuser comes to a shelter or a service centre for homeless people only when their physical or mental condition has deteriorated so much that friends no longer accept the person as a member of their community (taken from an interview with shelter providers, Leijo).

Homelessness of single women (as indeed of men) does not, however, need to be a consequence of personal problems or lifestyle. Even if single women are more welcomed by landlords than single men, the economic resources of a single woman frequently make it impossible for her to enter the private housing market. Half the households queuing for social housing consist of single people, and only a fraction are able to get a dwelling (Ikonen et al, 2000).

Homelessness and substance abuse problems of women

The problem of homelessness seems to be changing rapidly among women. Homeless women are now much younger than previously and are more likely to be substance abusers. In Spring 2000, nearly half of the clients aged under 25 of the City of Helsinki Special Social Welfare Office (which is responsible for services for homeless people) were women. Nor is this a pattern confined to the metropolitan region of Helsinki. Evidence from a recent meeting with the providers of shelters and service centres in the six biggest cities (November 2000) suggests that, at that time, considerably more than half of their service users were women aged under 25. Among these clients alcohol is being superseded by drugs and related problems, including HIV and prostitution, as the main problem linked to homelessness. The Special Social Welfare Office in Helsinki expects that by 2005 the composition of clients will perhaps be totally changed (interview, Leijo).

All indicators of the drug phenomenon have been on the increase in Finland throughout the 1990s. Because the initial level was relatively low, the problem has not been as large as in Central Europe. Quite recently, particularly during the year 2000, the drug problem among young people has become a topical issue in public debate as well as in the work of public authorities.

Surveys of services and treatment centres for substance abuse in different parts of Finland (undertaken by STAKES in 1987, 1995 and 1997) demonstrates that the number of female clients seeking services for substance abuse has increased considerably. While in the 1987 survey women accounted for 16%, by 1999 a quarter of clients were women. Female clients are younger than their male counterparts in all types of drug abuse services, regardless of the type of drugs involved. The disadvantaged situation of substance abusers is obvious: only one tenth of them are employed. Two thirds of them live in ordinary housing, the rest live in supported housing, in hostels, institutions, or they are roofless (Nuorvala et al, 2000). Among the female clients in the 1999 survey, one in ten was homeless, roofless or lived in a shelter, but many women said they were staying with friends. One woman in three was living with a person who also had drug problems (Partanen, 1999).

While alcohol is still the dominant intoxicant (nine out of ten clients), the proportion of clients who just use alcohol has fallen since 1987 to 62%, while the number of substance abusers who do not use alcohol at all has increased. Different kinds of intoxicants are being mixed. Little more than a fifth of the clients abused medication. Recently the number of HIV and hepatitis C patients has increased; 40% of hepatitis C patients in 1999 were women and, once again, young women dominated. (*Kansanterveys, 2/2000*).

Problems in the chain of services: new services needed

Medical care and treatment and detoxification have traditionally been a crucial part of the substance abuse services. The survey of services and treatment centres undertaken in 1999 (Nuorvala et al, 2000) reveals that a significant change in the structure of substance abuse services has been implemented in the 1990s. Institutional treatment was reduced considerably and a greater reliance is being placed on open care services. However, these open care services have not been able to fill the gap created by the closure of institutional treatment centres. The services targeted at the underprivileged have expanded as the number of clients asking for substance abuse services has increased overall. Under this category the survey counts day centres for homeless people and substance abusers, housing services (that is, supported housing) as well emergency shelters (Nuorvala et al, 2000; Kaukonen, 2000).

The survey also reveals that visits to psychiatric hospitals due to substance abuse problems have increased by more that 40% between 1995-2000, while, during the same period, vacancies in psychiatric hospitals declined by half compared to the level of the early 1990s. Women in particular have increasingly sought help for their substance abuse problems from psychiatric hospitals (Nuorvala et al, 2000).

New services, particularly low threshold services, have recently been opened for homeless people and for homeless women. Traditional hostel accommodation is changing. In Helsinki, for example, a new hostel for women has been established which provides single rooms for women who formerly lived in a large mixed-sex hostel (Viljamaa, 1999). Hostels also provide projects and services for women; special projects for women with substance abuse problems and mental health problems have been organised in some hostels for homeless women. Furthermore, service centres for substance abusers also now offer housing services; there are now several units which provide accommodation for women after a period of care while supported housing or mainstream housing is arranged. Both the municipalities and the organisations providing substance abuse services have housing, including supported housing, for this purpose. The Helsinki Special Welfare Office has 1,700 dwellings in total; however, demand far exceeds supply, especially in the Helsinki region.

The most pressing question among service providers today is how to deal with this new generation of homeless people? Existing service provision was designed for old-fashioned substance abusers, who drink alcohol. Providing services and, in particular, housing for young people with drug abuse problems, calls for special solutions and support measures (meetings with the shelter/service providers, interview, Leijo). Different kinds of services are needed, such as open care and low threshold support units, as well as supported housing and treatment units targeted at young drug users.

The service provision for homeless women appears to be in a transition phase in seeking the right approach. New accommodation is being built, in the form of single small flats, designed to meet women's needs for safety and privacy (Viljamaa, 1999). However, support by a 'special' person is also needed; women who have a positive relationship with a support person report high levels of satisfaction when help is received. Granfelt (1998) uses the concept 'holding environment', which gives a person safe, sustainable boundaries and enough liberty to enable them to feel safe.

Despite these successes the development of services focusing on women and on women with substance abuse problems is hindered by lack of resources. Equally, however, there is a need to provide increased levels of professional staffing for such services than was normal in traditional hostel accommodation for homeless people. This requires a new understanding from service providers to allocate more resources to these activities (Viljamaa, 1999).

The experiences of violence and sexual abuse which make it difficult for women to seek services that are mainly meant for men has been described elsewhere. While this is true for all women, it is even more evident in services for women with substance abuse problems. Research suggests that the status of excluded women with substance abuse problems is poor both within the culture of substance abusers and within the service provision. Within drinking circles women are easily subordinated and subjected to violence and sexual abuse. After such experiences there is a high threshold barrier for women to overcome in seeking services that are mainly meant for men. For this group, as for all homeless women, services designed to protect them from sexual exploitation and stigmatisation are needed. Daytime services, particularly, are usually planned according to the needs of men. Homeless women need services providing emotional as well as practical support in their everyday problems (Mecklin and Sonninen, 1998).

The importance of permanent housing in enabling people to manage their substance abuse problems has been emphasised in research (Mecklin and Sonninen, 1998). This is especially true for women who, despite having substance abuse problems, still have a need for private space and demonstrate the common basic urge of all women to turn a house into a home. However, most women with a substance abuse problem require support to access housing and to sustain a tenancy. Because of the lack of such support, Granfelt (1998) observed that the marginalised, single women she interviewed had 'unreasonable' dreams of getting a tenancy. One of the most important tasks of housing policy and social work is to provide the support necessary to enable these people to have a home even if they can not live independently (Granfelt, 1998). However, this task of coordination, which is difficult enough, is made even more difficult in a context where the housing market is overheating as a result of demand exceeding supply especially in the metropolitan region of Helsinki.

Conclusions

Extreme forms of social exclusion have been, and remain, more evident among men than among women. While middle-aged single men with drinking problems are seen as the least deserving group in Finnish society, homeless single women with severe substance abuse problems are also seen as belonging to this 'undeserving' group. Although support measures for women are being discussed more than support for men, the deficiencies in the provision and coordination of all services are evident.

The Finnish welfare society, which is said to be woman-friendly (Anttonen, 1996), has succeeded rather well in taking care of the well-being of mothers who live with their children and it endeavours to do so even in the most extreme circumstances. These preventive measures do not cater so well for single women or women who are no longer taking care of their children. This is particularly true of substance abusers, who often end up in the same circle of short treatment periods, homelessness and substandard accommodation as men.

Deficiencies in the housing policy concern single, young, low-income women in particular. Many of them cannot afford a rental dwelling on the free housing market in the growth cities, yet the lack of affordable dwellings in social housing forces many of them onto the free market.

The structure of substance abuse services has changed significantly in the 1990s. Institutional treatment has been reduced considerably and greater reliance is placed on open care services, which, however, have not been sufficient to replace the gap. Since women have increasingly sought help for their substance abuse problems from psychiatric hospitals, the reduction in such provision creates a need for alternative services and support. A hostel, at least in the Helsinki region, is more often the only option for accommodation after a treatment period in a hospital or in an institution for substance abusers. The chain of services, otherwise said to be typical for northern social welfare and health systems, seem to seriously falter here.

The survey of services and treatment for substance abuse uses the concept 'services for the underprivileged people'. These services have expanded as their number of the clients have increased. Emergency shelters, day centres and accommodation services, even supported housing, are counted under this title. Are these services considered to be a part of the system of professional substance abuse services or of ordinary social welfare services? There is a danger that housing will remain a marginal problem for professionals in the social welfare sector, while the issues of care and treatment are considered to be crucial. Is it appropriate that housing services for homeless people are dealt with as welfare services for underprivileged people? For a homeless woman, and especially one with substance abuse problems, having a house is more than an adjunct to the provision of welfare services; it is the base within which she can regain control of her life.

In the midst of these problems and unanswered questions of service provision, a new generation of young homeless women is emerging, who seem to be even more vulnerable than previous generations of older homeless women.

EXPERIENCES

SIXTEEN

Homeless women in Luxembourg: what do they expect of services?

Monique Pels

Introduction

All the available statistics on homelessness[1] indicate a substantial rise in the number of women in homeless shelters/intake centres since 1995. Annual surveys of intake agencies carried out since 1995 show that the number of women clients has doubled – they now make up 46% of the population living in homeless shelters.

Obviously, these figures are not the whole story, because they relate only to people – specifically, women – who have visited a homeless shelter/intake centre known to them in search of refuge. They reflect the population of welfare service users more than the total population of homeless women.

The questions 'who uses these services and why?' are key in studying the homeless community. Our aim in addressing them is two-fold: to identify particular causes of women's homelessness in Luxembourg; and to highlight the needs of homeless women in light of these causes.

This chapter is based on quantitative and qualitative data. The quantitative data were collected from a questionnaire sent out to 20 services and agencies with responsibilities for people in need. Of the 20 questionnaires sent out, 18 were returned, of which 16 were fully completed. The qualitative data were gleaned from 21 personal interviews or group discussions with women in housing need who agreed to talk frankly about their experiences, problems, their trials and tribulations, and the assistance they had sought, received, or were still looking for.

Why are women homeless?

No previous research has been done in Luxembourg on homeless women. The only information available is in the operational reports of homeless shelters/intake centres, and surveys or studies carried out for FEANTSA. Using the latter, we can identify the causes of women's homelessness as related to their position in society, in the labour market, and in the housing market.

Women's position in society and in the labour market

Women's employment rate in Luxembourg is very low and rising at a very slow pace – from 34% in 1988 to 37% in 1999. The labour force participation rate for all women aged 15-64 living in Luxembourg is 46.7% (Eurostat, 1996). Among women aged 24-49, it is 55.8%. Age-for-age, the French rate is 78.5% and the all–European Union (EU) rate 70.5%.

Not working in a paid job is more than just a personal issue for women in Luxembourg – it is a social fact, still deeply entrenched in attitudes. It is a situation long encouraged by government policies; there have been no incentives for women to work outside the home, or for women to return to work after maternity leave.

There are four key factors in women's fairly low participation rate. First, there is the lack of child care provision. A recent study by Lejealle (1998) forges a link between women's participation and the presence of dependent children. Economic activity declines sharply with increasing family size (from two and particularly three children upwards). Second, female participation also correlates closely with education – women with lower attainment levels have lower economic activity rates. Third, marriage is also a major depressant of labour force participation in Luxembourg – the activity rate of unmarried women aged 25-49 is 82.5%, compared to 49.2% for married women and 75.1% for widowed and divorced women. The gap in labour force participation in Luxembourg between married and unmarried women is one of the widest in Europe. The equivalent all-EU figures are 65.9% for married women, 81.5% for unmarried women, and 77.2% for widowed or divorced women. Fourth, there is nearly a 10-point gap between the participation rate of women aged 25-49 of Luxembourg nationality and that of women of the other EU countries in Luxembourg (Eurostat, 1996).

Women who do not work are dependent on their partner or family. Not having a paid job puts women at greater risk of homelessness in the event of partner abuse, or domestic violence, and holds back their integration or reintegration into society.

Most women interviewed for this study were not in paid work at the time they were in a partner relationship or seeking assistance from a welfare service or homeless shelter/intake centre. Either they had never worked or had stopped working to have children. This was not an issue until the moment they had to flee the conjugal or family home and face homelessness and all its attendant problems.

The Economic and Social Council estimates that:

> ... the labour needs of different sectors of the Luxembourg economy could be met by female labour. But to increase women's employment rate, there must be coherent social, family and tax policies, as well as a policy on the organisation of working time, which encourages what are often well-educated young women not to give up work and devote themselves solely to running their homes and raising their family. The same goes for women looking to return to work – there must be more, and better-targeted, specific training provision to help them re-enter the labour force. Also, community social and educational provision and activities must be substantially expanded and work organisation adapted to improve the family/work life balance. (Economic and Social Council, 2000)

Women's position in the housing market

The lack of comprehensive, reliable statistics makes it very hard to give a detailed picture of the housing market in Luxembourg. But official agencies, voluntary organisations and those looking to rent are all agreed that there is a chronic shortage of low-cost housing. The housing shortage is worse for rented social housing, where there are nearly 1,000 people on the waiting list each year. Women's general difficulty in accessing the housing market, therefore, is made worse by the housing shortage, especially in low-cost housing.

Applicants for Low-Cost Housing Fund accommodation must satisfy a number of conditions. For example, they may not apply for, or be allocated, low-rent housing if they own or have a life interest in other residential property in Luxembourg or abroad. Prospective tenants must also supply information about their household composition, income from all sources of the household members, current housing situation and the reasons for applying to be rehoused. When housing becomes available, the Fund first identifies all the households on its list for which that accommodation is appropriate and selects those with the lowest rent-to-income ratios. A decision is then taken between those pre-screened potential tenants on the basis of their current housing situation rather than by reference to other criteria. This means that women or single-parent families, for example, are not given priority.

In the private rented market, the practice of demanding key money (a rental guarantee, often of two or three months' rent) is another major barrier to housing access by women in need.

Identifying homeless women

From the replies to the questionnaire sent out to official agencies, some key attributes of homeless women living in shelters can be identified. These tie in with those of the women interviewed.

Most homeless women are young. In 1998, the 16 agencies concerned provided shelter or assistance to 191 women, 69% of them between the ages of 21 and 40. Other age categories were less well represented: 11% were under 21, and 20% over 40. All age categories were represented in the personal interviews, with the under-30s in the majority: 18–29 years (8 women), 30–39 years (5 women), 40–49 years (6 women) and 50–60 years (2 women).

Problems with families and partners play a key role in the life of homeless women. The quantitative data show that 45% of women are single, 35% are married, and the rest are separated or divorced. Two thirds had one or more children, who were an important and even decisive factor in the choices made by these women. The presence of children often proved an important if not the main reason for fleeing home to seek shelter in an intake centre. Of the women interviewed, 18 were separated or divorced, and only three were unmarried. One was childless; the others had one or more children.

Almost half the women in homeless shelters/intake centres were unemployed; only 25% of the sample had a job, the others were living on social security or social assistance benefits. The fairly low female labour market participation rate was reflected among the women interviewed. Only three women were in work; the others were registered with the employment service as job seekers. The vast majority of the registered job seekers were on guaranteed minimum income benefit

(GMI), but some were ineligible on the grounds of age (too young) or nationality. GMI is available for Luxembourg women aged over 30 in need, but not for those aged under 30 with less than 10 years' residency in the country.

The women interviewed had experienced a range of problems: partner abuse or domestic violence (5 women), family breakdown (2 women), relationship breakdown or separation or divorce (2 women), debt or eviction (7 women), discharge from hospital (1 woman). Relationship breakdown–separation–divorce often go hand in hand with debt and eviction. In the 7 cases of eviction, relationship breakdown, separation, divorce and debt problems had led to a build-up of rent arrears and eviction. Clearly, then, family problems and relationship breakdown are key causes of women's homelessness.

The needs of homeless women

Twenty-one personal interviews were conducted with women in varying degrees of housing need. They were unstructured interviews in which the women told their stories, aired their problems, solutions and plans, gave their views on the services provided and put forward proposals for improving or changing existing provision. The interviews were not just with women in refuges. Obviously, they were heavily represented, but we also met women in other forms of intake agency and service, such as drop-in centres, a street outreach service, a day centre, a supportive or supervised housing service and a family placement service.

The qualitative interviews with homeless women add an extra dimension to the studies carried out to date and help give a more realistic gloss to the needs as they express them. What we conclude from our analysis of what these women told us is that independence or autonomy and access to housing are key needs.

Independence and autonomy

Economic or financial independence is seen as very important by the women interviewed. Financial dependence on the partner can close off all avenues to women who are fleeing partner abuse or contending with non-violent relationship breakdown and leave them no other choice than to drift into homelessness. Not having a job has been the source of a series of problems and difficulties. Typical comments in this context were:

> "I wanted to get away from my violent husband, but how could I, with no money or job...?"

> "The police repeatedly told me I ought to leave my husband, because I was at risk; but every time he hit me, I went back home; I had nothing – no money, no job, no idea where to turn...."

These examples show how some women have to put up with violent partners because having no money of their own leaves them nowhere else to go. The only escape from violence for many is the street or a hostel. With no job or steady income, they are unable to find anywhere to live; institutional care is the only help on offer. Lack of an adequate income and a job deprives women of coping strategies.

What often stops many women getting a job is a lack of basic education. Updating and/or further training will often be needed to get them access to work. Most of those who do work earn only the minimum living wage, which makes it difficult to find somewhere suitable to live. As one interviewee observed: "I've signed up to train as a home health aide. It's what I've always wanted to do. It'll make it easier for me to find a job", "On what I earn, I'd never be able to afford rent and childcare. What will I have left to live on?" Hence, the problem is much wider than unemployment; women also need job-readiness training and access to decently paid jobs.

The women interviewed mentioned other dependency issues: how, for example, alcohol and drug dependency create a downward spiral of personal, social and financial problems which can push some women into homelessness. A more thorough-going analysis with more representative data is needed to determine whether alcohol- or drug-dependency is a cause or consequence of homelessness.

Some women, as the following quote indicates, drift from one dependency state to another, and until they have achieved a degree of autonomy, they will stay vulnerable and at-risk.

> "I've been dependent one way or another all my life. The first was when I was dependent on my step-father [rape]. When I was a teenager, I took to drink and drugs to forget it. When I got married, I was dependent on my violent husband. To try and cope with that, I went into therapy, which left me dependent on the psychiatrist,

not forgetting my dependence on the social services. I'm still dependent on a social service. I don't know if I will ever be my own person...."

Access to housing

Having their own, permanent place to live is an essential need which is, sadly, not being met for all women. As a result, the women turn to other solutions, such as support or intake by different services such as centres or hostels. Women's hostels and refuges provide day and night shelter for women with and without children. They give primary continuum-of-care to women and their children in the form of shelter, meals, hygiene services, medical care and educational, social and psychological guidance and support. After a settling-in phase, they can go on for a limited period to so-called 'transitional housing', supportively monitored by homeless shelter/intake centre staff.

The night shelter is accessible to all homeless people. Five women in our sample had stayed there before moving on to other care provision services.

The women interviewed reported a series of needs linked to homeless shelters/intake centres, not least the need for more places and more information about them. Despite the annual expansion of hostel/centre provision, demand continues to outstrip supply. In 1998, 346 women with 390 children were taken into homeless shelters/intake centres officially approved by the Ministry for the Advancement of Women. Another 283 applications were not followed up, either due to a shortage of places or because they withdrew their applications. Applicants may have to wait several days or weeks, or go to a different centre than that chosen. As one interviewee observed: "I spent a night in the police station because there was no room in any of the shelters and I couldn't go back home".

The women interviewed stressed the importance of having straightforward, detailed information about their rights and the forms of assistance available. Lack of information was part of the reason why six of the 21 women spent several weeks, if not several months, living on the streets before going into a shelter. Women who are not informed or are mis-informed are left utterly bereft. The following quotes demonstrate the helplessness they feel without information:

"When you're on the streets, you don't know where to turn for help. You feel so rotten, devalued and down that you can't think anyone will listen to you or help you."

"Shelters often have this negative image; it's completely undeserved, but if you don't know them, you don't realise that. You only go by hearsay. I didn't want to go there. I held out until the very last, when there was nothing and nowhere else; when in fact I got invaluable and vital help there."

Some groups of women find that their needs are not being recognised or addressed by intake centres. Women without children do not always fit into women's shelters which tend to focus on the needs of women with children, so single women may feel ill at ease. Women without children need a different type of assistance – more sympathetic attention, for example – and say they are not always finding it:

"I'm going to try to get out of the shelter as soon as I can. It's fine for women with children who are on their uppers, but my needs aren't the same, and they aren't being met. I don't know if there is a shelter which provides what I need."

Adapting to life in a shelter is not always easy, even for those who find it the best, and only, choice for them. Rules and regulations, community living, lack of space, may all be issues of life in a shelter which must be accepted, put up with and abided by:

"Having to tell somebody before you go out in the evening is not easy at my age...."

"Living in a community has its good side, there's always somebody to talk to; but there are also restrictions that you have to get used to...."

Immigrant women often lack access to shelters and services because they cannot make themselves understood. Yet, for immigrant women, regularising their status is very important. Without papers in order and an official address, they are blocked at every turn. Equally, women with psychiatric problems have difficulty finding a solution. It is no easier to carry out projects with and for them. They need referral to more specialised services, which are thin on the ground, and which rarely accept children.

Conclusions

Almost all the women interviewed had many personal plans. They are trying to cope, but many realise that achieving their aims will be a long, hard slog. These women need to regain their financial and personal independence to fulfil their plans. They want to learn to live without the assistance of institutions and social services. A job and affordable housing would in most cases help them reunite a family torn apart by previous problems.

The women are not short of ideas on how to improve their lot and that of other women in the same situation. Among the suggestions for the improved delivery of services for homeless women, and for women at risk of homelessness, are the following:

• More comprehensive information. Mount an information campaign to inform women, especially young women, about their rights, the opportunities for assistance and existing social services provision. Provide specific, detailed information rather than vague generalities. The women are in favour of information campaigns on welfare services and shelters/refuges which will deliver objective, positive information to dispel the negative image that homeless shelters/intake centres tend to have.

> "Everybody should know about these services, how they work and everything they can do to help women in need." "The information is available inside shelters, but it doesn't get to the outside public. That information has to come out. There are women who don't know their rights, don't know where to go or who to go to. Battered women don't know that they can live differently and re-build another life for themselves. They live in fear and know nothing else. They are afraid to speak out because they don't know that they can be helped."

• Build smaller, less showy, lower-cost housing than that currently built by the Low-Cost Housing Fund.
• Introduce housing benefit or rental assistance for families on the minimum living wage, along the lines of that paid to GMI recipients.

- Expand employment subsidies and training provision to bring employment opportunities within everyone's reach: "A job helps solve countless problems. Housing is easier to find with an income. A job gets you out of the house, gives you social contacts, feelings of self-worth. It lets you look forwards rather than always behind you".
- Give more help to single-parent families; they tend to get sidelined, when they should be given understanding, attention and help. It would avoid guilt feelings and a blame culture.
- Give women the time they need. Some shelters set maximum stay periods, but each woman moves forward at her own pace. Not being rushed is important if they are not to find themselves back at square one.

Two of these proposals have been taken up by public or private agencies. Rental assistance is one of the demands made by many voluntary organisations, and has been suggested and recommended by the Economic and Social Council. Information campaigns against partner abuse and domestic violence are run at regular intervals by the Ministry for the Advancement of Women and some voluntary organisations. However, these need to be brought to a wider audience and embrace issues other than violence. They should inform people about the existence of services and shelters, what they do and how they work, and be given the maximum possible exposure.

Note

[1] The only figures available to evaluate the extent of homelessness are those in operational reports of shelters/intake centres and sponsoring departments. It is hard to come up with precise figures, partly because not all homeless people will be seen by intake agencies, and partly due to double counting, because some will be seen by a series of shelters/intake centres within the space of a year.

SEVENTEEN

Women, exclusion and homelessness in Germany

Uta Enders-Dragässer

Introduction

In Western Germany, at the beginning of the 1980s, women working in welfare and social research made the homelessness and poverty of women visible by starting a gender-specific debate referring to the issues of the new women's movement, in particular, issues such as male violence against women, unequal opportunities, gender division of labour, sexism and gender role-stereotyping (Enders-Dragässer and Sellach, 1999). Because of the women's movement critique, the perception of women in the welfare system began to change. The discussion about the causes of the vulnerability of women began to shift from the debate about personal deficiencies to the debate about structural disadvantages, such as women's higher risks of poverty and violence (Geiger and Steinert, 1991; Enders-Dragässer, 1994). It was strongly argued that homeless women are a specific target group with specific needs different from those of homeless men, and that their access to service facilities of the support system is insufficient.

Pressure from the women's lobby, particularly following national conferences organised by the women's caucus of the NGO BAG Wohnungslosenhilfe (National Campaign for the Homeless), influenced the Federal Government to fund research and model projects. The first national study on homeless women was commissioned in the late 1980s (Geiger and Steinert, 1991). In 1995 the federal Government commissioned a first model project 'Support for single homeless women' and evaluation research (Enders-Dragässer and Sellach, 1999) and in 1998 it commissioned the consecutive model project 'Occupational qualification and training for homeless women' and evaluation research (Enders-Dragässer and Roscher, 1999).

The national study on homelessness among women and the two model projects considerably influenced the professional debate and have promoted innovative developments and research on homeless women. New services have been initiated exclusively for homeless women and exclusively staffed by women, working all over Germany, including: counselling agencies, day shelters, new schemes of housing and new schemes for occupational qualification and (re-)integration. The evaluation research brought the inequalities and deficits of the support system more strongly into view and influenced professional practice. The model projects have led to the creation of new services and new agencies.

Structural factors as causes for female homelessness

The first national research study into the situation of homeless women in Germany remains a landmark study because it made homeless women visible for the first time as a specific target group with specific needs. The research (Geiger and Steinert, 1991) is a very valuable contribution to the issue of open homelessness of women because of its rich material, its comprehensive data, and its insights into the complexities of the multi-dimensional situation of homeless women. Geiger and Steinert (1991) showed that the argument of individual deficiencies cannot explain the heterogeneity of the target group. They stressed the impact of structural factors, such as poverty, as a cause for homelessness. They made the competencies of homeless women visible and showed that women actively struggle to overcome their situation on their own by developing coping strategies – 'living in normality' being the main objective for them.

When analysing the situation of homeless women in the German Land Rheinland-Pfalz, Enders-Dragässer (1994) drew on the work of Geiger and Steinert (1991) concerning structural factors causing homelessness of women and identified four basic structures which influence women's daily life situations, eventually turning them into life risks resulting in poverty and homelessness:

- all forms of violence (harassment, battering, rape, prostitution, sexual abuse);

- the multi-dimensional causes and high risks of poverty for women (the gender division of labour, the infrastructural lack of child care and school provisions, women's unequal opportunities in education, occupation, social security and social welfare system);
- the various health problems of women;
- gender stereotypes and sexist prejudices (discriminations because of 'male quota' in culture, science, religion and politics, restricting women's participation).

Enders–Dragässer (1994) described a 'modernity trap' for women. No matter how they decide about their way of living, whether in dependency from a partner as 'breadwinner' or in trying to reconcile employment and family work to be independent, whether leaving a violent partner or staying with him, they bear high personal risks and have problems with social security, with economic resources and with housing. Enders–Dragässer (1994) also drew on the research of Golden (1992), who has shown that in the US homeless women create discomfort because there exists no category for a woman without family or home. Homeless women are dehumanised by fantasies and projections which have nothing to do with their real life situations. These fantasies, projections and myths determine how homeless women cope with their situation, how they are treated and how their needs are neglected.

Poverty and 'life positions' (*Lebenslagen*) of women

Enders–Dragässer and Sellach (Enders–Dragässer and Sellach, 1999) based their evaluation research on the categories and definitions of the 'Life position approach' (*Lebenslagen-Ansatz*) of the German-speaking poverty research. Categories such as income, education and occupational training, housing and health situation, communication and mobility, leisure and regeneration, and participation in society determine the 'life position' (*Lebenslage*) of individuals and restrict their scope of decisions and actions (Glatzer and Hübinger, 1990). They argued that the description of the 'life positions' (*Lebenslagen*) of women is incomplete and individualistic. It does not take into consideration specific life events and familial commitments of women, such as pregnancy, birth, care for children and family members, reconciliation of occupational and family work, partnership, marriage, separation, divorce, and bereavement. Women's scope of decisions and actions therefore greatly differs from that of men; women need specific resources such as child care and school provisions, health and social care services.

They argued that a further important factor neglected by poverty research is violence against women as a key in understanding crises and coping strategies of women. Abuse of alcohol, of prescription drugs, or of illegal drugs are often effects of violence. They increase the risks of economic and social poverty and social exclusion. Women with urgent need of housing lack public and private space for their empowerment where they are safe and protected against violence; where they can communicate and participate. Lacking housing, and hence a private space, they have to face prejudices and 'dehumanising sexualised' fantasies and projections which have nothing to do with their real life situation (Golden, 1992). This too contributes to social exclusion and their risks of poverty in hidden and subtle ways. Since women tend to live, in poverty and homelessness alike, as inconspicuously as possible there are more poor and homeless women than publicly perceived. Thus social exclusion of women is also hidden.

Coping strategies and the risk of homelessness

In pursuit of their main objective of 'living a decent and normal life', and/or because of the often total lack of support in Germany, women try to conceal their homelessness at all costs and seek private solutions outside the support system, risking dependency and violence. They try to stay with family members, neighbours, friends, or male 'acquaintances', in temporary, insufficient and often inadequate housing. Without knowing it, they also risk their entitlement for support. If they find short-term housing, for instance, in the flat of an 'acquaintance', they are no longer considered to be homeless. Because of their competency in avoiding sleeping rough, they fall outside the two legal definitions of need: 'homelessness' (*Obdachlosigkeit*) or 'people with no fixed abode' (*Nichtsesshaftigkeit*) – and the local welfare agencies argue, therefore, that they are not 'homeless'. This ignores the fact that women are legally entitled to support if they are unable to overcome their social difficulties by their own means (Enders–Dragässer and Sellach, 1999).

Homeless women avoid mixed-sex support provisions if possible. Within such services, female social workers are rare and women do not get the appropriate support they need. In mixed-sex support provisions women fear male domination and the permanent risk of male harassment and violence. Protection against male violence is not provided, nor even considered necessary. This applies to both female clients and female personnel. Therefore they are not places where women can speak out about their experiences with male violence and abuse. This situation is an issue of social exclusion and unequal opportunities. The often hopeless situation of homeless women and their experiences with the mixed-sex support provisions show that women as a specific needs group are neglected and disadvantaged. Therefore the women's debate considers this as an issue of sex discrimination with regard to both accessibility of support and satisfaction of needs (Enders–Dragässer and Sellach, 1999).

Enders–Dragässer and Sellach (1999) have emphasised that, because of their determination to cope, the extreme poverty and needs of women are perceived too late and are tackled too late. That leads to a double consequence. After a long time of suffering, only a minority of the women become visibly homeless, mostly on the street. These women are assumed to be the 'typical' homeless women perceived as typically destitute, suffering from mental illness, helpless and difficult people 'with no fixed abode', whose numbers are small. However, this presumption is wrong. Further, because the hidden homelessness of women does not happen within the 'gender-neutral' mainstream debate, subtle and hidden discriminations impede the women's access to support. The mainstream debate is gender-'blind' with regard to homeless women, their life situations and the male dominance within the support system with all its consequences for the women asking for support.

The homelessness of women and the women who are homeless

The National Campaign for the Homeless (BAG Wohnungslosenhilfe) estimated that, in 1999, about 30% (160,000) of all homeless people were women (BAG Informationen, 1999). Research data, from the national study and from the federally funded pilot projects, indicated an enormous extent of hidden homelessness and thus confirmed the importance of the issue of 'hidden homelessness'. Therefore Enders–Dragässer and Sellach developed a new definition scheme for the homelessness of women (Enders–Dragässer and Sellach, 1999), defining three groups of women in urgent need of housing, being either 'open' or 'hidden' or 'latent' homeless. These three definitions replace the two-fold categorisation of previous research of either 'manifest' or 'latent' homeless.

'Open' homeless are women sleeping rough, living on the street or in institutions of the support system (homeless hostels). Although they are the minority of the homeless women, according to the research evidence, they are perceived as the 'typical' homeless women. Their appearance still dominates the public perceptions and images of homeless women and the public debates about female homelessness.

'Hidden' homeless are the majority of homeless women, because they conceal their situation of homelessness for as long as possible. They live in temporary accommodation, for example, and are without a secure housing situation. In reality it is these women who are the 'typical' homeless women.

'Latent' homeless refers to women who are without legal disposition of their housing and/or are in immediate danger either of losing their home, or of having to flee it at any time because they are living in violent relationships. Due to a new legal regulation they are now entitled for support when this happens.

The survey data of 450 women, in the model projects, showed that 31% of women lived within their own unsecured social nets and 30% in facilities of the support system. This means that 61% of all women were without a secure housing situation. Thirteen per cent were sleeping rough, while 26% of the women lived in their own flat. More than half of the women (55%) had neither finished school nor vocational training. Taking together the women who were registered unemployed (45%) with the women who were unemployed but not registered, about two thirds of all women were without employment. The clients reported various physical or mental disabilities or illnesses. They had often been in institutions, in particular psychiatric institutions or institiutions for alcohol or drug dependents. It remains an open question whether their housing problems made them sick or addicted or vice versa.

The most important cause for the loss of housing was conflict with family or partners. All other reasons were of lesser importance. Half of all women spoke about experiences of violence. Considering that women who did not voice this issue may nevertheless have had similar experiences, it has to be assumed that violence is a very important risk leading to homelessness, and the most important cause as to why women avoid mixed-sex support facilities. Questionnaire evidence and interviews showed that the housing biographies of the homeless women were nothing less than the women's relationship biographies. This explains why the important triggers of sudden homelessness and sudden poverty of women are family breakdown – rejection, separation, divorce, loss of care for children, death of family members, and acts of violence.

The individual data of the 450 women made evident the structural risks which women bear. They are held responsible for relationships and domestic work. It is their problem how to reconcile occupational and family work. They show, to some extent, educational and occupational deficiencies too, and have difficulties with child care and school provisions due to the deficits of municipal infrastructure. Homelessness of women has two main causes, which are structural and not individual: women's higher risk of poverty and of (domestic) violence. The definitions of the German welfare legislation do not acknowledge the specific life situations of women, and miss the nature and the extent of female homelessness and of the need situation of homeless women.

Gender-specific requirements for support facilities

Homeless women are not victims but actively try to overcome their difficult situation and insufficient resources on their own, aiming at living in 'normality'. Their wish is accommodation 'of their own', with their own kitchen and their own bathroom (Enders-Dragässer and Sellach, 1999). Thus, another important aspect which emerged from the evaluation research of the model projects is that, as a rule, the women have been responsible for a household and for the needs of others (children, partners, other members of the family). They may have lost children to the care of others and grieve this. Their strong desire is to return to the normality of their own household. Their coping strategies are aimed at that end, and at being independent from others: from men and, especially, from social welfare.

As the experiences of the experts and the data show, homeless women have considerable self-care competencies and relationship skills which are very important for them. With appropriate support from women social workers, homeless women are very successful in re-establishing a 'normal' life unless illness or other factors intervene. The work of the projects has proved that it needs professional work of women and a 'women's room' in its literal and metaphorical sense to reach women with urgent need of housing at earlier stages and in hidden homelessness.

Evidence from the evaluation research of the first model project 'Support for single homeless women' (Enders-Dragässer and Sellach, 1999) demonstrates the importance of services run by women and targeted at women's needs. With their acceptance of the new services the women clients showed their need for support facilities exclusively for women. Respondents of the interviews often remarked that the projects were 'quiet', 'bright' and 'friendly'. When questioned they all concurred that the projects were 'quiet' because of the absence of men.

Important for contact were small personal networks, the clients' 'scenes'; thus the services provided also reach other women with urgent need of housing. Support provisions giving access to (re-)housing and self-care possibilities were of greatest interest. Self-care interests and household competencies of the clients were good starting points for the successful work of the projects.

The projects, contacted by women living in all forms of homelessness, proved to support their clients with adequate support and opened new perspectives. The housing situation of the clients as well as their health situation improved considerably. It was possible to reach those living in hidden homelessness at quite early stages of their homelessness (Enders-Dragässer and Sellach, 1999).

Enders-Dragässer and Sellach (1999) described requirements of good practice for support facilities for women in homelessness or in urgent need of housing, to enlarge the scope for their decisions and actions and to meet their specific need in acceptable and supportive ways. They also formulated these requirements as rights of homeless women (Enders-Dragässer and Sellach, 1999) and as requirements for quality management (Sellach, 1998) as outlined below.

The rights of women with urgent need of housing and examples of good practice

- Homeless women have the right to be protected against harassment and violence and against exploitation of their interactional and housekeeping competencies.
- Homeless women have the right to be supported by women experts working in the field of social work. They have the right of unrestricted communication of their experiences especially with regard to sexual violence.
- Homeless women are entitled to a 'women's room', in its metaphorical sense, as room for empowerment, as an alternative to traditional gender roles.
- Homeless women are entitled to a 'women's room', in its literal sense, as a room with protection, with an infrastructure for women, for communication, for body care, intimacy, respect and dignity; living and working rooms as places of social life, for everyday work, where they can care for themselves and can develop new perspectives with regard to children and family, education, social and cultural

participation; where they can qualify for employment and independence.

- Social work with homeless women also needs a 'women's room' in order to be able to discuss and to develop all aspects of social work for women.

Good practice services should operate according to these rights of homeless women to be able to guarantee their protection against harassment, violence and exploitation. In Germany models of good practice have been developed in various ways, combined with personal support and an exclusively female staff. The main models range from day centres to permanent rehousing solutions. Examples include:

- Day shelters for women only with sanitary facilities, a kitchen, washing, ironing and sewing facilities, perhaps additional computers, combined with counselling and personal support from female social workers, possibly with emergency night shelter.
- Temporary housing in a women's hostel (*Frauenpension*) with flats for not more than two women, each equipped with two individual rooms, and a living-room, kitchen and bathroom for shared use, combined with temporary personal support from female social workers (*Betreutes Wohnen*), linked to a day shelter with a counselling service.
- Short-term assessment service leading to permanent rehousing. The first and very successful model service operates in Munich ('Karla 51'). This service can accommodate about 40 women. The women have a room of their own for four weeks. During this time the staff assess their situation, try to rehouse them, and start the process of necessary personal support.
- Permanent (re-)housing of women within flats of their own or rooms of their own in flats for two to three women at a maximum, sharing kitchen and sanitary facilities, combined with temporary personal support by female social workers (*Betreutes Wohnen*, non-institutionalised).

There is also an example of a prevention service which can be considered to be an important model for future good practice. This is the counselling service 'Frauen in Not', operating in the city of Kassel for women endangered by violence and loss of their home. The women can consult the service before drastic situations have occurred, are supported if they wish to be rehoused and leave their partners, can start or change employment and can find new nurseries and schooling for their children.

Parallel non-violent and women-inclusive mixed-sex services will be necessary for women with partners, where their dignity and autonomy is respected and where the female staff are working with them without the partner being present.

In the near or distant future services of good practice for homeless women with or without children will have to live up to another very important expectation: to enable their women clients to earn a living on their own, thus securing permanent rehousing. These are the experiences with the new model project 'Occupational qualification and training for homeless women'.

Evaluation research on 'Occupational qualification and training for homeless women'

The model project 'Support for single homeless women' made apparent that homeless women have a requirement for occupational qualifications and seek work in order to (re-)integrate into the labour force. From the beginning this was expressed by the clients in Eastern Germany, but it emerged too, in a less expressive way, as a matter of concern for the women in Western Germany. This experience sparked the consecutive model project for homeless women: 'Occupational qualification and training for homeless women'.

This project covers occupational qualification and training schemes exclusively for women. It operates on the basis of Section 72 of the 1996 Federal Welfare Act and aims at (re-)integration of women in priority need for housing into the labour force. Thus the project combines the two most important issues for women (and men) with or without children with urgent need of housing: earning a living on their own and, thus, securing permanent rehousing. This model project therefore has to be considered as a very important contribution to social work for women (and men) and for the development of social policies for women and men with urgent housing need (Federal Welfare Act), of equal opportunity policies and of employment policies for women.

Occupational qualification and training work for disadvantaged women can draw on a rich tradition in Germany because of the collective re-entry of women into the labour force in Western Germany during the 1970s and the 1980s. However, homeless women were excluded from measures for (re-)integration into the labour market. It needed the reform of Section 72 of the Federal Welfare Act in 1996 to give them equal access. Nevertheless, there are still severe obstacles to overcome. They are not yet perceived as a target group for occupational training, qualification and (re-)integration into the labour market, by labour agencies and social administration agencies.

Therefore the project works on a structural and an individual level. Three of the four facilities are agencies for social work, one is an agency for occupational qualification and training. The three facilities undertaking social work cooperate with agencies for occupational qualification, training and employment. They give clients personal support while the women are qualified and trained by the cooperation partners. The agency for occupational qualification and training cooperates locally with agencies and organisations involved in social work for women.

Meanwhile the success of the model project lies in the demonstration that, as a group, women in urgent need of housing can successfully qualify and train for employment and successfully enter the labour force. Individually there may be serious problems which have to be dealt with by social work services. Therefore the experiences within the model projects will be very valuable.

A major problem seems to be the cooperation of both labour agencies and welfare agencies. Their inter-departmental cooperation has to be improved considerably to provide the clients with appropriate qualification and training schemes, either as individual or group measures in order to make their (re-)integration possible after successful qualification and training measures, and thus enable them to become independent from social welfare, which is the political objective. There is a considerable need to revise or to re-establish procedures and regulations within each administration and likewise between both administrations. However, a forthcoming law will prescribe the cooperation of labour and welfare agencies in the near future.

Conclusions

In Germany, professional debate and actual developments within the field of work for homeless women and men are determined, to a considerable extent, by perceptions and presumptions which are gender-blind, gender-stereotyped and sexualised. The hidden importance of the issue of gender as a driving force or impeding force goes unnoticed. Whereas the women's debate has brought about dynamic developments, the gender-neutral or gender-blind debate invalidates issues of both homeless women and men.

Two important questions remain to be perceived and to be solved in Germany. The first question is how to improve the accessibility of the support system for women with urgent housing need and how to support them with accessible and appropriate services relating to their specific life situations.

This is not yet an issue within the mainstream debate of both welfare administrations and the voluntary sector. The mainstream debate's gender-blindness results directly in deficits of service provisions. With its gender-specific exclusiveness it prevents gender- or women-inclusive definitions and argument, but instead disregards and trivialises the differing life situations and the gender-specific needs of women and hence of men.

The second important question to be perceived and to be solved is even less visible. This is the issue of how to improve the mixed-sex support agencies according to the gender-specific needs of women and men, protecting both women and men against male violence, and setting up more easily accessible and appropriate services that can give support much earlier to both sexes. The women's debate and the developments within social work for women are excellent bases on which to tackle both issues.

EIGHTEEN

(In-)visibility and shame: the stigma of being a woman and homeless in Sweden

Catharina Thörn

Introduction

The political discourse on homelessness in Sweden characterises homeless people as individuals who live 'outside of society', 'in the dark', or 'in the abyss'. They are pictured as unclean, drug abusers and as suffering from mental illness, and if they are women they are often referred to as prostitutes. This chapter discusses what these images of homeless people mean to homeless women and reflect on how they relate to the specificity of women's homelessness.

The analysis is based on 14 tape-recorded and transcribed in-depth interviews with women who are or have been homeless[1]. The ages of the interviewees ranged from 26 to 56 years. Seven of the women had had experience of sleeping rough. At the time of the interviews they had been homeless from a few months up to several years; one of them stated that she had never had a home of her own; half of the interviewees had spent time in prison; two were staying in single rooms in emergency housing; four were staying in various types of training flats; and one was accommodated in a family home. The women lived in different towns and cities. All names are fictitious to protect the interviewee's anonymity.

The construction of the hidden homeless woman

The debate on homelessness in Sweden in recent years has focused on homeless women and the ways their experience of homelessness differs from that of homeless men. The most striking feature to emerge is that, while men's homelessness is public and visible, women's homelessness tends to be private and hidden (Sahlin and Thörn, 2000). This invisibility has several implications. First, in demonstrating that there are many more homeless women than are reported in the official statistics, it reflects women's ability to 'solve' their housing problems through staying with friends, relatives or male acquaintances (Hanström, 1991; Järvinen, 1993). This observation is, implicitly and sometimes explicitly, tied to the widespread presumption that women, in order to get a place to stay, often have to 'pay with sex' (NBHW, 2000, p 105; ESO, 1999, p 27). This supposed sexual exploitation leads to the second dimension of women's hidden homelessness, that homeless women feel ashamed of their situation and adopt a variety of strategies to conceal their homelessness (NBHW, 2000, p 105). Even reactions otherwise described as typically male, such as being aggressive, are explained in terms of their trying to conceal sexual exploitation and shame (Beijer, 1998, p 110). Accordingly, when women exhaust alternative strategies and are left with no option than to seek accommodation in homeless shelters, their problems are held to be more severe than they are for men. The third aspect of women's hidden situation is, as argued by Beijer (1998), that homeless women, for a long time, have had to live on men's terms in shelters or in supported housing; their specific needs have not been sufficiently addressed.

Taken together, these aspects of women's hidden homelessness imply that homeless women are different from homeless men in terms of being more vulnerable and dependent, a condition frequently reinforced by their subordinate relationships with homeless 'boyfriends' (Mulinari, 1996); relationships which are pictured as even more oppressive than the male dominance experienced by some housed women. These differences have led to calls for activities and supported housing that target women alone, in order that their specific needs will be attended to. These needs are often identified as the provision of female activities (such as baking, applying cosmetics/make-up, sewing and weaving), a focus on their problems of guilt, shame and poor self-esteem and, finally, the need for assistance in breaking up from men who abuse them. A consequence of this construction is that it is generally argued that, because of their severe problems, treatment must come before any sort of housing, and that it is very difficult for couples to receive treatment and/or housing together. A paradoxical aspect of this interpretation is the focus on traditional female activities. Rather than breaking with traditional gender roles, they reinforce them by directing homeless women towards a certain image of womanhood. The homeless woman is conceived of as an 'unaccommodated woman' in the sense that she lacks shelter as well as the will or capacity to accommodate the dominant image of womanhood (Wardhaugh, 2000).

Reasons to hide? Women's experiences

Homelessness as a stigma

The public image of 'homeless women' in Swedish society is one which is formed and reformed in numerous investigations by various social authorities; it is a social construction presented as part of a discourse which purports to identify the reason for homelessness and the types of problems experienced by homeless women. All the women interviewed for this report related to this image; sometimes it was incorporated into their own histories, on other occasions they reacted against it. The women's personal narratives can, therefore, be seen as a kind of negotiation between how the authorities talk to, with and about them, (their notions of how homelessness is portrayed in the official public discourse), and how they talk about their own situation with other homeless people. Common to most of the interviewees was an understanding and acceptance of homelessness as a stigma. When asked about the house where she temporarily stayed, Becky explained:

> "It is housing for the excluded. It is not regular housing – that is something completely different.... It is a notorious area.... It has been called all those names – I don't even know them all. So you easily get a stigma from living there and that is not good."

Originally stigma meant a bodily mark that was cut or burned into the body in order to bring attention to and warn the public about the stigmatised individual (Goffman, 1963). The stigma was consequently both a warning sign and a punishment – all stigmatised people were socially marginalised criminals or traitors. Accordingly, there was a connection between the body sign and the person's moral inferiority. The current meaning of stigma is something deeply discrediting that spoils an individual's identity. Furthermore, it reduces an individual to what the stigma stands for. 'Homeless' is treated today, by the media and social authorities, as an identity, a personal characteristic, rather than as a condition relating to the housing market. To be female and homeless contains much more significance than just lacking accommodation – such as being poor, vulnerable and sexually exploited. Several of the women interviewed were offended when they were asked them if they were homeless, replying that they were "not like *that*", and accordingly distanced themselves from the label 'homeless'. The hidden dimension of women's homelessness can thus be seen from another perspective – as a deliberate defence against being stigmatised by the various images of homeless women that exist in the official discourse of the authorities and in the media discourse. The rest of this chapter is devoted to a discussion of the different meanings of being visible and invisible and the reasons women hide.

Invisibility and cleanliness

Those who cannot conceal their homelessness are often well aware that they cause a reaction – that they will not pass unnoticed. People keep a physical distance and avoid looking them in the eye. In the interviewees' narratives concerning their daily life, homelessness was frequently connected with uncleanliness. Mimmi did not see herself as homeless:

> "I have never slept in toilets or anything like that. Most of the time I have had a boarding room or a tent so I have seldom needed to sleep in sleazy places, you know, dirty toilets and places like that."

Since Mimmi was not dirty and had not slept in dirty places she could not identify herself as homeless. She said that she took a shower every morning. "You don't want it to show how poorly you live" she explained. In distancing themselves from the stigma of being homeless, to be clean seemed to be of crucial importance for several of the women. By being clean when they moved around in public spaces, they believed that they would not be regarded as homeless and, consequently, in a way become 'invisible'. Anna put it this way:

> "We are very anxious to do that [take showers]. I think that we are even more cautious about our personal care, you know. Because many think that if you are homeless then you wear torn jeans and are dirty, you know. But it is actually the other way around. You always wear new clothes. And if you can't do laundry you have to steal something new.... That is our thing ... that is the *only thing that we can do*. So there is absolutely no one who sees me downtown

and thinks 'she has no housing'. That is the only time I can melt into the crowd."

By being clean, Anna turned the public space into a *temporary refuge* from being seen as homeless – she became an anonymous stranger among other strangers. Sofia also underlined the importance of being clean, otherwise "you really feel like you are an outsider". By being clean the women felt like 'normal' people, and Anna also believed it made 'normal' people more tolerant towards the presence of homeless individuals in their basements or staircases:

> "But if they see that we are normal people too, that we can conduct ourselves and don't muck up or infect the environment. When they see that, that we too can keep things nice and clean I think that they would become more humane and show us some empathy."

Visibility and shame

An important aspect of the interaction between people is the creation of different social spaces. Goffman (1959) argues that we play different roles when presenting ourselves to other people. He makes a distinction between 'front-stage' and 'back-stage'. Front-stage is public space where we present ourselves to others and are mindful that we can be watched. Back-stage, on the other hand, refers to private spaces where we can relax and do whatever we like and prepare ourselves for presentations in the front-stage. Back-stage also includes those spaces where bodily needs can be taken care of. To distinguish between these two regions and to keep the body clean in the front-stage is, according to Young (1990), to demonstrate respectability. This means:

> ... conforming to the norms that repress sexuality, bodily functions, and emotional expression.... The body should be clean in all respects, and cleaned of its aspects that betoken its fleshiness – fluids, dirt, smells. The enviroment in which respectable people dwell must also be clean, purified: no dirt, no dust, no garbage, and all signs of bodily function – eating, excreting, sex, birthing – *should be hidden behind closed doors.* (Young 1990, pp 136-137; emphasis added)

Those who cannot hide behind closed doors have no option but to live their private lives in other people's front-stages, where they risk being seen in situations which they would rather hide from other people's gaze. They become dirt in the sense of Douglas (1966), that is, out of place. Wright (1997, p 40) argues that homeless people's mere presence in the city, and their activities such as sleeping and eating on the streets, urinating in parks and so forth, signal that they are in the 'wrong' place doing the 'wrong' things. Therefore, homeless people are a kind of symbolic dirt in public spaces and they are also often described as dirty.

When identified as homeless, the women interviewees felt both exposed and vulnerable. Public spaces can, then, be viewed as both places of potential refuge from the stigma of homelessness and as a *critical milieu*, where homeless women risk violation of their self-esteem and feelings of shame about themselves and their situation (Johansson, 1997, p 95).

Even when the women interviewees had strategies designed to hide their homelessness, there were situations when it was impossible, such as at night-time when they tried to sleep in someone's basement or in a public toilet. Anna tried to find places where she knew that she could be alone, such as old air-raid shelters. It did occur to her that she could sleep in public toilets, but she did not like that idea, "you just want to hide yourself", she explained. Mia said that she had tried to sleep in staircases, but that "then they consider you shabby. They almost chased you with a broom". According to Mia, if you are homeless you have to be prepared to be treated as dirt, something which has to be "cleaned away". Lillian also used this metaphor for an event when she slept in a basement and a man poured a bucket of water over her. In these situations of exposed homelessness it does not matter whether women are clean or not, because the symbolic dirt they constitute cannot be washed off.

Pride and prejudice

"Well, just imagine if you are homeless and need to stay with somebody, it implies that you have to pay with something and it is often with your body. To get liquor and drugs. So they are exploited." (Interview with social worker)

"For a homeless woman there is always somewhere to sleep. If she pays." (Poster for the City Mission with a picture of a used condom)

Women with no homes are frequently presumed to be sexually exploited in order to secure a roof over their head. In the social worker's discourse this presumption is combined with the idea that this condition gives women a reason to conceal their homelessness. The women interviewed in this report were well aware of this official image and it made it difficult for them in their contacts with the social authorities. Mia said:

"Many times when I came to the social services office they had preconceived ideas that I prostituted myself just to have somewhere to stay. But that was out of the question and I got so angry that they could even think something like that."

When asked about her feelings of being exposed as a homeless woman Sofia was offended, as if the question had some implicit intention. She said,

"I would *never* go to bed with someone – not on those premises. *Never* – that's not the way I am."

Presumptions of prostitution can also lead to homeless women avoiding shelters. Sandra said that she would "rather sleep in a tent" than go to a shelter, because she feared acquiring the stigma of being a homeless woman including suspicions of selling sex in order to have a roof over her head. Consequently, *images* of homeless women as prostitutes can imply that some of them deny their homelessness. According to Lillian:

"It has always been clear to me that I have to say 'no I am not homeless'. Or else you have to explain that you are really *not* a prostitute."

In order to avoid the stigma of being homeless several women deny their situation and avoid places where they could be identified as homeless. So shelters, and even the local authority office, are perceived by women as a critical milieu.

The ambivalent value of the other's gaze

The interviewed women talked about other people's gaze with ambivalence. They expressed, on the one hand, that they did not want to be seen as homeless but as 'normal' people and, on the other hand, how humiliating it could be to be ignored when asking for help. It seems that feelings of shame are intimately related to not being viewed by another person as an equal. Sara, for example, never managed to find a shower when she lived in the street for two months and she felt she became a nobody during this time:

> "You could see really quickly that you did not belong to society anymore. You could see that from my looks. I was surprised, really scared, when I looked in the mirror. Just to go in somewhere to shop and then you meet a shop-assistant – all these kinds of meetings become incredibly difficult because you could see exactly who I was. Like a traditional beggar – but a woman, and that is even worse."

Shame is related to other people's gaze as it is closely tied to feelings of inferiority and vulnerability (Katz, 1999). Sara's shame was related to a feeling of not belonging anymore, and the feeling that it was obvious from the way she looked. She said that other people viewed her with a distant look and seemed bothered: "It was like I didn't exist anymore". Sara felt invisible; she felt that people ignored her because they identified her as homeless. The shame that Sara felt made it very difficult for her to meet people and even harder for her to ask for help. But she also said that when she got desperate for a place to stay she went out to bars in the evening and asked women for help, but was often refused. To ask for help and show your vulnerability and to be denied help, reinforces feelings of shame and a sense that no one *sees* you. On the other hand, being seen and helped, but being treated as a victim, can also cause shame, the shame of being viewed as helpless. Lillian avoided a day centre for homeless women for this reason.

> "You become what people treat you like, and if they treat me like a homeless vulnerable woman I feel like that. And even if that's the way it is – if you don't live according to that it does not feel that hard."

To be treated as a victim, argues psychiatrist Lifton (1996), is further victimisation, as you are no longer treated as an individual but as a 'living dead', a symbol for the circumstances you have been through. In this way people distance themselves from the designated victims.

Being seen is related to being trusted. Several of the women interviewed used the expression 'worthless' when they described how they felt about their situation. Sandra linked this sense of being worthless to a feeling of not being able to do the right thing, namely, to have a house.

> "My God, I am a grown-up and I didn't even have a flat. The self-esteem got really low. You felt really worthless.... Worthless when you can't even have a home."

Sandra argued that the only thing that can release her from shame would be to be *trusted*. She wanted to be *seen* as a normal, grown up woman who can take care of her own life and handle her own housing situation.

The right to 'hide behind the door'

In his 1992 article Sommerville argues that homelessness can be characterised as material poverty and lack of a private sphere. Those who are homeless have no access to a room of their own, in its double sense – material and psychological – but have to live under circumstances that they cannot control. This means that when they find somewhere to live – at a friend's place, in a basement or in supported housing, they may lose this place. And even though several women did not identify themselves as homeless, no one felt that they had a home. When the women interviewees were asked what a home meant to them, it was not surprising that a recurrent theme was to do with feelings of control and power. None of the women associated home, in the first instance, with family, husband or sense of community, but rather with a place of their own. The home was described as a place where they could be protected from the chaos 'out there', where they could feel safe from other people's intrusion on their privacy – a place in which they and only they had control. Home was described first and foremost in terms of exclusion – as a place where you can exclude other people. To Susan this was the fundamental principle of home:

> "In your own home you can ask people to leave. I almost never do that but that is your right."

To describe 'home' in this way can be seen both in terms of the women's experience – all of them had been or are excluded from other people's homes – and in terms of their wish for rooms of their own, where they have the power to exclude others. Homeless people lack this right; but it was of symbolic importance for them to have the right to draw boundaries around their own selves. The right to a home was expressed by the women as the right to a 'back-stage', and many women used the door as a metaphor for being at home. Anna, for example, said:

> "Home for me is when you open a door and lock the door. Then you are at home. Home is safety – it is your territory – there I can do whatever I want to."

The locked door represented Anna's ability to control and execute power over her private sphere. She described it as a place where she herself could set the limits of what she could or could not do. To be able to decide who could enter the home seemed to be of crucial importance. If they did not have that control over the door they didn't feel that they had a home. Simmel (1994) argues that the door is a symbol for human freedom. Since the door can be closed and opened, it represents power and control as well as generosity and solidarity. The last thing Sara said before she left the interview was:"Freedom, that is a door". The explicit connection of home to a door may be interpreted as a wish for a private sphere, which a closed door offers, and at the same time for the opportunity to be able to invite people in, something else which homeless people are denied. Their own home is consequently the place were they can 'hide' from other people's gaze, a back-stage where they are in control and can be alone.

Conclusions

This chapter has focused on women's experiences of homelessness and two interrelated and recurrent themes in the discourse on homeless women – that women 'hide' and 'feel' shame. The narratives of the interviewed women express an ongoing struggle with this representation of homeless women. In opposition to the notion that women conceal their homelessness out of shame of their behaviour, we have argued that concealment should be seen as a deliberate strategy designed to avoid the stigma of being homeless. The women are reacting to the official and public image of homeless women as prostitutes, as dirty, or as victims. Two main strategies that the women use to conceal their homelessness have been considered – being clean and avoiding shelters and day-centres for homeless women. Public space and shelters are, although in different ways, experienced as critical milieus where they feel humiliated and ashamed. Their shame is thus directly related to experiences of being identified as a homeless woman, an identity that they perceive as degrading. At the same time they want to be recognised and accepted as individuals who have no place of their own – which for many is something different from being homeless. They want help to get housing and they want to be respected as individuals, with a right to privacy, and to be trusted to take care of themselves. But these expressed needs are not in line with what the social authorities define as their 'special needs'. In today's discourses on homeless people, and homeless women in particular, rights are replaced by needs – which are implied in the construction of homeless women as sexually exploited, with severe problems due to the long concealment of their situation and their low self-esteem and feelings of shame. In this discourse, the women's own expressed needs for housing and of being in control of their own lives remain unheard, and, as Lillian stated, "... a home of one's own should be a right, not a privilege".

Note

[1] The interviews were completed for a dissertation concerning women's experiences of home and homelessness. The idea for the dissertation grew out of a two-year research project about young homeless women and the concept of 'being an outsider'. The results from this project are discussed in Thörn (2000).

NINETEEN

Conclusions

Bill Edgar and Joe Doherty

Introduction

The research evidence presented in this report has illustrated the scale of homelessness among women in the European Union and suggests an intriguing consistency between member states. First, all the national reports indicate that the typical form of homelessness among women is 'hidden' homelessness. Second, while the evidence drawn from each country demonstrates that rooflessness remains a predominantly male problem, up to a fifth of the street homeless and around a third of all homeless people are women. Third, data from homeless service provider records indicate that over recent years, in most countries, women represent an increasing proportion of users. Fourth, and perhaps most significantly, there is an observable change in the composition of the female homelessness population reflected in increases in younger women and in women from ethnic minority groups or immigrant backgrounds.

The national reports also clearly demonstrate the multiplicity of the causes of women's homelessness. While relationship factors represent key variables in the description of homelessness among women, they are not a sufficient explanation. In a context where women's access to housing is becoming less dependent on a male breadwinner, it is to be expected that the importance of relationship factors will diminish and their nature will change. In both strong and weak male breadwinner societies, structural changes define a social and economic context which leaves female-headed households vulnerable to the vagaries of the housing market and undermines the capacity of women to maintain independent autonomous households.

The national reports describe a pattern of service provision available to homeless women which, through most European states, shares a common genesis. Each of the national reports questions the effectiveness and appropriateness of these services in meeting the needs of homeless women, especially their effectiveness in preventing homelessness, in alleviating the stresses of homelessness and in facilitating the permanent resettlement of homeless women. Services for homeless people throughout Europe have historically been modelled on the provision for an archetypal homeless male and, even today, they display little gender sensitivity and are unresponsive to the changing needs of a growing and heterogeneous population of homeless women.

Pathways to homelessness

The view that a woman's housing history can be described simply by her relationship history does not reflect either the changed familial situation of European women during the last quarter of a century, nor the growing heterogeneity of their socio-economic circumstances. Explanations of the vulnerability of women and female-headed households in the housing market, and their susceptibility to homelessness, require an understanding of the way structural, relationship and personal factors interact in often quite complex ways. Within the context of the changed structural characteristics of both the labour market and the housing market across Europe, the vulnerability of women to the risk of homelessness reflects a combination of their economic, family, parental and ethnic status. Women whose economic position in the labour market is weak are particularly vulnerable; a vulnerability compounded by the erosion of the mediating role of family support and the inadequacy of social protection systems.

The preceding chapters have demonstrated the prevalence of a wide diversity of circumstances with regard to the role of the family in providing support to vulnerable women. In Mediterranean countries (Portugal, Spain and Greece) and in some continental European countries (Belgium, Luxembourg, France, Germany) the support role of the family, if less secure than in the recent past, is still evident. In other countries (Scandinavia, the UK and, more recently, Ireland), as women have become commodified and entered the labour market in increasing numbers, the social and welfare support role of the family has diminished. The commodification of women, however, has often been characterised by low paid and insecure employment that does not provide sufficient resources for the maintenance of autonomous households. Nor does it secure adequate access to social insurance or welfare protection sufficient to guarantee access to decent and permanent accommodation, particularly in circumstances where the provision of affordable social housing is diminishing. Through a process of defamilialisation the state has absorbed some of the risks previously accounted for within the family, but this process has been uneven: a near universal provision in Denmark and Sweden, it has been much more selective in the UK and Ireland as well as in many continental countries, while in other countries, mostly Mediterranean, it is virtually absent.

While the impact of social protection systems varies across welfare regimes, the evidence presented in this book indicates that it is women with children who are most likely to be protected in most countries. Protection is weakest for women with children in countries where there is a lack of social rented housing and in strong male breadwinner societies (and especially where there is a concurrence of the two). Lone parents, especially younger mothers, are more likely to be reliant on family support or confessional services in countries such as Ireland, Spain and Greece, while in social-democratic regime countries single mothers benefit most from state protection. Changes in the efficacy of family support together with the uneven landscape of social protection combine to mean that it is mainly young and older single women without children (or who have lost the custody of their children) and immigrant women who are least likely to find protection from vulnerability in the housing market.

Such explanations need to be framed within the (family) life-course stage of women – youth, adult or old age – if they are to be effective in guiding policy solutions. The relevance of the life course concept, in the development of an understanding of the causes of homelessness among women, is not so much the insight which it provides with regard to the stresses and needs which women experience at different stages in their lives, but rather that it emphasises the 'transition phases' in women's lives when they may be more vulnerable. This is not to imply that homelessness among women will be episodic or of short duration, but rather that their vulnerability may be greater at key life stages – for example, leaving home, the birth of a child, the break-up of a relationship. Equally women's needs and the efficacy of services in meeting those needs may be different at each of these stages of transition.

Service provision and women's experiences of homelessness

While the structural, societal and governance changes described in this book have contributed to the housing vulnerability of those female-headed households who are in a weak economic and labour market situation, there has not been a concomitant recorded increase in street homelessness among women. Homelessness among women typically remains hidden. Several explanations are posited for this situation. Firstly, it is argued (Sahlin and Thörn, 2000, ch 18) that women wish to avoid the stigma attached to being homeless. This stigma is variously attributed to the loss of status as a mother, carer or homemaker or to the popular mythology or perception of homeless women as 'fallen' women and prostitutes. Secondly, it is argued that women are more resourceful in managing their precarious housing circumstances using well-developed coping strategies which involve reliance on extended social networks or male dependency (Pels, 2000, ch 16). Finally, it is argued that women avoid using homeless services which tend to be male dominated and in which they risk exposure to violence and abuse (Enders–Dragässer, 2000, ch 17).

The 'hidden' nature of homelessness among women is also explained, in part, by the availability of specialist, targeted services – which are not everywhere classified as homeless services – for victims of relationship break-ups and for lone parents. Women fleeing domestic violence and vulnerable young single mothers avoid being recorded as homeless in that they can access specialist service support and accommodation (albeit temporary) even if, in some countries and in some areas, there is an under-provision of such services. The increase in the use of homelessness services by women in recent years has thus mainly been among young single women (under 24 years of age) and among women of immigrant and ethnic origin. However, it is also frequently reported that there remains a 'residual' population of older homeless women who are frequently characterised as having mental health problems.

In all European states, and thus in all the welfare regime types, there is evidence of some similarity in the patterns of service provision for homeless women and for women at risk of homelessness. In the formative welfare regimes the pattern of service provision is epitomised by Portugal, where Baptista and Bruto da Costa (2000) describe the development of services for young single mothers from a confessional origin, the evolution of services for women fleeing domestic violence from a feminist lobby and general services from a philanthropic tradition.

In the Continental regimes a distinction between mother and child services, women's refuges and general services is described in almost all countries. In the Netherlands, for example, there is a clear distinction between women's shelters (*FIOM*) for vulnerable single mothers and women's refuges (*Blijf van mijn Lijfhuizen*) for women fleeing domestic violence. In Germany, the development of services from the feminist movement was so strong that refuges for women fleeing domestic violence form a distinctive sector of service provision operationally and ideologically separated from homelessness services. In the Liberal/ Atlantic regime a diversity of situations prevail. In Ireland the prevalence of confessional services suggests comparisons with Mediterranean countries, while in the UK the origins and funding of services via the Women's Aid movement suggests similarities with the pattern of service provision in Germany and the Netherlands. In the Nordic countries, on the other hand, where levels of single-parent households are relatively low (with the exception of Finland), and where social protection systems for women with children are adequate, homeless services for vulnerable single mothers are less evident. On the other hand, while the proportion of single female-headed households is relatively high in the Nordic countries social protection systems are not attuned to mediate the vulnerability they may face in the housing market.

The genesis of service development in Europe suggests a bifurcation of service provision in which women-oriented services are under-provided and generalist services lack gender sensitivity. Women-oriented services have typically emerged chronologically, first to meet the needs of young vulnerable single mothers and then to meet the needs of women fleeing domestic violence. This leaves a gap in service provision for other groups of women (young single women and older women) or throws them back on reliance on generalist services which have a strong male orientation. However, there is some evidence that women's services are beginning to diversify with women's shelters, for example, beginning to open up to meet the needs of groups of women other than those fleeing domestic violence. On the other hand, there is other evidence to suggest that the continued enforcement of strict rules of access continue to exclude some groups of women (for example, those involved in drug abuse) from specialist services such as women's refuges. Both situations suggest the lack of an holistic approach to the needs of women who may be vulnerable in the housing market.

Prevention

In so far as the majority of women at risk of homelessness remain living in precarious housing circumstances, in temporary accommodation, living with family and friends, cohabiting or sharing involuntarily, then we need to consider whether (or to what extent) strategies of prevention enable them to move into independent accommodation without recourse to homelessness services. Tosi (2000a) suggests that, in Italy, women are the main clients, and the largest growing group of clients, at offices for adults in difficulty. However, there is little evidence in the research presented in this book to indicate that existing services are directed at hidden homeless women or designed to meet their needs. Enders-Dragässer (2000) describes a number of innovative pilot projects in Germany which have developed women-focused services involving a range of services from advice and day centres to support and housing which are run by women and for women. However, the pilot nature of these projects is indicative of their absence among existing service provision. Elsewhere evidence suggests that there is a limited understanding or perception of the extent or nature of hidden homelessness among women; even in the most benign circumstances we can conclude that services are not geared to the needs of women whose housing situation remains hidden homelessness.

Alleviation

The evidence that women are underrepresented in generalist homelessness services, together with the argument that they avoid male-dominated services, suggests that there is an absence of gender-sensitive services to alleviate the effects of homelessness among women. Where gender-specific services have emerged – in relation to the (confessional) services for young single mothers and the (feminist-inspired) services for women fleeing domestic violence – they have been limited in scope and targeted at specific groups. The problem of the absence of gender-directed services is further compounded by evidence (for example, from Belgium; see Chapter Eight) which suggests that in those circumstances where services meet the support needs of women, then women tend to remain in those services for longer periods and turnover is low. Hence other homeless women must have recourse to traditional hostel services or are excluded from services altogether and remain hidden homeless. This dilemma leads to a conundrum where lack of capacity of gender-specific support reinforces the perception that there is only a limited need. The need for gender-specific and gender-sensitive services is, arguably, more urgent where services for homeless people are characterised by traditional hostel and emergency services. Where services provide self-contained housing with support, then gender issues such as that of privacy and the fear of violence and abuse should disappear.

Resettlement

There is considerable evidence from the national reports that women respond positively to the provision of gender-sensitive support and housing. However, the evidence which is available on the outcomes of supported (gender-specific) services shows that a high proportion of women return to live with a (former) partner rather than establish their own household in permanent housing. Part of the reason for this is suggested by Enders-Dragässer (2000; see also Chapter Seventeen) who indicates that service provision (in Germany) to meet the employment and training needs of women (who are often in a weak labour market position) is largely absent from existing service provision for homeless women. She further suggests that the coordination of existing services to meet these needs is fraught with difficulties and is only weakly developed. Novak and Schoibl's discussion of services in Austria (Chapter Ten), corroborates Enders-Dragässer's arguments. Given the evidence about the feminisation of poverty and the immiserisation of female-headed households, the inadequacy of joined-up policies in this arena is inexcusable.

It is evidence such as this which suggests that there are clear weaknesses in the existing landscape of service provision for women whether we view the picture from a macro-level or micro-level of analysis. Service provision is weakest at the structural level in meeting women's needs for appropriate training or employment support and in enabling them to gain access to and maintain permanent, independent accommodation. Overall there is a lack of gender-specific and gender-sensitive services that address the needs of homeless women and those services that do exist tend to be insufficiently focused on women's felt and experienced needs. These deficiencies point to a need for a greater range of services – low threshold as well as supported housing – that address issues of prevention and resettlement as well as alleviation. It is clear also that services need to adapt to meet the changing profile of women who are vulnerable in the housing market. Women's aid refuges have been successful because they have focused services to a particular need based on a clear understanding of the nature of that need. Services for young women and for women from ethnic minority groups need to be similarly focused and more widely available.

Further research

This book has, for the first time, provided a picture of the nature and causes of homelessness among women across the European member states. However, the evidence accumulated here is patchy and uneven and a fuller understanding of the nature of homelessness among women and the formulation of appropriate policy instruments requires considerably more research. In conclusion we identify a number of potentially fruitful areas of investigation.

While there is some evidence that homelessness, and the risk of homelessness, has been increasing in many countries, the more important feature is the changing composition of female service users. The reasons for the increasing proportion of young women among service users are not clearly understood on the basis of the evidence presented here. Equally, the implications of this trend can be interpreted in different ways as we argue Chapter Three. This points to the need for longitudinal research focused on the pathways into and out of homelessness for young women. Such research would also need to focus on their experiences of services particularly in so far as this may be related to repeat homelessness.

The emergence, in some countries, of women from ethnic minority groups as a significant element among the female homeless also suggests that further research needs to focus on a hitherto relatively neglected issue of culture in framing adequate explanations of homelessness among women. The evidence from Italy (Chapter Thirteen) and the Netherlands (Chapter Fourteen) presented in this book clearly demonstrates that issues of economic dependency, levels of single parenthood and cohabitation vary hugely from one ethnic community (for example, West Indian versus Islamic) to another.

The research evidence confirms the persistence of relationship breakdown as a trigger to homelessness. There is mention also, in a number of countries, of the persistence of a cluster of older women among the homeless population. However, rather than focusing on the circumstances of particular groups of women, in the case history approach adopted in many previous studies, research could more fruitfully compare the triggers to homelessness at different life course transition stages.

The arguments underlying many of the chapters in this book present the case for gender-sensitive as well as gender-specific service provision and for the improved coordination of services to meet the specific needs of women. The need for gender-sensitive services to alleviate homelessness is argued for from two distinct perspectives: that women have specific and distinct needs, and that specialist services are needed to protect women from abuse and exploitation. Enders-Dragässer (2000) argues that women's needs are distinctive to the extent that the cause of their homelessness arises from an abusive relationship, that their need for support emanates from their caring responsibilities and that their physiology requires privacy and the provision of specific health services. The absence of services which cater for such needs is seen as one of the reasons, perhaps the main reason, why women adopt a range of strategies to avoid homelessness services. Evidence points also to the fact that even those existing services that demonstrate some sensitivity to issues of gender are struggling to cope with the (often changing) needs of particular groups of women – women from ethnic minority groups 4and young drug users, for example. This indicates the need for research focused on the needs and experiences of female service users generally and for the improved dissemination of best practice in addressing the needs of specific groups of women.

References

Abrahamson, P. (1999) 'The welfare modelling business', *Social Policy and Administration*, vol 33, no 4, pp 394-415.

Ackers, L. (1998) *Shifting spaces: Women, citizenship and migration within the European Union*, Bristol: The Policy Press.

Agee, M.L. and Walker, R.W. (1990) 'Is there any truth to the buzz words "feminisation of poverty"?', *International Journal of Social Economics*, vol 17, no 5, pp 18-30.

Alberdi, J. (1993) 'La familia, propiedad y aspectos jurídicos', in L. Garrido and E. Gil Calvo (eds) *Estrategias Familiares*, Madrid: Alianza.

Aldridge, R. (2000) *Women, exclusion and homelessness*, National Report 1999 for the European Observatory on Homelessness, Brussels: FEANTSA.

Alexander K. (1999) *Homelessness factfile 1998-99*, London: London Research Centre and Crisis.

An Garda Siochana (1999) *Annual report of the Garda Siochana*, Dublin: Government Publications.

Andersen, J. (2000) *Jyllandsposten*, 16 January.

Anderson, I. (1995) *National inquiry into youth homelessness*, London: CHAR.

Anderson, I. and Tulloch, D. (2000) *Pathways through homelessness: A review of the research evidence*, Homelessness Task Force Research Series, Edinburgh: Scottish Homes.

Anderson, I., Kemp, P. and Quilgars, N. (1993) *Single homeless people*, London: HMSO.

Anttonen, A. (1996) 'The welfare state, women and social citizenship in Finland', in U.-M. Perttula and J. Sipilä (eds) *Social policy in Scandinavia: Essays on history, gender and future changes*, Series C 8/1996, Tampere: Department of Social Policy, University of Tampere.

APAV (Associação Portuguesa de Apoio à Vítima) (1997) *Manual ALCIPE para Atendimento de Mulheres Vitimas de Vislência*, Lison: APAV.

Ariño Villarroya, A. (1995) 'La doble marginación', in S. Sarasa, and L. Moreno, *El Estado de Bienestar en la Europa del Sur*, Madrid: CSIC.

Arnmark, L. and Raun, M. (1998) *Solidaritet i det moderne samfund. Speciale*, Copenhagen: Institut for Statskundskab, Københavns Universitet.

Asukasvalintatyöryhmän muistio (1999) Suomen ympäristö 276, Asuminen, Helsinki: Ympäristöministeriö.

Avramov, D. (1995) *Homelessness in the European Union – Social and legal context of housing exclusion in the 1990s*, Brussels: FEANTSA.

BAG Wohnungslosenhilfe (1999) *BAG Informationen Weibliche Wohnungsnot*, Bielefeld.

Balchin, P. (ed) (1996) *Housing policy in Europe*, London: Routledge.

Ball, M. and Harloe, M. (1998) 'Uncertainty in European housing markets', in M. Kleinman, W. Matznetter and M. Stephens (eds) *European integration and housing policy*, London: Routledge.

Ball, M. and Wood, A. (1999) 'Housing investment: long run international trends and volatility', *Housing Studies*, vol 14, no 2, pp 185-209.

Bang, H., Jensen, P.H. and Pfau-Effinger, B. (2000) 'Gender and European welfare states', in S. Duncan and B. Pfau-Effinger (eds) *Gender, economy and culture in the European Union*, London: Routledge, pp 115-42.

Baptista, I. and Bruto da Costa, A. (2000) *Women, exclusion and homelessness*, National Report 1999 for the European Observatory on Homelessness, Brussels: FEANTSA.

Barlow, J. (1998) 'Planning, housing and the European Union', in M. Kleinman, W. Matznetter and M. Stephens (eds) *European integration and housing policy*, London: Routledge, pp 113-24.

Barroso, R. and Martín Símón, F. (1994) *Intervención social con transeúntes en Extremadura*, Departamento de Psicología y Sociología de la Educación, Universidad de Extremadura, Sin publicar.

Bateman, R., de Graaf, L., Oudijk, C. and Poortvliet, N. (1999) *Dak-en thuisloze vrouwen in Rotterdam, Vlaardingen en Spijkenisse*, Rotterdam: COS.

Bauman, Z. (1996) *Work, consumerism and the new poor*, Buckingham: Open University Press.

Beck, U. (1992) *Risk society*, London: Sage Publications.

Behrens, L. H. and Raal, K. (1999a) *Kortlægning. Kvinder og børn fra etniske minoriteter på krisecentre*, Esbjerg: Formidlingscenteret for Socialt arbejde.

Behrens, L.H. and Raal, K. (1999b) *Man kan mærke, når hun er i huset, KRIB-puljen – delrapport 2*, Esbjerg: Formidlingscenteret for Socialt arbejde.

Beijer, U. (1998) *Hemlösa kvinnor i Stockholm*, FoU-rapport 1998:7, Stockholm: Research and Development Department, Social Services.

Bell, J. (1989) *Women and children first*, Report by the National Campaign for the Homeless, Dublin.

Bellah, R. (1986) *Habits of the heart: Individualism and commitment in American Life*, New York, NY: Harper Row.

Bento, A., Barreto, E. and Pires, T. (1996) *Os Sem-abrigo nas ruas de Lisboa*, Lisbon: SCML.

Berlingske Tidende (1996) *Psykisk syge lokkes på stoffer*, Tema 8, 14 April.

Blangiardo, G. and Terzera, L. (1997) *L'immigrazione straniera nell'area milanese*, Provincia di Milano, Ismu, Milano.

Blasi, G.L. (1990) 'Social policy and social science research on homelessness', *Journal of Social Issues*, vol 46, no 4, pp 207-19.

Boelhouwer, P. and van der Heijden, H. (1992) *Housing systems in Europe, Part 1:A comparative study of housing policy*, Delft: Delft University Press.

Boelhouwer, P., van der Heijden, H. and Priemus, H. (1996) 'The Netherlands', in P. Balchin (ed) *Housing policy in Europe*, London: Routledge.

Borchorst, A. (1998) 'Køn, velfærdsstatsmodeller og familiepolitik', in B. Larsen and H. Møller (eds) *Socialpolitik*, Copenhagen: Munksgård.

Borges, G. (1995) *Caracterização sócio-económica dos Utilizadores do Refeitório dos Anjos*, Lisbon: SCML.

Børner Stax, T. (1997a) *Om hjemløshed: Begreber, typer, tal og metoder*, arbejdspapir, Copenhagen: Socialforskningsinstituttet.

Børner Stax, T. (1997b) *Youth homelessness in Denmark: National Report 1996*, Brussels: FEANTSA.

Børner Stax, T. (1998) *From shelter to dwelling: A re-integrative project at Mændenes Hjem*, Brussels: FEANTSA.

Børner Stax, T. (2000a) *Én gang socialt marginaliseret – altid ...?*, Copenhagen: The Danish National Institute for Social Research.

Børner Stax, T. (2000b) 'Understandings of homelessness and social policy in Denmark', in V. Polakow and C. Guillean (eds) *Homelessness*, Westport, CT: Greenwood Publishing Group, INC.

Børner Stax, T. and Kæmpe, J. (1999) *Support and housing: Two complementary aspects of a social policy*, Brussels: FEANTSA.

Børner Stax, T. and Koch-Nielsen, I. (1996) *National Report 1995: Homelessness in Denmark*, Brussels: FEANTSA.

Bramley, G. (1994) 'An affordability crisis in British housing: dimensions, causes and policy impact', *Housing Studies*, vol 9, no 1, pp 103-24.

Brandt, P. (1992) *Yngre hjemløse i København*, Copenhagen: FADL's forlag.

Burrows, R., Pleace, N. and Quilgars, D. (1997) *Homelessness and social policy*, London: Routledge.

Byudvalget (1994) *Rapport nr 2 fra Byudvalget*, Juni, Copenhagen.

Cabrera, P. J. (1998) *Huéspedes del aire: Sociología de las personas sin hogar en Madrid*, Madrid: UPCO.

Cabrera, P. (2000) *Women, exclusion and homelessness in Spain*, National Report 1999 for the European Observatory on Homelessness, Brussels: FEANTSA.

Callan, T. (1999) *Monitoring poverty trends data from the 1997 Living in Ireland Survey*, Dublin: Economic and Social Research Institute/ Department of Family Community and Family Affairs.

Cantillon, B. (1999) 'Vrouwen-armoede: de prijs voor een onvoltooide emancipatie', in B. Cantillon (ed) *De welvaartsstaat in de kering*, Kapellen: Pelckmans, pp 195-216.

Cantillon, B., De Lathouwer, L., Marx, I., Van Dam, R. and Van den Bosch, K. (1999) *Sociale indicatoren: 1976-1997*, Antwerpen: Centrum voor Sociaal Beleid.

Carchedi, F., De Filippo, E., Morlicchio, E., Morniroli, A., Orientale, G., Pugliese, E. and Tagliacozzo, C. (1999) 'Povertà e immigrazione', in E. Mingione (ed) *Le sfide dell'esclusione: Metodi, luoghi, soggetti*, Bologna: Il Mulino.

Caritas (1990) *Annual report*, Madrid.

Caritas di Roma (1999) *Immigrazione. Dossier statistico 1999*, Roma: Anterem.

Caritas di Roma (2000) *Immigrazione. Dossier statistico 2000*, Roma: Anterem.

Caritas Italiana and Fondazione Zancan (1997) *I bisogni dimenticati. Rapporto 1996 su emarginazione ed esclusione sociale*, Milano: Feltrinelli.

Carlson, H. (1990) 'Women and homelessness in Ireland', *The Irish Journal of Psychology*, vol 11, no 1, pp 68-76.

Casanova, L., Lucas, J., Alves, N., Mata, J. and Bettencourt, N. (1998) *Dar voz aos utentes*, Lisbon: SCML.

Castel, R. (1993) 'Plus d'un français sur deux redoute d'être exclu', *La Rue*, no 2, pp 13-14.

CECS (1999) *Informe España 1998*, Madrid: Fundación Encuentro.

Centrepoint (1998) 'Women's homelessness reaching record levels', *National Development News*.

Christiansen, A. (1993) *Bedre bebyggelser -bedre liv?*, SBI-byplanlægning 65, Hørsholm: Statens Byggeforskningsinstitut.

Christensen, A. and Koch-Nielsen, I. (1992) *Vold ude og hjemme*, SFI, 92:4, Copenhagen: Levevilkår i Danmark.

Coles, B., Rugg, J. and Seavers, J. (1999) 'Young adults living in the parental home: the implications of extended youth transitions for housing and social policy', in J. Rugg (ed) *Young people, housing and social policy*, London: Routledge,

Comité de las Regiones, Unión Europea (1999) *Dictamen sobre 'El problema de los "sin techo" y la vivienda'*, Brussels, 2-3 de junio, CDR 376/98 fin.

Commission for Racial Equality (1990) *Sorry it's gone: Testing for racial discrimination in the private rented housing sector*, London: CRE.

Commissione per le politiche di integrazione degli immigrati (2000) *Secondo rapporto sull'integrazione degli immigrati in Italia*, Rome: Dipartimento per gli Affari Sociali, Presidenza del Consiglio dei Ministri.

Cook, G. and McCashin, A. (1997) 'Male breadwinner: a case study of gender and social security', in A. Byrne and M. Leonard (eds) *Women and Irish society: A sociological reader*, Belfast: Beyond the Pale Publications, pp 167-80.

Corbillon, M. and Dulery, A. (1996) *Education familiale en Centres maternels*, intervention 5th EUSARF European Congress, London, 13 September.

Cortés Alcalá, L. and Paniagua Caparrós, J.L. (1997) 'La vivienda como factor de exclusión social', *Documentación Social*, vol 106, pp 93-147.

Council for the Homeless Northern Ireland (1999) *Homelessness in Northern Ireland April 1998-March 1999*, Belfast: Council for the Homeless.

Cousins, C. (1999) *Society, work and welfare in Europe*, Basingstoke: Macmillan.

Cousins, M. (1995) *The Irish social welfare system: Law and policy*, Dublin: Roundhall Press.

Cousins, M. (1997) 'Ireland's place in the worlds of welfare capitalism', *Journal of European Social Policy*, vol 7, no 3, pp 223-35.

Cox, G. and Lawless, M. (1999) *Wherever I lay my hat.... A study of out of home drug users*, Dublin: Merchant's Quay Project.

Crane, M. (1997) *Homeless truths: Challenging myths about older homeless people*, London: Crisis and Help the Aged.

CRASH (Construction Industry Relief and Assistance for the Single Homeless) (1995 and 1996) *Statistics on London winter shelters*, London: CRASH.

CREDOC (1999) *L'accueil en urgence des personnes en difficulté sociale*, Recueils et documents, no 1, FNARS – CREDOC, February.

Croes, M., Huijts, G., Mastenbroek, M. and Römkens, R. (1990) *Opvangvoorzieningen en mishandelde vrouwen*, Utrecht: NIZW.

DARES (1999) 'Emploi et salaires: les inégalités entre femmes et hommes en mars 1998', *Premières informations premières sythèses*, no 32.2, août.

Davies, J. and Lyle, S. (1996) *Discounted voices: Homelessness amongst young black and minority ethnic people in England*, Leeds: University of Leeds.

De Bruijn, J.G.M., Derksen, L.D. and Hoeberichts, C.M.J. (eds) (1993) *The women's movement: History and theory*, Aldershot: Avebury.

De Decker, P. (1998) *The rise of social rental agencies in Belgium*, Brussels: FEANTSA.

De Decker, P. (2000) *Women, exclusion and homelessness: Access to services and opportunities*, Brussels: FEANTSA.

De Decker, P. and Raes, K. (1996) *Access to housing, processes of exclusion and tenure (in)security in Belgium*, Brussels: FEANTSA.

De Decker, P. and Serriën, L. (1997) *Trends in housing and (youth) homelessness*, Brussels: FEANTSA.

De Decker, P. and Geurts, V. (2000) 'Wonen: residualiseert de huursector?', in J. Vranken (ed) *Armoede en sociale uitsluiting. Jaarboek 2000*, Leuven: Acco, pp 193-204.

De Decker, P., Meulemans, B. and Geurts, V. (1997) 'Trouble in paradise? On rising housing problems in Belgium', *Netherlands Journal of Housing and the Built Environment*, vol 12, no 3, pp 281-306.

de Elejabeitia, C. (1996) 'Feminización de la Pobreza', *Documentación Social*, vol 105.

de Feijter, H. (2000) *Women, exclusion and homelessness*, National Report 1999 for the European Observatory on Homelessness, Brussels: FEANTSA.

De Haes, V. (1994) *Leven van de bijstand: Een onderzoek naar de persistentie van de armoede in Vlaanderen*, Brussels: CBSG.

De Miguel, C. (1993) 'Profesión y género', in L. Garrido and E. Gil Calvo, *Estrategias Familiares*, Madrid: Alianza, pp 13-22.

De Miguel, J. (1998) *Estructura y cambio social en España*, Madrid: Alianza.

de Ussel, I. (1998) *La familia y el cambio político en España*, Madrid: Tecnos.

Deben, L., Rensen, P. and Bronkhorst, M. (1999) 'Telonderzoek', in D. J. Korf, L. Deben, S. Diemel, P. Rensen and H. Riper (eds) *Een sleutel voor de toekomst*, Amsterdam: Thela thesis, pp 13-42.

Defensor del Pueblo (1998) *Informe sobre 'La violencia doméstica contra las mujeres'*, Madrid: Oficina del Defensor del Pueblo.

DEPOS (1989) *Condition and trends in the housing market in large urban areas in Greece, Volume 1. Basic elements of the survey*, Athens: Public Corporation for Housing and Urban Development (DEPOS), August [in Greek].

DEPOS (1990) *Condition and trends in the housing market in large urban areas in Greece, Volume 2, Discrepancies according to social categories and groups of households*, Athens: Public Corporation for Housing and Urban Development (DEPOS), March [in Greek].

DEPOS (1994) *The housing problems of multi-membered nuclear families*, Athens: DEPOS, Department of Research [in Greek].

DEPOS (1996) *Housing conditions of the lower income classes in Greece*, Athens: DEPOS, Department of Research [in Greek].

Derrida, J. (1976) *Of grammatology*, Baltimore, MD: Johns Hopkins University Press.

DETR (Department of the Environment, Transport and the Regions) (2000) *Statutory homelessness*, Statistical release, London: DETR.

DETR (2000) *Quality and choice: A decent home for all*, Housing Green Paper, London: The Stationery Office.

Dibblin, J. (1991) *Wherever I lay my hat: Young women and homelessness*, London: Shelter.

DoE (Department of the Environment) (1996) *Study of single homeless applicants*, London: The Stationery Office.

Douglas, M. (1966) *Purity and danger: An analysis of the concepts of pollution and taboo*, London: Routledge.

Driessen, K. and Smekens, E. (1996) 'Wie zijn de armste vrouwen? Een beeld van hun denk- en ervaringswereld', in M. Vanegendoren and R. Vanherck (eds) *Arme vrouwen. Vrouwen in de keijker van het armoedeonderzoek*, Diepenbeck: Steunpunt Women's Studies, pp 45-104.

Duncan, S. (2000) 'Theorising comparative gender inequality', in S. Duncan and B. Pfau-Effinger (eds) *Gender, economy and culture in the European Union*, London: Routledge, pp 1-24.

Economic and Social Council (2000) *Evolution economique financiere et sociale du pays 2000*, Annual Opinion, ESC, Luxembourg.

Economou, D. and Sapounakis, A. (1993) 'Housing policy and social exclusion', study included in research on social exclusion organised by the National Centre of Social Research (EKKE), Athens (to be published).

EDIS (1998) *Las condiciones de vida de la población pobre en España: Informe general*, Madrid: Fundación Foessa.

Eitel, G. and Schoibl, H. (1999) *Grundlagenerhebung zur Wohnungslosensituation in Ôsterich*, Wohnungslosigkeit und Wien: Wohnungslosenhilfe unter besonderer Berücksichtigung der Situation von Familien und Jugendlichen.

Emke-Poulopoulou, H. (1994) *The demographic problem*, Athens [in Greek].

Enders-Dragässer, U. (1994) *Frauen in Wohnungsnot*, Endbericht der Studie 'Zur Situation alleinstehender wohnungsloser Frauen in Rheinland-Pfalz', Mainz: Ministerium für die Gleichstellung von Frau und Mann.

Enders-Dragässer, U. (2000) *Women, exclusion and homelessness in Germany*, National Report 1999 for the European Observatory on Homelessness, Brussels: FEANTSA.

Enders-Dragässer, U. and Roscher, S. (1999) *Berufsförderung und (Re)Integration für Frauen in der Wohnungslosenhilfe*, Bundesmodellprojekt 'Berufliche Förderung von alleinstehenden wohnungslosen Frauen', im Auftrag des Bundesministeriums für Familie, Senioren, Frauen und Jugend, wohnungslos 3/1999.

Enders-Dragässer, U. and Sellach, B. (1999) '"Der Lebenslagen-Ansatz" aus der Perspektive der Frauenforschung', *Zeitschrift für Frauenforschung*, 17 Jahrgang, Heft 4/99, pp 56–68.

EOP (1992) unpublished extracts of the survey on social and economic parameters conducted in 1991 in Greece by the National Technical University of Athens (EMP) for the National Organisation of Welfare (EOP), Athens.

Ermisch, J. (1996) 'The economic environment and family formation', in D. Coleman (ed) *Europe's population in the 1990s*, Oxford: Oxford University Press.

Eskelinen, L. (1994) *Socialt Udstødte i Københavns Kommune*, Copenhagen: Amternes og Kommunernes Forskningsinstitut.

ESO (1999) *Bostad sökes*, Ds 1999:46, Stockholm: Finansdepartementet.

Esping-Andersen, G. (1990) *The three worlds of welfare capitalism*, Cambridge: Polity Press.

Esping-Andersen, G. (1999) *Social foundations of post-industrial economies*, Oxford: Oxford University Press.

ESYE (National Statistical Agency) (1994) *Population, employment and housing survey*, Athens [in Greek].

Etzioni, A. (1994) *The spirit of community: The reinvention of American society*, New York, NY: Touchstone.

European Commission (1996) *European Observatory on National Family Policies: A synthesis of National Family Policies 1995*, York: University of York.

European Commision (1997) *Equal opportunities for women and men in the European Union*, Annual Report, Brussels: European Commission.

European Commission (2001a) *The social situation in the European Union*, Brussels: European Commission.

European Commission (2001b) *Employment in Europe 2000*, Brussels: European Commission.

Eurostat (1996) *European Labour Force Survey 1996*, Luxembourg: Eurostat.

Eurostat (2000) *ECHP Data Quality, Working Group European Community Household Panel*, Doc PAN 108/99 Revised, Luxembourg: Eurostat.

Fahey, T. (1992) 'State, family and compulsory schooling in Ireland', *Economic and Social Review*, vol 23, no 4, pp 369-95.

Fahey, T. (1998) 'The Catholic Church and social policy', in S. Healy and B. Reynolds (eds) *Social policy in Ireland: Principles, practice and problems*, Dublin: Oaktress Press, pp 411-30.

Fahey, T. (2000) 'The agrarian dimension in the history of the welfare state: a case study' (unpublished manuscript).

Fahey, T. and McLaughlin, E. (1999) 'Family and state', in A.F. Heath, R. Breen, and C.T. Whelan (eds) *Ireland north and south: Perspectives from social science*, Oxford: Oxford University Press, pp 117-40.

Fahey, T. and Watson, D. (1995) 'An analysis of social housing need', *General Research Series*, Paper No 168, Dublin: Economic and Social Research Institute.

FAWOS (1996) *Fachstelle für Wohnungssicherung, 'Eine Wohnung ist nicht alles, aber ohne Wohnung ist alles nichts'*, Wien: Delogieringsprävention und Wohnungssicherung.

Federatie Opvang (2000) *De Maatschappelijke Opvang: Ciifers en Trends 1998* (derde concept), Ultrecht: Federati Opvang.

Federici, N., Oppenheim-Mason, K. and Sogner, S. (1993) *Women's position and demographic change*, Oxford: Clarendon Press.

Fest, K.K. (1996) *Vrouwenhulpverlening in Stichting Blijf-van-mijn-Liif-Nijmegen*, Nijmegen: Wetenschapswinkel.

Figueira, A., Santos, A., Frias, M.J. and Martins, P. (1995) *Caracterização de Sem Abrigo na Cidade de Lisboa*, Lisbon: Câmara Municipal de Lisboa.

Finne, E. (1999) *Statistik över missbrukare, hemlösa och psykiskt störda i Stockholm år 1997*, Fou-rapport 1999:12, Stockholm: Research and Development Department, Social Services.

Fischer, P.J. and Breakey, R.B. (1991) 'The epidemiology of alcohol, drug and mental disorders among homeless persons', *American Psychologist*, vol 46, no 11, pp 1115-28.

Fitzpatrick, S., Kemp P., and Klinker, S. (2000) *Single homelessness: An overview of research*, Bristol/York: The Policy Press/Joseph Rowntree Foundation.

Forssén, K. (1998) *Children, families and the welfare state: Studies on the outcomes of the Finnish family policy*, STAKES Research Report 92, Jyväskylä: STAKES.

Foucault, M. (1972) *The archaeology of knowledge*, New York, NY: Pantheon.

García Roca, J. (1998) *Exclusión social y contracultura de la solidaridad: Prácticas, discursos y narraciones*, Madrid: HOAC.

Garrett, G.R. and Bahr, H.M. (1976) 'The family backgrounds of skid row women', *Signs: Journal of Women in Culture and Society*, vol 2, no 2, pp 369-81.

Gazzola, A. (1997) *Gli abitanti dei nonluoghi. I 'sneza fissa dimora' a Genova*, Roma: Bulzoni.

Geiger, M. and Steinert, E. (1991) *Unter Mitarbeit von Carola Schweitzer: Alleinstehende Frauen ohne Wohnung*, Soziale Hintergründe, Lebensmilieus, Bewältigungsstrategien, Hilfeangebote, Köln: Schriftenreihe des Bundesministers für Frauen und Jugend, Band 5.

Giddens, A. (1990) *The consequences of modernity*, Stanford, CA: Stanford University Press.

Giddens, A. (1991) *Modernity and self-identity*, Stanford, CA: Stanford University Press.

Gill, B. (1996) *Psychiatric morbidity among homeless older people*, London: ONS.

Gilroy, R. and Woods, R. (1994) *Housing women*, London: Routledge.

Glasgow City Council (1999) *Her stories: Young women and homelessness in Glasgow 1990-1999, Rough Sleeping Initiative in Glasgow*, Glasgow: City Council.

Glasgow Council for Single Homeless (1998) *Women and homelessness in Glasgow*, Glasgow: GCSH.

Glasgow Council for Single Homeless (1999) 'Women and homelessness update', *GCSH Newspage*, May.

Glatzer, W. and Hubinger, W. (1990) 'Lebenslagen und Armut', in D. Doring, W. Hanesch and E. Huster (eds) *Armut und Wohlstand*, Frankfurt am Main.

Gleerup, J. (1987) *Fire § 105-institutioner på Fyn*, Fyns Amtskommune: Social- og sundhedsforvaltningen.

Glendinning, C. and Millar, J. (1992) *Women and poverty in Britain in the 1990s*, London: Harvester Wheatsheaf.

Goffman, E. (1959) *The presentation of self in everyday life*. New York, NY: Anchor/Doubleday.

Goffman, E. (1963) *Stigma. Notes on the managment of spoiled identity*, Brunswick, NJ: Prentice Hall.

Golden, S. (1992) *The women outside: Meanings and myths of homelessness*, Berkeley, CA: University of California Press.

González López, M.J. and Pairó, M.S. (1998) 'Households and families: changing living arrangements and gender relations', in S. Duncan and B. Pfau–Effinger (eds) *Gender, economy and culture in the European Union*, London: Routledge, pp 49-86.

González López, M.J. and Solsona, M. (2000) 'Households and families: changing living arrangements and gender relations', in S. Duncan and B. Pfau–Effinger (eds) *Gender, economy and culture in the European Union*, London: Routledge, pp 49-86.

Government of Ireland (1937) *Constitution of Ireland*, Dublin: Stationery Office.

Granfelt, R. (1992) *Asuntolan naisen elämää*, Helsinki: Helsingin yliopisto, Sosiaalipolitiikan laitos, tutkimuksia 1/1992.

Granfelt, R. (1998) *Kertomuksia naisten kodittomuudesta*, Pieksämäki: Suomalaisen Kirjallisuuden Seuran toimituksia 702.

Greve, J. (1990) *Homelessness in Britain*, York: Joseph Rowntree Foundation.

Gundelach, P. and Riis, O. (1992) *Danskernes værdier*, Copenhagen: Forlaget Sociologi.

Gupta, N.D. and Rothstein, D.S. (2000) 'The impact of worker and establishment-level characteristics on male-female wage differentials: evidence from Danish matched employee–employer data', Paper presented to first EALE/SOLE World conference, Catholic University of the Sacred Heart, Milan, Italy, 22-25 June.

Habitat Actualité (2000) *Logement et instabilité familiale*, January, ANIL.

Haffner, M.E.A. (1991) *Fiscal treatment of owner-occupiers in the EEC*, Delft: OTB.

Haffner, M.E.A. and Dol, C.P. (2000) *Housing statistics in the European Union*, Delft: Delft University of Technology.

Hanström, M.-B. (1991) *På glänt? Bostads- och boendeförhållanden för kvinnor med missbruksproblem*, Report R52, Stockholm: Byggforskningsrådet.

Hart, I. (1978) *Dublin Simon Community 1971-1976: An exploration*, Dublin: Economic and Social Research Institute.

Harvey, B. (1993) 'Homelessness in Europe – national housing policies and leal rights', *Scandinavian Housing and Planning Research*, vol 10, pp 115-19.

Haut Comité pour le Logement des Personnes Défavorisées (1997) *Lever les obstacles au logement des personnes défavorisées*, 4ème Rapport, Paris.

Healey, P. and Williams, R. (1993) 'European planning systems: diversity and convergence', *Urban Studies*, vol 30, no 4/5, pp 701-20.

Health, S. and Miret, P. (1996) *Living in and out of the parental home in Spain and Great Britain: A comparative approach*, Cambridge Group for the History of Population and Social Structure, Working Paper Series 2, Cambridge: Cambridge University Press.

Heikkilä, M. and Uusitalo, H. (1997) *Leikkausten hinta, Tutkimuksia sosiaaliturvan leikkauksista ja niiden vaikutuksista 1990-luvun Suomessa*, Raportteja 208, Helsinki: STAKES, Saarijärvi [English summary].

Heydendael, P., Nuy, M. and Brouwer, H. (1990) *Plott. Rapport eerste fase*, Nijmegen: Instituut voor Sociale Geneeskunde.

Holohan, T. (1997) *Health status, health service utilisation and barriers to health service utilisation among the adult homeless population of Dublin*, Dublin: Eastern Health Board.

Hummelgaard, H. (1997) *Udsatte boligområder i Danmark*, AKF-Rapport, Copenhagen: Amternes og kommunernes forskningsinstitut.

Ianello, A. (1997) 'Donne senza dimora: marginalità e servizi', *TRA*, vol 29, pp 12-14.

Iglesias de Ussel, J. (1998) *La familia y el cambio político en España*, Madrid: Tecnos.

Iivari, J. and Karjalainen, J. (1999) *Diakonian köyhät, Epävirallinen apu perusturvan paikkaajana*, Raportteja 235, Helsinki: STAKES, Saarijärvi [English summary].

Ikonen, M.-L., Lehtinen, O. and Tiitinen, V. (2000) *Väestö- ja asuntomarkkinatietoja 2000*, Helsinki: ARA Valtion Asuntorahasto, Selvityksiä 5/2000.

Inside Housing (2000) 'Wake up call', 17 March.

INSEE (1995) *Les femmes*, série Contours et Caractères.

Järvinen, M. (1991) *Den sociale ressourceopgørelse januar 1990*, Social sikring og retsvæsen 1991:7, Copenhagen.

Järvinen, M. (1992) 'Hemlöshetsforskning i Norden', in M. Järvinen and C. Tigerstedt (eds) *Hemlöshet i Norden*, no 22, Helsingfors: NAD-publikation.

Järvinen, M. (1993) *De nye hjemløse: Kvinder, fattigdom og vold*, Holte: Socpol.

Jensen, M.K. (1995) *Hjemløse med og uden egen bolig*, Copenhagen: SFI (95:6).

Jensen, M.K. (1997) *Sociale boformer, boformer for psykisk syge, alkohol- og stofmisbrugere samt socialt udstødte og hjemløse*, Hørsholm: SBI (281).

Johansson, T. (1997) *Den skulpterade kroppen*, Stockholm: Carlsson.

Jokinen, A. (1996) 'Asunnottomat miehet ja kodittomat naise, Asunnottomuuden sukupuolisidonnaiset tulkinnat', *Janus*, 1996, no 7, pp 97-117 [English summary].

Jones. A. (1999) *Out of sight, out of mind? Homeless women speak out*, London: Crisis.

Jones, G. and Gilliland, L. (1993) *Young people in and out of the housing market*, Edinburgh: Scottish Council for Single Homeless (SCSH) with Centre for Educational Sociology, University of Edinburgh.

Joseph Rowntree Foundation (1991) 'Homelessness amongst under 25s', *Findings* no 48, York: Joseph Rowntree Foundation.

Juul, S. (1998) *Fællesskab og solidaritet i Danmark*, Working Paper, Copenhagen: The Danish National Institute for Social Research.

Kærn, J. (1999) 'Boligselskabernes rolle i forhold til de udstødte', Paper at the Conference of Socially Excluded and Threatened Groups, Odense 22-23 November.

Kansanterveys (2000) *2/2000*, Kansanterveyslaitoksen tiedotuslehti, huhtikuu.

Kärkkäinen, S. (2000) *Women, exclusion and homelessness in Finland*, National Report 1999 for the European Observatory on Homelessness, Brussels: FEANTSA.

Katz, J. (1999) *How emotions work*, Chicago, IL: Chicago University Press.

Kaukonen, O. (2000) *Päihdepalvelut jakautuneessa hyvinvointivaltiossa*, Tutkimuksia 107, Helsinki: STAKES, Saarijärvi [Summary].

Kelleher, C., Kelleher, P. and McCarthy, P. (1992) *Patterns of hostel use in Dublin and the implications for accommodation provision*, Dublin: Focus Point Publication.

Kelleher, P. (1995) *Making the links: Towards an integrated strategy for the elimination of violence against women in intimate relationships with men*, Dublin: Women's Aid.

Kennedy, S. (1985) *But where can I go? Homeless women in Dublin*, Dublin: Arlen House.

Kilkey, M. and Bradshaw, J. (1999) 'Lone mothers, economic well being and politics', in D. Sainsbury (ed) *Gender and welfare state regimes*, Oxford: Oxford University Press, pp 147-84.

Kleinman, M. (1998) 'Western European housing policies: convergence or collapse?', in M. Kleinman, W. Matznetter and M. Stephens (eds) *European integration and housing policy*, London: Routledge.

Kleinman, M., Matznetter, W. and Stephens, M. (1998) *European integration and housing policy*, London: Routledge.

Koch-Nielsen, I. (1996) 'Hvem er de svage?', in *Socialforskning*, Særnummer, August, Copenhagen.

Koch-Nielsen, I. and Børner Stax, T. (1999) 'The heterogeneity of homelessness and the consequences for service provision', in D. Avramov (ed) *Coping with homelessness: Issues to be tackled and best practices in Europe*, Aldershot: Ashgate.

Korf, D.J., Diemel, S. and Riper, H. (1999) 'Consumentenonderzoek', in D.J. Korf, L. Deben, S. Diemel, P. Rensen and H. Riper, *Ein sleutel voor de toekomst*, Amsterdam: Thela Thesis, pp 43-162.

Kouveli, A. (1991a) Consolidated report of the results from the housing survey in large urban areas, volume 1: Survey on housing and private housing construction enterprises in Greece, National Centre of Social Research (EKKE) in collaboration with the Ministry of Environment and Physical Planning and the ESYE in 1986-87, Athens, August [in Greek].

Kouveli, A. (1991b) Housing typology of housing in large urban areas, volumes 1 and 2: Survey on housing and private housing construction enterprises in Greece, National Centre of Social Research (EKKE) in collaboration with the Ministry of Environment and Physical Planning and the Statistical Agency of Greece in 1986-87, Athens, December [in Greek].

Kouveli A. (1993) Socio-economic inequalities in housing in large urban areas; Survey on housing and private housing construction enterprises in Greece, National Centre of Social Research (EKKE) in collaboration with the Ministry of Environment and Physical Planning and the Statistical Agency of Greece in 1986-87, Athens, August [in Greek].

Kristensen, C.J. (1994) *Nye fattige: Unge hjemløse kvinder i København*, Copenhagen: Forlaget Sociologi.

Laceur, B. (1999) *A chance to change*, Gent: Stad Gent.

Laparra, M., Gaviria, M. and Aguilar, M. (1996) 'Peculiaridades de la exclusión en España', *Pobreza, necesidad y discriminación* (II Simposio sobre Igualdad y Distribución de la Renta), Madrid: Fundación Argentaria.

Lasch, C. (1995) *Eliternes oprør – og forræderiet mod demokratiet*, Copenhagen: Hovedland.

Leahy, A. (1974) *Medical care for the vagrant in Ireland*, Simon Ireland Report.

Leal, J. (1998) *La vivienda de apoyo en España*, Informe para FEANTSA.

Leinikki, P. and Holmström, E. (2000) 'Huumeisiin liittyvät hepatiitti- ja HIV - infektiot lisääntyivät huolestuttavasti', *Kansanterveys, kansanterveyslaitoksen tiedotuslehti*, nro 2, April, pp 3-4.

Lejealle, B. (1998) 'Les femmes et le marché de l'emploi', *Population et emploi*, no 3, CEPS/I.

Lescrauwaet, D. (2000) *Thuislozen krijgen (nog) geen voet aan huis in de sociale huisvesting*, Berchem: Steunpunt Algemeen Welzijnswerk.

Lesthaeghe, R. (1995) 'The second demographic transition in western countries: an interpretation', in K. Oppenheim-Mason and A.M. Jensen (eds) *Gender and family change in industrialising countries*, Oxford: Oxford University Press, pp 17-62.

Lewis, J. (1992) 'Gender and the development of welfare regimes', *Journal of European Social Policy*, vol 2, no 3, pp 159-73.

Lifton, R.J. (1996) 'Victims and survivors', in B. Giam and J. Grunberg (eds) *Beyond homelessness: Frames of reference*, Iowa City, IA: University of Iowa Press.

Lindberg, G. (1971) 'Segregationsprocesser', in G. Lindberg, *Urbana processer. Studier i social ekologi*, Lund: Glerups Bokförlag, pp 133-55.

Lissenburgh, S.T. (2000) 'Causes of the gender pay gap in the 1990s: an analysis of British national survey data', Paper presented to first EALE/SOLE World conference, Catholic University of the Sacred Heart, Milan, Italy, 22-25 June.

Lister, R. (1994) '"She has other duties": women, citizenship and social security', in S. Baldwin and J. Falkingham (eds) *Social security and social change: New challenges to the Beveridge model*, Hemel Hempstead: Harvester Wheatsheaf, pp 31-44.

Lucas, R. (1995) 'Prevalencia de sintomatología psicótica y habitos tóxicos en una mustra de Homeless', *Revista de Psiquitria de la Facultad de Medicina de Barcelona*, vol 22, pp 18-24.

Luddy, M. (1995) *Women and philanthropy in nineteenth-century Ireland*, Cambridge: Cambridge University Press.

MacLennan, D., Stephens, M. and Kemp, P. (1996) *Housing policy in the EU member states*, Report to the European Parliament, PE166-328, Brussels: European Commision.

Madigan, R. and Munro, M. (1993) 'Privacy in the private sphere', *Housing Studies*, vol 8, no 1, pp 29-45.

Madigan, R., Munro, M. and Smith, S.J. (1990) 'Gender and the meaning of the home', *International Journal of Urban and Regional Research*, vol 14, pp 625-47

Madruga Torremocha, I. and Mota López, R. (2000) *Las condiciones de vida de los hogares pobres encabezados por una mujer: Pobreza y género*, Madrid: Caritas Española.

Mahon, E. (1987) 'Women's rights and Catholicism in Ireland', *New Left Review*, no 166, pp 53-77.

Mahon, E. (1995) 'From democracy to femocracy: the women's movement in the Republic of Ireland', in P. Clancy, S. Drudy, K. Lynch and L. O'Dowd (eds) *Irish society: Sociological perspectives*, Dublin: Institute of Public Administration in association with the Sociological Association of Ireland, pp 675-708.

Malos, E. and Hague, G. (1997) 'Women, housing, homelessness and domestic violence', *Women's Studies International Forum*, vol 20, no 3, pp 397-409.

Maloutas, T. (1990) 'Athens, housing, family: analysis of the post-war housing practice', Athens: Exantas [in Greek].

Marpsat, M. (1999) 'Un avantage sous contrainte: le risque moindre pour les femmes de se trouver sans abri', *Population*, vol 54, no 6, pp 885-932.

Marpsat, M. and Firdion, J.M. (1998) 'Sans domicile à Paris : une typologie de l'utilisation des services et du mode d'hébergement', *Sociétés Contemporaines*, no 30, pp 111-55.

Martens, E.P. (1999) *Minderheden in beeld*, Rotterdam: ISEO.

Martínez, R. (1996) 'Feminización de la pobreza ¿un proceso inevitable?', in *La pobreza entre Nosotros. Interpelación a la sociedad y a la Iglesia*, Secretariado Social Diocesano, Escuela Social de la Iglesia Asturiana, Materiales de Trabajo 3.

Marx, I., Cantillon, B., Gijselinck, C. and Tan, B. (1999) 'De sluipende marginalisering van laaggeschoolden', in B. Cantillon, L. de Lathouwer, I. Marx, R. Van Dam and K. Van den Bosch (eds) *Sociale indicatoren: 1976-1997*, Antwerpen: Centrum voor Sociaal Beleid, pp 175-94.

Maselli, F. (1999) 'La comunità delle Missionarie della Carità', in P. Guidicini and G. Pieretti (eds) *Città globale e città degli esclusi*, Milano: Franco Angeli.

Maunuksela, A. and Salminen, K. (1994) *Se mitä toiseksi luulit, Asuntoloissa Eläneiden naisten tarinoita*, Järvenpään Diakonissaopisto (unpublished).

McCrone, G. and Stephens, M. (1996) *Housing policy in Britain and Europe*, London: UCL Press.

McLaughlin, E. and Yeates, N. (1999) 'The biopolitics of welfare in Ireland', *Irish Journal of Feminist Studies*, vol 3, no 2, pp 49-69.

Mecklin, P. and Sonninen, E. (1998) *Dooriksen Dokumentti, Faktoja ja fiktioita päihdeongelmaisten naisten elämästä, asumisesta ja osallistumisesta*, Marraskuu: Mikkelin ammatti-instituutti (unpublished).

Meert, H. (2000) La ville des 'résidents de la rue', in E. Corijn, and W. De Lannoy (eds) *Crossing Brussels. La qualité de la différence*, Brussels: VUB Press, pp 107-21.

Meo, A. (1997) *Donne senza dimora: alcune ipotesi di lettura*, relazione al convegno FIO, psd, 28 febbraio, Bergamo.

MEPAT (1999) *HABITAT II – Plano Nacional de Acção – Habitação*, Lisbon: MEPAT - Secretaria de Estado da Habitação e Comunicações.

Meulemans, B., Geurts, V. and De Decker, P. (1996) *Wonen in Vlaanderen. Onderzoek naar de doelgroepen van het huisvestingsbeleid*, Brussels: Ministerie van de Vlaamse Gemeenschap, Administratie LIN, Afdeling Woonbeleid.

Meurs, D. and Ponthieux, S. (2000) 'Components of the gender wage gap in 12 EU countries', Paper presented to first EALE/SOLE World conference, Catholic University of the Sacred Heart, Milan Italy, 22-25 June.

Middleton, S., Ashworth, K. and Braithwaite, I. (1997) *Small fortunes, spending on children, childhood poverty and parental sacrifice,* York: Joseph Rowntree Foundation.

Millar, J. and Glendinning, C. (1989) 'Gender and poverty', *Journal of Social Policy,* vol 18, no 3, pp 363-81.

Ministry of Housing and Urban Environment (1999a) *Housing, building and urban affairs in Denmark,* Copenhagen: By og Boligministeriet.

Ministry of Housing and Urban Environment (1999b) *By- og boligpolitisk oversigt 1998 - 99,* Copenhagen: By og Boligministeriet.

Ministry of Housing and Urban Environment (1999c) *Skæve huse til skæve eks*istenser, 5 August, Copenhagen.

Ministry of Housing, Environment and Public Works (1995) 'National report for Greece', Document prepared by DEPOS in view of the Habitat II Conference in Istanbul in June 1996.

Muehlberger, U. (2000) 'Women's labour force attachment in Europe: an analytical framework and empirical evidence for the households', Paper to the European Network of Housing Research, Gävle, Sweden, June.

Muestreo-estudio sobre casas refugio, Comisión para la Investigación de Malos Tratos a Mujeres, Instituto de la Mujer, Madrid, 1995-96.

Mujeres en cifras, L. (1997) *Instituto de la Mujer,* Madrid: Ministerio de Trabajo y Asuntos Sociales.

Mulinari, D. (1996), 'Kvinnoprojekt och feminism', in I. Sahlin (ed) *Projektets paradoxer,* Lund: Studentlitteratur.

Munk, A. (1998) *Forfalds- og fornyelsesprocesser i ældre bykvarterer,* SBI-rapport 305, Hørsholm: Statens Byggeforskningsinstitut.

Munk, A. (1999) *Den boligsociale indsats,* SFI-rapport 319, SBI- rapport 319, Hørsholm: Statens Byggeforskningsinstitut.

Munk-Jørgensen, P. (1992) *Hjemløse psykisk syge,* Århus: Institut for psykiatrisk demografi.

Muñoz, M. and Vázquez, C. (1998) 'Las personas sin hogar: aspectos psicosociales de la situación española', *Intervención Psicosocial,* vol 7, no 1, pp 7-26.

Myers, D. Peiser, R., Schwann, G. and Pitkin, J. (1992) 'Retreat from homeownership: a comparison of the generations and the states', *Housing Policy Debate*, vol 3, no 4, pp 945-75.

NBHW (2000) *Hemlösa i Sverige 1999. Vilka är de och vilken hjälp får de?*, Socialstyrelsen följer upp och utvärderar, no 1, Stockholm: NBHW.

Neale, J. (1997) 'Homelessness and theory reconsidered', *Housing Studies*, vol 12, no 1, pp 47-61.

Nolan, B. (1999) 'Income inequality in Ireland', in A. McCashin, and E. O'Sullivan (eds) *Irish Social Policy Review, 1999*, Dublin: Institute of Public Administration, pp 78-92.

Nolan, B. and Watson, D. (1999) *Women and poverty in Ireland*. Dublin: Oaktree Press.

Nolan, B. and Whelan, C.T. (1996) *Resources, deprivation and poverty*, Oxford: Clarendon Press.

Novac, S., Brown, J. and Bourbonnais, B.A. (1996) *No room of her own: A literature review on women and homelessness*, Toronto: Canadian Housing Information Centre.

Nuorvala, Y., Metso L., Kaukonen, O. and Haavisto, K. (2000) 'Päihde-ehtoinen asiointi sosiaali- ja terveyshuollossa: vuosien 1995 ja 1999 päihdetapauslaskentojen vertailu', STAKES, *Yhteiskuntapolitiikka*, no 3, pp 246-54.

O'Cinneide, S. and Mooney, P. (1972) *Simon survey of the homeless*, the Simon Community of Ireland supported by the Medico-Social Research Board.

O'Connor, J. (1999) *States, markets, families. Gender, liberalism and social policy in Australia, Canada, Great Britain and the United States*, Cambridge: Cambridge University Press.

O'Connor, P. (1998) *Emerging voices: Women in contemporary Irish society*, Dublin: Institute of Public Administration.

O'Sullivan, E. (1996) *Homelessness and social policy in the Republic of Ireland*, Occasional Paper No 5, Dublin: Department of Social Studies, Trinity College, University of Dublin.

O'Sullivan, E. and Higgins, M. (2000) *Women, exclusion and homelessness*, National Report 1999 for the European Observatory on Homelessness, Brussels: FEANTSA.

Offe, C. (1996) *Modernity and the state: East, West,* Cambridge: Polity Press.

Office of An Tanaiste (1997) *Report of the Task Force on Violence against Women,* Dublin: Stationery Office.

OECD (Organisation for Economic Co-operation and Development) (1999) *Ireland,* Paris: OECD.

OECD (2000) *Employment outlook,* Paris: OECD.

Orloff, A.S. (1993) 'Gender and the social rights of citizenship: the comparative analysis of gender relations and welfare states', *American Sociological Review,* vol 58, pp 303-28.

Orloff, A.S. (1996) 'Gender in the welfare state', *Annual Review of Sociology,* vol 22, pp 51-78.

Pais, E. (1998) *Homicídio Conjugal em Portugal – Rupturas violentas da conjugalidade,* Lisbon: Hugin.

Pannecoucke, I., Guerts, V., van Dam, R., De Decker, P., Goosens, L. and Cantillon, B. (2001) *Profiel van de sociale huurder en subjectueve beleving van de relaties van de sociale huisvesting,* Antwerp: OASeS/CSB, UFSIA.

Partanen, A. (1999) *Selvitys päihdehuollon huumeasiakkaista 1998, Pompiudou-huumetiedonkeruu,* Helsinki: STAKES, Tilastoraportteja 29/1999.

Pascall, G. (1997) *Social policy: A new feminist analysis,* London: Routledge.

Passaro, J. (1996) *The unequal homeless: Men on the streets, women in their place,* London: Routledge.

Paugam, S. (1996) 'La constitution d'un paradigme', in S. Paugam (ed) *L'Exclusion: L'état des savoirs,* Paris: Éditions la Découverte.

Pels, M. (2000) *Women, social exclusion and homelessness in Luxembourg,* National Report, Brussels: FEANTSA.

Pereira, A.P. and Silva, D.S. (1999) *Os Sem-Abrigo da Cicade de Lisboa – Riscos de Viver (n)a Cicade,* Lisbon: Laboratorio Nacional de Engenharia Civil.

Pereira, A., Barreto, P. and Fernandes, G. (2000) *Análise longitudinal dos sem-abrigo em Lisboa: A situação em 2000,* Lisbon: Laboratório Nacional de Engenharia Civil.

Perista, H. and Perista, P. (1998) *A mulher e a riqueza: o poder de a gerar, a impossibilidade de a gerir*, Lisbon: DMPS.

Perista, H., Gomes, M.E. and Silva, M. (1993) *A pobreza no feminino na cidade de Lisboa*, Lisbon: ONG's do Conselho Consultivo da CIDM.

Pfau-Effinger, B. (1998) 'Gender, culture and gender arrangement – a theoretical framework for cross-national gender research', *Innovations: The European Journal of the Social Sciences*, vol 11, no 2, pp 147-66.

Planer, M., Steltzer-Orthofer, C. and Weitzer, B. (1994) *Wohnungslose Frauen – Entstehungsbedingungen und Verlaufsformen von Wohnungslosigkeit im weiblichen Lebenszusammenhang*, Linz.

Pleace, N., Ford, J., Wilcox, S. and Burrows, R. (1999) *Lettings and sales by Registered Social Landlords, 1996/1997*, London: Housing Corporation.

Pollo, M. (1995) 'I senza fissa dimora in Italia', in G. Pochettino (ed) *I senza fissa dimora*, Piemme: Casale M.

Provincia di Milano and Ismu (1999) *L'immigrazione straniera nell'area milanese*, Rapporto statistico dell'Osservatorio Fondazione Cariplo-Ismu-Provincia di Milano.

Raftery, M. and O'Sullivan, E. (1999) *Suffer the little children: The inside story of Ireland's industrial schools*, Dublin: New Island Books.

Ritokallio, V.-M. (2000) 'Tuloerot ja köyhyys kansainvälisessä vertailussa 1980-1995', in M. Heikkilä and J. Karjalainen (ed) *Köyhyys ja hyvinvointivaltion murros*, Helsinki: Gaudeamus, pp 17-42.

Rollet, A., Norvez, F., Mollo, M., Donati, S. and De Luca, J. (1995) *Les centres maternels: Utopies et réalités éducatives d'hier et d'aujourd'hui*, Université de Versailles Saint-Quentin-en-Yvelines.

Room, G. (2000) *Social mobility, social exclusion and social welfare: Comparative dynamics* (mimeo).

Ruiz Becerril, D. (1999) *Después del divorcio. Los efectos de la ruptura matrimonial en España*, CIS 169, Madrid.

Ruspini, E. (1998) 'Genere e povertà in Italia', *Pari e dispari*, Milano: FrancoAngeli.

Sahlin, I. and Thörn, C. (2000) *Women, exclusion and homelessness in Sweden*, National Report 1999 for the European Observatory on Homelessness, Brussels: FEANTSA.

Sainsbury, D. (1996) *Gender, equality and welfare states*, Cambridge: Cambridge University Press.

Sainsbury, D. (1999) *Gender and welfare states regimes*, Oxford: Oxford University Press.

SAM (1999) *Le persone senza dimora, Rapporto 1999*, Milano.

Sánchez Morales, D. and Mª del Rosario (1999) *La población 'sin techo' en España: Un caso extremo de exclusión social*, Madrid: Editorial Sistema.

Sandeman, A., Doherty, J. and Edgar, W. (2000) *CORE: Lettings and sales by registered social landlords in England*, London: Housing Corporation.

Sapounakis, A. (2000) *Women, exclusion and homelessness in Greece*, National Report 1999 for the European Observatory on Homelessness, Brussels: FEANTSA,

Schmid, G., O'Reilley, J. and Schoman, K. (eds) 1996 *International handbook of labour market policy and evaluation*, Cheltenham: Edward Elgar.

Schoibl, H. and Novak, C. (2000) *Women, exclusion and homelessness in Austria*, National Report 1999 for the European Observatory on Homelessness, Brussels: FEANTSA.

Scottish Executive (2000) *Report of Homelessness Task Force*, Edinburgh.

Scottish Poverty Information Unit (1998) *Women, family and poverty*, March.

Scottish Poverty Information Unit (1999) *Poverty in Scotland 1999*, Glasgow: Caledonian University.

Scottish Women's Aid (1999) *Briefing: Housing*, Edinburgh.

Sellach, B. (1998) 'Qualitätsstandards in der Wohnungslosenhilfe für Frauen aus der Perspektive der Frauenforschung', *Wohnungslos* 2/98.

Shaw, I., Bloor, M. and Roberts, S. (1996*) Without shelter: Estimating rooflessness in Scotland*, Edinburgh: Scottish Office.

Shelter UK (1999) *Making connections*, London: Shelter.

Shelter UK (2000) *Statistics from Shelterline*, London.

Siikanen, A., Säylä, M. and Tahvanainen, M. (1999) *Suomalaisten asumismenot*, Helsinki: Suomen Ympöministeriö, ympäristö, Asuminen 330.

Sijses, B. and Bekkers, B. (1990) *Allochtone vrouwen in opvangcentra*, Amsterdam: Stichting Averroès.

Simmel, G. (1994) 'Bridges and doors', *Theory, Culture & Society*, vol 11, no 1, pp 11-17.

Skifter Andersen, H. (1999) *Byudvalgets indsats 1993 - 98. Sammenfattende evaluering*, SBI-rapport 320, Hørsholm: Statens Byggeforskningsinstitut.

Skifter Andersen, H. and Als, J.K. (1986) *Boligbyggeriet og kommunernes befolknings-udvikling*, SBI-rapport 181, Hørsholm: Statens Byggeforskningsinstitut.

Smith, E.M. and North, C.S. (1994) 'Not all homeless women are alike: effects of motherhood and the presence of children', *Community Mental Health Journal*, vol 30, no 6, pp 601-10.

Smith, J., Gilford, S. and O'Sullivan, A. (1998) *The family background of homeless young people*, London: Family Policy Studies Centre.

Smith, J. (1999) 'Gender and homelessness', in S. Hutson and D. Clapham (eds) *Homelessness: Public policies and private troubles*, London: Cassell, pp 108-32.

Sociaal en Cultureel Planbureau en Centraal Bureau voor de Statistiek (1999) *Armoedemonitor 1999*, Den Haag: SCP Socialkonstruktivisme: Bidrag til en kritisk diskussion, Copenhagen: Hans Reitzels Forlag.

Söderholm, S. (2000) *Hulttioita ja vilpittömiä vanhuksia, Helsingin kaupungin omistamien kiinteistöjen henkilöstön ja sosiaalityöntekijöiden näkemyksiä häädöistä ja häädetyistä* (unpublished manuscript).

Sommerville, P. (1992) 'Homelessness and the meaning of home: rooflessness or rootlessness?', *International Journal of Urban and Regional Research*, vol 16, pp 529-39.

Spanish Institute of Statistics (1991) *Population Census*, Madrid.

Specht-Kittler, T. (1999) 'Die Schätzung der Zahl der Wohnungslosen in Deutschland 1994-1999', *Wohnungslos*, March 2000, pp 93-100.

Statistics Denmark (1996C) 'Den sociale ressourceopgørelse januar 1996, kommunefordelte opgørelser for ældreområdet mv', *Socialstatistik 1996*, vol 12 (Statistikservice) Copenhagen: Statistics Denmark.

Steinert, E. (1991) 'Wohnungslose Frauen im Spiegel des Selbst: Problemgenese des Wohnungsverlustes, soziale Orientierungen und Bewältigungsstgrategien', in M. Geiger and E. Steinert (eds) *Alleinstehende Frauen ohne Wohnung*, Köln: Schriftenreihe des Bundesministers für Frauen und Jugend.

Stoner, M.R. (1983) 'The plight of homeless women', *Social Service Review*, vol 57, pp 565-81.

Strauss, M., Gelles, R. and Steinmetz, S. (1980) *Behind closed doors: Violence in the American family*, London: Sage Publications.

Svahnstrom, H. (1996) *Femmes sans adresses: Réflexion sur l'itinérance au féminin*, Centre de Chaligny, mémoire DSTS.

Tagliaferri, G. (1999a) 'Cooperativa Parella di Torino', *Intervista*, 29 November.

Tartinville, S. (2000) *Women, exclusion and homelessness in France*, National Report 1999 for the European Observatory on Homelessness, Brussels: FEANTSA.

Taylor, G. (1985) *Pride, shame and guilt: Emotions of self-assesment*, Oxford: Clarendon Press.

Taylor, I. (1992) *Discharged with care*, Edinburgh: SCSH, Lothian Health Board.

Tezanos, J.F. (1998) *Tendencias en exclusión social en las sociedades tecnológicas: El caso español*, Madrid: Fundación Sistema.

The Scottish Office (1998) *Women's issues*, London: The Stationery Office.

Thomas, A. and Dittmar, H. (1995) 'The experience of homeless women: an exploration of housing histories and the meaning of home', *Housing Studies*, vol 10, no 4, pp 493-515.

Thomsen, N. (1997) *Registreret partnerskab, samliv og velsignelse*, Rapport fra et af biskoppene nedsat udvalg vedrørende kirkelig velsignelse af registeret partnerskab.

Thörn, C. (2000) 'Utan hem – utanför samhället?', *Hemlöshet – Olika perspektiv och förklaringsmodeller*, Stockholm: Carlssons Förlag.

Tiitinen, V. (2000) *Asunnottomat 1999*, Helsinki: ARA Valtion Asuntorahasto, Selvityksiä, 6/2000.

Tobío, C. (1996) *Estrategias de compatibilización familia-empleo*, Madrid: Instituto de la Mujer.

Torode, R. and O'Sullivan, E. (1999) 'The impact of Dear Daughter', *Irish Journal of Feminist Studies*, vol 3, no 2, pp 85-97.

Tosi, A. (1993) *Immigrati e senza casa. I problemi, i progetti, le politiche*, Milano: Franco Angeli.

Tosi, A. (1999) 'Homelessness and the housing factor: learning from the debate on homelessness and poverty', in D. Avramov (ed) *Coping with homelessness*, Aldershot: Ashgate, pp 15-24.

Tosi, A. (2000a) *Women, exclusion and homelessness in Italy, National Report 1999*, European Observatory on Homelessness, Brussels: FEANTSA.

Tosi, A. (2000b) 'The integration of immigrants: housing and cities', in C. Marcetti, N. Solimano and A. Tosi, *Le culture dell'abitare*, Brussels: FEANTSA.

Tosi, A. and Ranci, C. (1999) *Support in housing in Italy, National Report 1998*, Brussels: FEANTSA.

van der Heijden, H. and Haffner, M. (2000) 'Housing expenditure and housing policy in the West European rental sector', *Journal of Housing and the Built Environment*, vol 15, no 1, pp 71-92.

Van Gils, M. (1994) *Vrouwenopvang in Nederland*, Utrecht: Stichting Vrouwenvang.

Van Haegendoren, M. (1996) 'Woord vooraf', in M. Van Haegendoren, and R. Vanherck (eds) *Arme vrouwen. Vrouwen in de kijker van het armoedeonderzoek*, Diepenbeek: Steunpunt Women's Studies, pp 7-10.

Van Solinge, H. and Plomp, R. (1997) 'Armoede en demografisch gedrag', in N. van Nimwegen and G. Beets (eds) *Bevolkingsvraagstukken in Nederland anno 1997*, Den Haag: NIDI.

Vega González, L.S. (1996) *Salud mental en población sin hogar*, Oviedo: Servicio de Publicaciones del Principado de Asturias

Viljamaa, L. (1999) 'Että naisille pitäis löytää jotain parempaa paikkaa', *Kartoitus asunnottomien naisten palvelutarpeista Helsingissä*, Helsinki: Helsingin Diakonissalaitos.

Vranken, J. and Geldof, D. (1994) *Armoede en Sociale Uitsluiting*, Jaarboek 1994, Leuven: Acco.

Vranken, J., Geldof, D. and Van Menxel, G. (1997) *Armoede en Sociale Uitsluiting*, Jaarboek 1997, Leuven: Acco.

VVAA (1999) *La Población y los hogares madrileños según la zonificación de servicios sociales,* Madrid: Comunidad de Madrid.

Waldfogel, J. (1998) 'Understanding the family gap in pay for women with children,' *Journal of Economic Perspectives,* vol 12, no 1, pp 137-46.

Wardhaugh, J. (1999) 'The unaccommodated woman: home, homelessness and identity', *Sociological Review,* vol 47, no 1, pp 91-109.

Wardhaugh, J. (2000) *Sub city: Young people, homelessness and crime,* Aldershot: Ashgate.

Watson, S. (1984) 'Definitions of homelessness: a feminist perspective', *Critical Social Policy,* vol 11, no 1, pp 60-72.

Watson, S. (1988) *Accommodating inequality: Gender and housing,* Sydney: Allen & Unwin.

Watson, S. (1999) 'A home is where the heart is: engendered notions of homelessness', in P. Kennett and A. Marsh, (eds) *Homelessness: Exploring the new terrain,* Bristol: The Policy Press, pp 81-100.

Watson, S. and Austerberry, H. (1981) 'A woman's place: a feminist approach to housing in Britain', *Feminist Review,* vol 13, p v.

Watson, S. and Austerberry, H. (1986) *Housing and homelessness: A feminist perspective,* London: Routledge and Kegan Paul.

Webb, S., (1994) *My address is not my home: Hidden homelessness and single women in Scotland,* Edinburgh: Scottish Council for Single Homeless / Glasgow Council for Single Homeless.

Webster, D. (2000) 'Lone parenthood: two views and their consequences', in I. Anderson and D. Sim (eds) *Social exclusion and housing,* London: Chartered Institiute of Housing.

Williams, J. and O'Connor, M. (1999) *Counted in: The report of the 1999 assessment of homelessness in Dublin, Kildare and Wicklow,* Dublin: Economic and Social Research Institute/Homeless Initiative.

Wilson, D. (1996) *We will need to take you in,* Edinburgh: Scottish Council for Single Homeless, Age Concern Scotland.

Wolf, J., Elling, A. and de Graaf, I. (2000) *Monitor Maatschappelijke Opvang,* Utrecht: Trimbos Institute,

Women's Aid (2000) *25 years of listening to women*, Edinburgh: Women's Aid in Scotland.

Women's National Commission (1995) *Women in the 90s*, London.

Wright, T. (1997) *Out of place: Homeless mobilizations, subcities, and contested landscapes*, Albany, NY: State University of New York Press.

Yeates, N. (1997a) 'Familism and selectivism in community care for the elderly: A comparison of the Republic of Ireland and the UK', in M. May, E. Brunsdon, and G. Craig (eds) *Social Policy Review 9*, London: Social Policy Association, London Guildhall University, pp 290–316.

Yeates, N. (1997b) 'Gender and the development of the Irish social welfare system', in A. Byrne, and M. Leonard (eds) *Women and Irish society: A sociological reader*, Belfast: Beyond the Pale Publications, pp 145-66.

Yeates, N. (1999) 'Gender, familism and housing: matrimonial and property rights in Ireland', *Women's Studies International Forum*, vol 22, no 6, pp 607-18.

Young, I. M. (1990) *Justice and the politics of difference*, Princeton, NY: Princeton University Press.

Index

Page references for figures and tables are in italics; those for notes are followed by n.

Sellach, B. 207, 209, 210-11, 213, 214
service provision 6-7, 44, 47, 48, 231-2, 234-8, 239
  Austria 129, 130, 134-8, 140
  Finland 189-91, 192-3
  France 142-3, 146-50
  Germany 208, 213-16, 217, 218
  Greece 155, 160
  Italy 164, 165, 168-9
  Luxembourg 203-5
  Netherlands 177-9, 181-2
  Portugal 53-7, *54*, 61-3
  Sweden 220
Seville 70
sexual abuse 84, 191, 220
shame 137-8, 220, 223-4, 225-7, 228-9
Shaw, I. 33, 96
Simmel, G. 228
single parents *see* lone parents
single women 26, 27, 30
  Belgium 107-10, 112
  Finland 188
  France 149
  Germany 32
  Ireland 85
  UK 92
single-person households 27-8, *28*
  Denmark 116-17
  Netherlands 176
  Spain 67
sleeping rough *see* rough sleeping
Smekens, E. 105, 107
Smith, J. 3
social exclusion 8, 65-6, *66*
  Denmark 115, 118-19, 121-2, 124
  Italy 164
  Spain 66-8
social housing 12, 23-4, 28, 29-30
  Belgium 108-9, 112
  Denmark 119-20
  Finland 35, 185-6
  France 145-6
  Greece 155
  Italy 172
  Luxembourg 199-200
social protection 5, 43-4, 232, 233

social security *see* welfare state
society *see* position in society
Söderholm, S. 185, 186
Sommerville, P. 227
Sonninen, E. 185, 187, 188, 191
Spain 48, 65-6, 74-5
  domestic violence 71-2
  education 68
  employment *25*, 67-8
  family support 66-7
  homelessness *39*
  housing 23, *23*, 29, *29*
  lone parents 73-4
  older women 42
  poverty 26
  single-person households *28*
  unemployment 26
  welfare state typology 13-14
  women's homelessness 37-8, 39, 68-70
squatters 159
Steinert, E. 32, 207, 208
step parents 93
Stephens, M. 22, 23, 175
stigma 137-8, 221-2, 225, 228, 234
Stoner, M.R. 77
street homeless *see* rough sleeping
subsidiarity 79, 89n
substance abuse
  Finland 183, 186, 187-9, 190, 191, 192
  Germany 212
  see also alcohol; drug addiction
Sundholm (Denmark) 122, 124-5n
Sweden 49, 80, 219, 228-9
  employment *25*
  hidden homelessness 219-21
  home 227-8
  housing 23, *23*, 29, *29*
  immigrants 40
  lone parents 28
  poverty 26-7
  single-person households *28*
  unemployment 26
  women's experiences 221-7
  women's homelessness 35-6